COSMIC UNDERSTANDING

COSMIC
UNDERSTANDING

o o o

*Philosophy and Science of
the Universe*

Milton K. Munitz

*Princeton University Press
Princeton, New Jersey*

Contents

Preface

The progress made during the past several decades by the science of cosmology in understanding the overall structure of the universe has been the most far-reaching and intellectually momentous in the entire history of this perennial topic of human interest.

Along with very many others who have been intrigued by these developments, I was sufficiently stimulated to publish, in 1957, two books on the subject. One was an anthology of important writings in the field of cosmology, *Theories of the Universe: From Babylonian Myth to Modern Science* (Free Press, 1957); the other, *Space, Time, and Creation: Philosophical Aspects of Scientific Cosmology* (Free Press, 1957), was an attempt, from a philosopher's perspective, to see what these impressive scientific advances signified. (A second edition of the latter book was reprinted recently by Dover Publications.) In the intervening decades, the field of cosmology has grown enormously, as judged not only by sheer quantity of technical papers and books, but by the quality, richness, and innovative character of its results. The challenge to digest this fresh material and to come to terms with it intellectually continues to be an exciting and important one.

If, as the cosmologist tells us, the universe had a beginning some 15 billion years ago and will meet its own death in the far-off, yet foreseeable future, would not the assimilation of these claims have the most profound bearing on our overall world view? What changes, if any, would they bring about in our notions of (1) the scope and limits of cosmological knowledge, (2) the relation of the physical universe to what we may think of as the nature of ultimate reality, and (3) our own place as human beings in the entire scheme of things? My general purpose in the present book is to explore these issues—to assess the broader philosophic bearings of the recent discoveries and investigations of the cosmologist.

In connection with the first of the above themes—the scope of cosmological knowledge—I undertake (in Chapters 3 and 5) to show the advantages of taking a broadly pragmatist perspective. In support of this approach, detailed analyses are given of the following: the several meanings of the expressions "the universe" and "the universe *as a whole*"; the role of cosmological models in achieving intelligibility; different types of observable and conceptual horizons in cosmology; the scientific efforts at identifying or explaining the origin of the universe.

To give the necessary scientific background and illustrative materials for the philosophical points made, I give a brief account, in Chapter 4, of the chief empirical findings and theories of recent cosmology. A reading of this chapter may be postponed for those readers who prefer to reach, more rapidly, the other philosophical topics treated in later chapters. Its careful perusal, however, would not only be of service in judging the merit of my philosophical analyses, but it might also help to stimulate philosophical thinking along lines alternative to my own.

In Chapter 6, I examine the second type of question mentioned above—that which recalls disputes of a traditional metaphysical character. In discussing this theme, I align myself broadly with a number of viewpoints (developed in the West as well as in the East) that recognize the need to include in our world view a place for the dimension of the Transcendent. The term I adopt for this dimension is "Boundless Existence." Without thinking of this dimension in conventional theistic terms, I briefly explore the kind of intensified awareness of it available to us—an awareness that is without conceptual bounds or horizons of the sort found in cosmology.

The discussion, in Chapter 7, of the contribution current cosmology makes to an understanding of the status of human life in the cosmos begins with an analysis of the Anthropic Principle. I argue for rejecting an interpretation of this principle in teleologic terms. At the same time, it is shown we need not invoke a philosophy of nihilism that despairs of all search for meaning in life. This search is considered from two angles: (1) the natural conditions of human existence and the goods these make possible, and (2) the contribution of an intensified awareness of the "wholly other" character of Boundless Existence.

Interspersed among the foregoing analytical discussions are accounts of the relevant views of some pre-Socratics and of Spinoza and Wittgenstein.

My book is intended for those readers—whether students, scientists, or the wider class of thoughtful laymen—for whom the efforts at bridging the "two-culture" gap between the language of the technical specialist and the humanist are important and worth making.

In my account of the empirical findings and theories of contemporary cosmology, I have been guided by the classic writings of Einstein, Edwin Hubble, R. C. Tolman, and H. P. Robertson, as well as by the recent contributions of John A. Wheeler, Charles W. Misner, Steven Weinberg, Dennis Sciama, and Stephen Hawking, among others. For their critical comments on reading the manuscript of my book, I am also much indebted to George Gale and an anonymous reader. I also wish to thank Alice Calaprice, Gretchen Oberfranc, and Sanford G. Thatcher of Princeton University Press for their skilled editorial guidance. Finally, I wish to record my gratitude to Marilyn Ehrlich, as well as to my wife, Lenore, and to my sons, Charles and Andrew, for their help and encouragement in bringing the project of writing this book to fruition.

Scarborough, New York
February 1986

COSMIC UNDERSTANDING

ONE

The Search for Cosmic Understanding

COSMOLOGY

Every living creature interacts with its environment, its world, in ways that are appropriate to its capacities, needs, and resources. Every organism seeks to "comprehend" (in some way to take in) its world in the effort to meet its needs. These needs are of different kinds. Some are typical of the species, others idiosyncratic. Some are recurrent and persistent, others transitory and occasional. Put a puppy in a room and it explores that world in order to find out as much as it can, to test experimentally whether its ways of grasping or sensing might give it satisfaction. The interactions of human beings with their world are carried out in more complicated and diverse ways, on different levels, and in different directions. As distinguished from other organisms, a characteristic capacity of human beings for dealing with their world is to use understanding and practical intelligence, and thereby gain more effective control. Here again, the special forms in which this will be achieved will vary widely.

In the above paragraph, the term "world" was used somewhat loosely. Since it can also be given different special senses, let me single out a group of meanings—indeed a subclass of these—that will be of special interest to us in what follows. There is an entire class of metaphorical uses that, once noted, we shall put aside as not relevant to our present concern. Thus the term "world" may

be employed to refer to some special domain of interest or preoccupation. It was this type of use that was involved in my earlier reference to the room in which a puppy is placed as its "world." It is
this metaphorical sense, too, that appears, for example, in such
expressions as "the business world," "the art world," "the com-
puter world," "the world of international affairs," and so on.
When used in this way, a person normally participates in several
different "worlds." Thus there is nothing to prevent someone from
being a participant in "the world of mathematics," "the tennis
world," and "the world of chamber music," among others. However, this metaphoric use of "world," though enjoying widespread
everyday usage, is one I shall largely ignore in the present investigation.

We come closer to our special interest by confining attention to
the use of the expression "world" in astronomical contexts. Here
we find that in ordinary usage the term still enjoys a certain multiplicity of senses, since it is used interchangeably with various distinct, more technical astronomical expressions. For example, the
term "world" may be employed as a name for our planet Earth or
as a designation for any other planet in the solar system. The term
"world" is also sometimes used to refer to a star, or, still more in-
clusively, to a galaxy. Finally, the term "world" may be used to
designate the most comprehensive astronomical system of all—*the
world as a whole*. The preferred technical expression for this most
inclusive astronomical system is *"the universe."* It is this last astronomical meaning of the term "world" with which we shall be principally concerned in this book. So understood, the world (the universe) is the primary subject matter for *cosmology*. The term
"cosmology," as its etymology indicates, is an inquiry into or discourse about the cosmos. Since the expressions "cosmos," "the
universe," and "the world as a whole" are frequently interchanged
in popular astronomical usage, we may define cosmology—in a
preliminary, rough way—as an inquiry into or discourse about the
world as a whole.

One of the characteristic, persistent, and irrepressible needs of
the human mind is to have a cosmology. It consists in the interest

of being able to describe and understand the large-scale, global structure of the universe in which we live. An interest in cosmology, as just briefly described, is to be found in virtually every period and culture of recorded history. When seen in this broad perspective, contemporary scientific cosmology is a very special illustration of this persistent human interest. In one form or another, human beings had sought to satisfy it long before science emerged. Cosmology had been pursued, and for certain cultures is still pursued, under a variety of nonscientific auspices. Men will call upon whatever resources, methods, and faculties they are prepared to rely on in obtaining a satisfactory description of the world. Their acceptance of a cosmological scheme will accordingly vary with the different, often conflicting and rival methods for acquiring and justifying beliefs. Where creative imagination and the power of thought are not exercised in a controlled and critical way, as they are in science, men will fall back on the imaginative appeal of some poetic myth, an unquestioning faith in a sacred religious text, or some purely philosophical scheme of thought.

Contrasted with the foregoing is the method for warranting beliefs held in science. In the case of contemporary scientific cosmology, this method rests on the use of detailed observation, the interpretation of empirical data by theories of physics, and the use of mathematical or other modes of logical reasoning contained in these theories. The task of the cosmologist is to explain relevant astronomical and other empirical data, and in so doing, to give an account of the spatial, temporal, and compositional structure of the universe. He does this by constructing a conceptual system, a model of the universe. It is through the mediation of an accepted cosmological model that he claims to possess an understanding of the universe.

Whether pursued as a scientific discipline or in some other way, the need to have a cosmology, an acceptable picture of the universe, generally derives from two principal motives. One is curiosity, a purely intellectual craving and sense of wonder that prompts the asking of certain questions. To accommodate all the various methods used in obtaining and sanctioning a cosmology

5

mentioned above, we can identify four major types of questions that human beings typically and repeatedly have raised in expressing their curiosity about the world. As ordinarily phrased, they ask: (1) "Did the universe have a beginning, or was it always in existence?" (2) "Is there a spatial limit to the universe, or is it of infinite spatial extent?" (3) "What are the basic materials and major units of which the universe is composed?" (4) "Is there a purpose or design to the universe that would explain both its existence and its various structural features?" These are questions about the temporal, spatial, compositional, and teleologic properties of the universe. Scientific approaches to cosmology have generally confined themselves to the first three types of questions, whereas cosmologies that are based on myth, religion, and some metaphysical speculations have also sought to give answers, of one sort or another, to the teleologic question.

A second motive underlying the search for a satisfying cosmology derives from the human need to "situate" the life of human beings in the universe. We wish to know our "place," where we fit in among all the other entities that make up the universe. What forces, powers, and causes brought us into existence and sustain us? What should be our goals, purposes, and values? Is there some cosmic design of which our lives are a part? Being able to answer these kinds of questions is one way of responding to what is frequently referred to as a search for the meaning of life.

The combination of these two motives—that of sheer curiosity and that of finding the broader cosmic pattern of which our lives are a part and that would contribute to finding a meaning in life— has been the principal sustaining incentive in the pursuit of cosmology. For some individuals, one or another motive may dominate; for example, the curiosity motive may be uppermost for some scientific cosmologists. At the same time, we must also recognize that not all human beings share an interest in cosmology to the same degree—some have only the most fleeting and superficial interest, whereas others may make it their dominant intellectual passion and preoccupation.

When cosmological questions are seen historically or on a large canvas that describes the intellectual life of an entire period or culture, there is also great variability in the amount of attention given to them. In some periods or in the life of some societies, the focus of attention may be so concentrated on more immediate problems of a practical sort—for example, on sheer survival or on economic or political problems—that an interest in the world on a cosmic scale is a remote and unavailable luxury, a luxury for which there is neither time nor energy. Or it may be, too, that when attention is given to it, the account accepted by the group and transmitted to the individual is of a perfunctory and traditional sort. Once learned, the standard account is accepted in an unquestioning spirit. In such periods and for such cultures, cosmology is not among the dominant or active foci of attention or radical change.

However, this is surely not the case at the present time, at least wherever science plays a major role in shaping the thought and beliefs of people. Indeed, along with revolutionary developments in other sciences—for example, particle physics or molecular biology—scientific cosmology has aroused a great amount of interest. Newspapers, books, and other media report to a wide audience the latest discoveries and theories of the cosmologist. The result has been to put scientific cosmology in the forefront of scientific disciplines that have engaged the attention of an increasing number of scientific specialists, at the same time that the fruits of that research, as communicated to a wider public, have aroused great interest and promise. In all of this ferment there is much fascination and a strong sense of anticipation, shared by active participants and interested bystanders alike, in the outcome of ongoing research. One cannot help wonder whether scientists are finally on the verge of solving the grandest riddle of all. Are they within striking distance of laying bare the real structure of the universe? Would not such an achievement be of momentous proportions and have the most profound consequences? There is understandable excitement in keeping abreast of the direction and details of current inquiries in cosmology.

This phenomenon is a relatively recent one. The proliferation and elaboration of various sophisticated models of the universe, based on the results of the most advanced data-gathering instruments and the interpretation of these findings by concepts of the most highly regarded and well-tested theories of mathematical physics, are a striking and important feature of contemporary cosmology. It is a phenomenon that is only several decades old, having begun in 1917 with Einstein's pioneering cosmological investigations, based on the theory of relativity, and with Edwin Hubble's important observational researches in the 1920s into the "realm of the nebulae." Progress ever since has been made possible by the introduction of increasingly more powerful instrumental and conceptual resources.

Optical and radio telescopes have probed the large-scale spatial depths of the universe to enormous distances of billions of light-years.[1] Some radio sources (and possibly also some quasars) are so many billions of light-years away that radiation from them, reaching us only now, has been traveling from a time when the universe was only 10 or 20 percent of its present age. The basic macroscopic units of the universe consist of clusters of galaxies. These range in size from relatively small clusters such as our own Local Group, numbering approximately twenty, and containing our own Milky Way Galaxy, to clusters having thousands of member galaxies. Light takes several million years to traverse a cluster of average dimensions. The largest clusters are 100 million light-years across.

In addition to its spatial properties, another, perhaps even more remarkable feature of the universe, as established by cosmology in our time, is that the universe, when considered from a large-scale temporal point of view, is not unchanging, but shows an underlying pattern of expansion. Already by the late 1920s, confirmation had been given to the idea that the universe is undergoing a systematic expansion. For a brief period, beginning in the late 1940s and continuing into the early 1960s, there was a lively debate between those who favored a steady-state ("continuous creation")

[1] A light-year is the distance that light, traveling at the rate of 300,000 kilometers per second, traverses in a year, or 9.46×10^{12} kilometers—approximately 10 trillion kilometers.

model of the expanding universe and those who argued for an evolutionary conception according to which the universe had a definite origin in the finite past. This debate was eventually settled in favor of the evolutionary conception.

The content of these latest scientific ideas is embodied in various models of an evolutionary expanding universe. One such account is "the standard hot big-bang model" of the expanding universe. It describes the early stages in the career of the universe and the subsequent evolutionary developments of its major constituents. The model incorporates basic concepts of the theory of relativity and other relevant branches of physics. It is supported by much observational evidence. According to this model, the universe had its origin approximately 15 billion years ago. Since then, the universe has already undergone or encompassed a variety of evolutionary and transformational processes—nuclear, atomic, molecular, galactic, stellar, planetary, biological, and human-cultural. It may be expected to undergo still further changes, and will eventually meet its own inevitable death in one form or another in the far off, yet foreseeable future.

The belief that the world as a whole possesses an inherently developmental structure has always exercised a strong imaginative and intellectual appeal. Men have repeatedly been attracted to the thought that if we could somehow establish that the underlying structure of the world consists of a beginning and distinct subsequent stages, then we should have the basic schema at hand for understanding its overall plan. Such a schema would be valued even if not all the details necessary to fill it out were known or perhaps even knowable. The attraction of this type of model in the search for cosmological intelligibility is exhibited from the earliest stages of human culture, where it takes the form of a widely assorted array of primitive myths and religious cosmogonies. It is found, too, in a number of proto-scientific cosmogonies proposed by several pre-Socratic Greek philosophers in the sixth and fifth centuries B.C. What is impressive, exciting, and conducive to the deepest thoughtful consideration is the fact that the same appeal to a developmental or evolutionary cosmology is also given strong support by the most responsible efforts of current scientific cosmology.

THE HUMAN SIGNIFICANCE OF CHANGES IN COSMOLOGY

Because of the great interest in, and significance of, these recent investigations in cosmology, we are faced with a situation that, in its possible widespread impact on our most fundamental human attitudes and beliefs, is comparable to earlier eras in which radical intellectual changes of a general sort were instigated by revolutionary scientific developments. A clear instance of this sort of phenomenon is to be found in the initial shock and later aftermath of the Copernican revolution. This momentous event marked one of the first major stages in the gradual dissolution of the medieval world picture, a way of thought that held sway for more than a thousand years. Let us pause, briefly, to recall some aspects of that earlier upheaval before considering our own present situation.

In shifting from a geocentric to a heliocentric conception of our planetary system, the major dislocation in man's cosmological outlook brought about by the Copernican revolution was initially only spatial in character. The Earth was displaced from its central position in the finite universe. This shift brought with it, however, major repercussions in a variety of directions, not the least of which was man's view of his own place in the entire scheme of things. According to the prevalent medieval world picture, the cosmos was centered on the Earth. Man, created in God's image, was the pinnacle of creation. He was placed on the Earth so that he may use all that it contains to work out his salvation and thereby fulfill God's providential and benevolent design. However, with the demotion of the Earth from its hitherto central astronomical position in the cosmos, doubts began to creep in about man's claim to a uniquely privileged status and role. In the ensuing centuries, this spatial reorientation forced a number of other modifications and encouraged the fashioning of new ways of thinking on a variety of fronts. Taken together, these changes brought about the eventual overthrow of some of the main pillars of the hitherto dominant medieval cosmology.

The main features of that cosmology consisted of three strands: Biblical cosmogony, Aristotelian physics, and Ptolemaic astronomy. Thus in Aquinas and Dante, as major spokesmen for the medieval outlook, we find each of these components.

The first strand in medieval cosmology, Biblical cosmogony, articulated the central theistic belief that God, as a transcendent, immaterial, eternal, and perfect Being, created *ex nihilo* the world and all that it contains. Much of traditional theology took the words of Genesis literally. It accepted as an article of faith the account there given of the act of Divine Creation of the world. The Creation was a unique event that took place in the finite past, an event of transcendent mystery. It linked the infinite omnipotence and goodness of God with the contingent existence of the world and all that it contains. For medieval man, various types of entities were thought of as manifesting different gradations and as occupying different locations in the great "chain of being." The chain stretched from the lowest, innermost circles of Hell, through the intermediate domain of man's temporary abode in an earthly vestibule between two eternities, to the highest zones of Heaven where dwell the blessed immortal souls of men, the angels, and the Infinite Mind of God.

The second strand in medieval cosmology, Aristotelian physics, involved a radical distinction between terrestrial and celestial physics. In order to describe the astronomic, cosmologic, and other physical details of the world as created, medieval theology fused, as best it could, the account of Genesis with the inherited dogmas of Aristotelianism and Ptolemaic astronomy. Terrestrial phenomena (those "below the sphere of the Moon") were constituted of, and depended on the distinctive properties and interrelations of, the four basic elements—earth, water, air, and fire. By contrast, celestial phenomena required an understanding only of the quintessential ethereal element, out of which all the perfect, unchanging heavenly bodies were thought to be composed.

The third pillar of medieval cosmology consisted of the paradigm that the various heavenly bodies (Sun, Moon, planets, and fixed stars) revolved around the fixed, central Earth. The geometric and kinematic patterns of their individually distinct motions were to be constructed out of circles in various combinations and patterns—deferents, equants, epicycles, and eccentrics.

All of this doctrine had been worked out in elaborate and polished detail. It was part of the common, inherited, and unquestioned intellectual and religious world picture of medieval man. To disturb even the purely astronomic and cosmologic framework of this world picture was to threaten the viability and coherence of the entire scheme. It could not be tolerated, and for a long time it was not. It suffices to remember the "crime" of Galileo in subscribing to the Copernican astronomy, and how it was the source of his condemnation by the Church. It is a historically clear and important example of how serious an offense it was for science to challenge traditional beliefs.

The principal immediate change intended and brought about by Copernicus, in his great work *De Revolutionibus Orbium Caelestium* (1543), affected only the geocentricity component in the Ptolemaic strand of medieval cosmology. He himself left intact not only the conception of a finite universe bounded by the sphere of the fixed stars and a commitment to the fundamental beliefs of theism, but also the exclusive reliance on a combination of circles to describe the orbits of the Earth, Moon, and planets. The abandonment of this last requirement was eventually accomplished by Kepler's proof that the planets move in elliptical orbits. The whole subsequent history of astronomy, down to the present day, achieved a wide-ranging enrichment and reorientation in our conception of the major astronomic components of the universe. In the next several centuries, attention shifted from a concentration on the problems of planetary astronomy to the details of stellar, and more recently of galactic astronomy.

Alongside these changes in observational astronomy, there had developed, already by the seventeenth century, a radical shift in scientists' conception of the scope of physical laws. As Descartes had argued, and as Newton and all subsequent scientists came to believe, abandonment of the dualistic qualitative physics of Aristotle and the medievals calls for a conception of physical laws that are universal in scope, whether the instances of these laws are found on the Earth or anywhere else in the universe. Physics achieved a unification in its understanding of physical phenomena by postulating that the same laws hold throughout the universe.

Since the days of Copernicus, various revisions in the purely scientific parts of the medieval world picture, to bring them in line with the advances of science over the centuries, have been incorporated in more sophisticated theologies. At the same time, the cardinal belief in God's existence as the transcendent Creator of the world (the component previously labeled "Biblical cosmogony") has remained, for many, a necessary principle in any acceptable world view.

If, now, we turn to the main features of modern scientific cosmology, as it is focused on the model of an expanding evolutionary universe, the impact on our general outlook is likely to be as great as that brought about by the Copernican revolution. While the initial center of disturbance introduced by the latter was essentially *spatial* in character, the fresh challenge to accustomed ways of thinking presented by recent cosmology is primarily *temporal* in its bearing.

As each of us knows only too well, our own individual life is bounded by its birth and death. Not only is temporal boundedness true of each human life, but it is true as well, and more widely, of any entity, living or otherwise, that comes into existence at a certain time, undergoes its generic as well as distinctively individual interactions and processes, and either has already gone out of existence or may be expected to do so. Temporal boundedness holds for individual galaxies, stars, molecular aggregations, living organisms, artefacts, and political or social groupings. Familiar examples of temporally bound entities are thus to be found everywhere *within* the universe and within the range of everyday experience. According to evolutionary cosmology, however, we must widen the scope of examples of temporal boundedness still further, indeed as widely as possible. For *the universe as a whole also had a beginning, pursues its own career, and will eventually come to an end.* The absorption and assessment of the wide-ranging implications of this last claim is one of the major challenges of recent investigations in scientific cosmology.

No more than with other intellectual upheavals brought about by science—for example, the Copernican or Darwinian revolutions—will the many consequences of the recent findings of evolutionary cosmology be sensed and made explicit all at once. The process of intellectual assimilation and digestion takes time. It works slowly yet inexorably. It calls for reflective analysis, a cooperative undertaking by different persons and specialists, working on different levels and in different directions. One of my purposes in the following pages, in surveying some of the main findings of contemporary cosmology, is to set the stage for raising some of the broader philosophical questions provoked by these developments, and to invite the reader to explore with me some possible replies to these difficult yet important questions.

Let us consider some examples of the sorts of questions that call for examination in an effort to meet this challenge.

The expression "the universe" is used on countless occasions and in combination with a great variety of other expressions throughout the literature of cosmology. This is to be expected, since cosmology has the universe as its subject matter: it is *about* the universe. While we may be inclined to take this for granted as a commonplace and noncontroversial starting point, nevertheless the use of the expression "the universe" calls for explicit analysis. It is by no means the case that all who use this expression understand it in the same way. To sort out some of its several uses turns out (not unexpectedly) to be of central importance in gauging the scope and possible achievements of cosmology.

To see the sort of thing I have in mind, let us focus on the use of the term "the universe" as ostensibly referring to an entity to which the properties of having a development, and in particular of having a beginning and end, are assigned. Consider the expressions "the beginning (or origin) of the universe," "the beginning of time," and "the end of the universe," as these are typically and frequently used in expositions of current evolutionary models of the expanding universe. How shall we understand these expressions? Are we clear about the meanings of the terms "beginning" and "end" as applied to the universe? What does it *mean* to say that the universe came into existence so-and-so many years ago, or that it will end at such-and-such a time in the future? What are the similarities in, or differences between, the use of these expressions as applied to the universe and the way these expressions are used in connection with other entities? In what respects is the universe similar to or different from other entities to which these descriptions are applicable? For example, is the universe at all like an organism or a star? The biologist describes the typical stages in the development of an amoeba or a whale from its earliest beginnings as a distinct individual to its death. The astronomer describes how a star emerges from a diffuse gaseous state, undergoes intermediate stages of transformation, and—depending on the type being described—comes to its end as a neutron star, black hole, supernova, or in some other way. Is the universe, too, an individual object like a living organism or a star? If we think of the universe as in some sense an individual, does this require—as in other standard applications of the notion of what it is to be an individual—that we be able to identify it against a background of other comparable cosmic entities? In the case of the universe, what sense can we make of this requirement? If one describes *this* universe as having had an origin and eventually an end, is this to be understood as allowing the possibility of there being *other* universes? If so, what does this mean?

Among other topics raised by these questions concerning the beginning and end of the universe are those which recall familiar metaphysical issues having to do with a belief in God, and the way in which such metaphysical concepts as Being, Reality, or Existence are related to the conception of the universe as a physical system. For example, in using the expressions "beginning of the universe" and "end of the universe," are we obliged to invoke the concept of "absolute nothing"? Does it follow that if the universe had an origin, it was "preceded" in some sense by Absolute Nothing? And if, similarly, the universe is to come to an end, does this also mean that it will be "succeeded" by Absolute Nothing? If not, what alternatives are there that would make sense of the claim that the universe did have a beginning and will have an end?

Another way of phrasing our central question highlights the broader notion of *intelligibility*. Through its models and theories, cosmology undertakes to make the universe intelligible by describing its overall structure. The evolutionary model is an example of how such intelligibility can be articulated. On what does the achievement of such intelligibility depend? Is the universe an independently existing entity, one that—antecedently to all inquiry—possesses a unique structure that awaits discovery and disclosure? What justifies this belief? How is it to be reconciled with the claim that all conceptual activity, including all science, represents a constructive contribution to the knowledge process, and that without this humanly creative contribution it makes no sense to say there is an independent, antecedently existing structure to be discovered? Shall we say, then, that man's creative conceptual powers *confer* intelligibility on the universe? If the latter, what is the universe "in itself," if—as we seem driven to presuppose—it is different from our humanly constructed models and theories? What is the connection between an accepted model of the universe and the subject matter to which that model is addressed? In what does *truth* about the universe consist? Does it consist in some form of *correspondence* between our thought and what exists apart from human language and inquiry?

Analysis of the concept of cosmic intelligibility also raises the question of determining the actual or possible *cognitive limits* in the search for intelligibility. This is the question of conceptual horizons. What kinds of limits or horizons are there to the human ambition to *understand* the universe? In what do these consist? What forms do they take? Are any of them flexible and surmountable? Are any fixed and irremovable so that even science cannot transcend them? For example, how are the concepts of "the beginning" and "the end" of the universe, related to possible limits to human knowledge? In ascribing a beginning and end to the universe is science confronting a permanent inability to discover anything "beyond"? Or is it the case that even if there are certain limits to knowledge, these are only temporary halting places? If they are only provisional barriers, encountered because of some insufficiency in available resources of physical theory or technological limitations of instrumentation, is it not reasonable to expect that, with further progress of science, these limits will be overcome and moved back? If so, is it not being prematurely dogmatic to suppose that science will never be able to get beyond what some theory calls the "beginning" or the "end" of the universe?

The questions I have posed—about the use of the expression "the universe," about intelligibility in the domain of cosmology, and about the kind of limits that confront the actual or possible realization of understanding in cosmology—are central to any philosophical interest in the scope of cosmology. They cannot be settled by reviewing the observational data, mathematical calculations, or physical theory used in support of this or that particular cosmological model. Cosmologists might enjoy a fair degree of consensus about these matters, communicate readily with one another by means of a shared technical vocabulary, and agree on a set of methodological criteria for judging the relative merits of competing models, and yet have divergent philosophic views on how to "interpret" the general significance of the scope or results of their inquiries.

One of the principal sustaining motivations in the pursuit of cosmology down the ages has been man's need to situate himself in the cosmos. In addition to understanding the physical, chemical, astronomic, and biological causes and conditions of human existence, men hanker for something more than simply a knowledge of these facts—they seek in some way to come to terms with them. Men look for the kind of wisdom, insight, and enlightenment that would help toward assessing their finitude and mortality. If the conceptual questions enumerated above can be collected and subsumed under the general heading of determining the *cognitive limits* of scientific cosmology, then the existential questions we are now pointing to can be subsumed under the heading of understanding the *limits of the human condition* in the light of what cosmology discloses about the nature of the universe.

Clearly, the belief that the universe had an assignable origin, moreover that, by virtue of its special initial conditions, the stage was set for subsequent developments of an atomic, molecular, astronomic, biological, and human sort, and that the universe will eventually meet its own death—all these claims, if sustained, would impinge directly on how we are to think of the origin and fate of mankind's existence. On a more personal level, it would permeate the way in which each of us might come to think of the possible values to be sought for and found in our individual lives. All of this would determine in the most intimate and profound way how we regard the actual or possible accomplishments of our collective and individual existence, and thereby the values or meaning of life. It would make us more deeply aware of what it means to refer to "the gift of life." It would help us, too, to come to terms with the inevitable death of mankind, the death of any other conscious beings there may be in other corners of the universe, and with our own personal death, when all of these are seen in the light of the origin and eventual death of the universe itself.

Thus far I have been stressing two main motivations in the study of cosmology—that which stems from a need to satisfy an intellectual curiosity (or sense of wonder) about the widest framework for understanding all that exists physically, and that which stems from an interest to "situate" ourselves as human beings among other entities within the world. There is, however, a third motive that not only encompasses the foregoing but is perhaps the most fundamental of all. It is what gives primary impetus to the study undertaken in this book. We may use the term "ontological" as a convenient label to mark this type of interest. Briefly stated, what it stands for is a primarily philosophic interest in having some reasonably clear grasp of how we are to understand such expressions as "reality," "existence," or "being." Every world view contains, explicitly or implicitly, some ontology—some conception of what it regards as the fundamental levels, kinds, categories, types, degrees, or modes of that which exists or has being.

Given the gradual erosion of a theistic world view in the modern era and the emergence of science as the primary seat of intellectual authority for an increasingly large segment of the population (along with an increasingly secular and naturalistic world view this inspires), we are led inevitably to raise the following question. In studying the properties of the universe and obtaining the best available account of it by science, are we not at the same time learning all there is to be known about existence? Are not the latest fruits of cosmology and subsidiary empirical sciences all that one needs to satisfy the quest for an ontology? Is not the universe, as described and understood in the most satisfactory scientific terms, the ultimate reality?

It will be one of the purposes of my investigation to show the shortcomings of this suggestion. Without reverting to one or another form of theism, I shall explore a dimension of existence—to be labeled "Boundless Existence"—that transcends the existence of the universe, an awareness of which is essential (so I shall maintain) for any sound ontology. While there are many routes to such an awareness, that which follows the cosmological route is perhaps one of the most rewarding.

By studying the materials of contemporary scientific cosmology, a principal goal of the present inquiry is accordingly to come within sight of the main outlines of an ontology (a world view) in which we can discern the principal lines of differentiation and interconnection among three crucial ontological dimensions of existence—namely, the universe as existent, human existence, and Boundless Existence.

TWO

Cosmology at the Dawn
of Western Thought

Before turning to an exploration of the central themes and questions arising out of the recent developments in cosmology, I propose to pause in order to examine a major example of the many-
sided pursuit of cosmology in an earlier epoch. This will take us
back to the very dawn of Western thought in ancient Greece of the
sixth and fifth centuries B.C. At that stage of history, science and
philosophy were not yet distinguished as separate disciplines or
types of inquiry. They existed in an undifferentiated matrix of curiosity, shrewd insight, and bold speculation that marked the
thought of the *physikoi*—students of Nature—whose observations,
explanations, arguments, and comprehensive visionary schemes
sought to encompass the whole range of natural phenomena.

Three of the most prominent, interesting, and influential rep-
resentatives of this period of pre-Socratic thought are Anaximander, Heraclitus, and Parmenides. Although, as we shall see, there
are important differences among them, they formed a relatively
homogeneous group. They based their individual schemes of
thought on certain shared premises and on a common orientation.
From that vantage point, they illuminate different aspects of man's
knowledge of, and situation in, the cosmos. Our return to the
thought of these thinkers is no mere act of piety nor an indulgence
of historical curiosity about the beliefs of our earliest intellectual
ancestors. In examining their writings, we intend neither to partic-
ipate in the work of textual scholarship nor to give a detailed ac-

count of all aspects of their thought. Rather, we shall recall what they said because their views at the interface between cosmology and philosophy have the unmistakable qualities of freshness, simplicity, and wisdom in a degree that assures them of abiding interest and importance.

Obviously, their reflections were not aroused by or directed toward the issues arising from present-day cosmologic theories. Nevertheless, the issues and options considered by this group of intellectual pioneers, and the conclusions they arrived at, have fascinating resonances with some of the topics we shall ourselves want to explore in this book. Their insights, speculations, and arguments merit careful scrutiny for the possible relevance and applicability to our own fund of questions.

Because there is a certain community and overlap of interest and doctrine among these thinkers, for all their differences in voice and approach, I shall select from the range of topics associated with each only some major ideas for special attention and analysis. Thus in Anaximander we shall find stated for the first time the very idea of an orderly universe, a world operating according to discoverable laws—in short, a cosmos. Anaximander also has some interesting things to say about the relation of the cosmos to what he calls *Apeiron*, the Boundless. Next, we shall turn to Heraclitus to learn something of the importance, as he sees it, for any enlightened human being to listen to the *logos*, and thereby have the kind of cosmic vision that saves a person's life from pettiness and narrowness. Finally, in the magisterial yet carefully reasoned arguments of Parmenides we shall find the principles and distinctions we do well to bear in mind in venturing on any discussion of Being and Nothing.

Anaximander: Discovering the Cosmos

Anaximander is the first and most important of the Milesian thinkers of the sixth century B.C. who entered upon an inquiry into Nature. That inquiry left behind an appeal to the mythic and anthropomorphic categories that dominated earlier thought. It relied instead on concepts and methods of reasoning that bear some obvious resemblance to, and continuity with, later developments in science and critical philosophy. Although only the barest hints remain of his teachings, enough survives and is reasonably well authenticated to allow some partial reconstruction of his thought. He can be credited with having arrived at a number of important pathbreaking insights and bold hypotheses in astronomy, meteorology, and the explanation of the emergence of life.

Let one example of this innovative substitution of naturalistic and scientific explanations for older mythic and anthropomorphic explanations suffice for our present purpose. Consider, for example, how, according to traditional Greek religion, one could explain the occurrence of thunderbolts. They were regarded as being the willful acts of Zeus, the lord of the sky, the cloud gatherer, the all-powerful weather god. To accomplish his purposes on a particular occasion, to express his displeasure and punishment, Zeus would hurl his thunderbolts at his targets. However dramatically or "morally" satisfying this type of account may have been thought to be, any attempt to explain or predict the occurrence of a thunderbolt, guided by such a scheme of thought, cannot be scientific. It does not rest on having discovered some lawful regularity in natural phenomena, operating causally and independently of a god's volitional agency. It is precisely this latter sort of naturalistic explanation, however, that is offered by Anaximander. According to one doxographical source, Anaximander gave the following explanation of thunderbolts:

> Concerning thunder, lightning, thunderbolt, fire-winds(?), whirlwinds: All these arise from wind. For, when it is enclosed in a thick cloud and bursts out violently because of its lightness and the fineness of its parts, then the tearing of the cloud produces the noise, the dilatation [or explosion] causes the flash, by contrast with the darkness of the cloud. [1]

[1] Quoted in Charles H. Kahn, *Anaximander and the Origins of Greek Cosmology* (New York: Columbia University Press, 1960), 100.

What is of interest, of course, in the foregoing explanation is not its truth or acceptability as judged by present-day scientific notions, but the fact that it is an exercise in scientific explanation at all. Gone are Zeus and an appeal to his willful, capricious acts. In its place we have the workings of clouds, the relative densities, compressions, and dilations of materials, and the way these interact with one another according to some rationally intelligible principle.

It is not, however, with the details of Anaximander's views in astronomy, meteorology, or biology that we shall hereinafter be concerned. Those details have long since either been entirely scrapped or, where suggestive and on the right track, have been enormously amplified and supported by the rich, sophisticated methods and resources of modern science. What is of permanent and continuing interest are some of the general ideas that Anaximander stressed in his approach to the questions of cosmology. That approach presupposes and rests upon the kind of scientific theorizing we have seen illustrated in Anaximander's explanation of thunderbolts.

Anaximander's cosmological ideas are summarized in a passage from Simplicius, an ancient doxographer, who includes what is apparently the only direct quotation from the otherwise lost writings of Anaximander. It is a quotation that points to a central theme in Anaximander's cosmology. Here is the passage:

Anaximander . . . declared the Boundless to be principle and element of existing things, having been the first to introduce this very term of "principle"; he says that "it is neither water nor any other of the so-called elements, but some different, boundless nature, from which all the heavens arise and the *kosmoi* within them; out of those things whence is the generation for existing things, into these again does their destruction take place, according to what must needs be; for they make amends and give reparation to one another for their offense, according to the ordinance of time," speaking of them thus in rather poetical terms. It is clear that, having observed the change of the four elements into one another, he did not think fit to make any one of these the material substratum, but something else besides these.[2]

When undertaking to make sense of a passage such as the foregoing and to derive from it some understanding of the outlines, at least, of Anaximander's cosmology, we are in a position not altogether unlike that of an archaeologist who, having found the mutilated, fragmentary jawbone of an extinct prehistoric animal, attempts to infer and reconstruct the entire body and mode of life of that animal. It is obviously an undertaking filled with much conjecture and allowing for rival interpretations. Despite these difficulties and risks, but with the best available scholarship as our guide, we may offer the following summary of Anaximander's cosmology.

At the heart of that cosmology is the very concept of a cosmos. The adaptation of the word *kosmos*—which for the Greeks in its ordinary usage signified a well-ordered arrangement—to apply to the world as a whole is a philosophic innovation that makes its appearance in sixth-century B.C. Milesian thought. It cannot be credited with assurance to any one thinker. As we may conjecture, for Anaximander it signified the orderly arrangement of the world when that arrangement is regarded both from a spatial point of view and with regard to the processes of change and transformation that belong to celestial, meteorological, and biological phenomena within the finite bounds of the heavens.

Insofar as we can reconstruct Anaximander's astronomical views, we can say that, in common with age-old beliefs resting on ordinary observational experience, he accepted the view of the world as spatially finite. Rather than believing, however, that the sky and its various heavenly bodies form a flat, rooflike structure over the Earth, Anaximander conceived the outer bounds of the world to be spherical, with the Earth freely suspended at its center. According to him, the Sun, Moon, and stars performed their cy-

---

[2] Based on the lost work of Theophrastus, *The Opinions of the Natural Philosophers (Physikon Doxai)*, fragment 2, in H. Diels, *Doxagraphi Graeci* (Berlin, 1879), 476; Kahn, *Anaximander*, 166.

clically regular, circular patterns of motion around the central fixed Earth. He took the Earth to have the stubby cylindrical shape of a drum, on one of whose flat surfaces we live. He also had the quaint view that the stars are closer to the Earth than the Sun and Moon. And he regarded the Sun, Moon, and stars to be not distinct bodies, but the impressions we obtain from looking through small apertures in surrounding rings of fire, as these exist at different distances from the Earth. Within this spherically bounded astronomical world, the main regions of the visible world—the fixed central Earth, terrestrial water, and the "air" that stretches from the Earth to the fiery circles of the Sun and stars—are situated.

Of equal importance with the spatial orderliness of the world is Anaximander's recognition of the broad temporal patterns of change and transformation that pervade the world on all its levels. The daily rounds of the Sun, the phases of the Moon, the rising and setting of the stars, the changes of the seasons, the birth, growth, and death of all living things—all the common facts of everyday experience—are incorporated in Anaximander's way of thinking as aspects of an underlying periodic cyclic balancing among the elemental powers of Nature. These powers, qualities, and forces are the Hot and the Cold, the Dry and the Wet, the Bright and the Dark. Their operations are illustrated in all types of natural phenomena: the changes of day and night, the rising of the mist, the drying of the land under the action of the Sun, drought and rainfall, the condensing of the rain cloud, and so on.

All exhibit the unceasing passage of one elemental power into another, "aggressing" into the province or domain of the other, yet forced eventually "according to the ordinance of Time" to make "reparation" for its "injustice" and pay the "penalty" for its aggression. As a result, it is invaded by its "opponent." Of course, the counteracting new invasion will in turn be "punished." When seen in broad perspective, the general outcome is the preservation of a periodic, renewable harmony or balance of Nature. During its lifetime, the cosmos is the scene of these unending cycles of ascendencies and declines, aggressions and counter-aggressions. It exhibits a ceaseless series of processes "on the way up" and "the way down."

I have used the phrase "the lifetime of the cosmos," and here we venture, with much uncertainty, on another aspect of Anaximander's cosmology. For it would be wholly consistent with the general character of his view of the cosmos to think of it as having an origin and a death. We have no secure evidence of how Anaximander conceived the process of cosmogony, the birth of the cosmos. There is simply his remark that "Something capable of generating Hot and Cold was separated off from the eternal [Boundless] in the formation of this world, and a sphere of fire from this source grew around the air about the earth like bark around a tree. When this sphere was torn off and closed up into certain circles, the sun and moon and stars came into being."[3]

As we know from the passage quoted earlier, Anaximander sharply distinguished the elemental powers operating in the cosmos (the primary Hot and Cold, the Wet and the Dry, etc.) from the Boundless. The Boundless is not one of the elemental powers. It is the unlimited, inexhaustible, permanent source from which the powers that belong to the cosmos are derived. All particular differentiated objects and phenomena result from the interactions and mixture of these elemental powers and qualities. At the death of the cosmos, both the fundamental elemental powers and all that is composed of them will cease to exist. The elemental powers underlying all phenomena will eventually return to the Boundless.

However, the Boundless—unlike the mortal cosmos—is immortal. It is not to be pictured as a god, although it is divine, for the mark of divinity is immortality. The Boundless that "encompasses" the cosmos is not to be taken as quantitatively infinite in spatial extent. It consists, rather, of that which has no geometrical shape, is qualitatively indeterminate, though it is the inexhaustible, eternal source of all that does have shape, quality, or form. The manner in which the Boundless gives birth to the cosmos—

[3] Kahn, *Anaximander*, 85.

how the process of initial "separation" takes place—is unknown to us. Anaximander offers no hypothesis to explain the power of the Boundless to generate a cosmos.

Though we have no strong textually secure ground for our next conjecture, it is a reasonable supposition that Anaximander subscribed to the doctrine of a plurality of worlds or *kosmoi*. For the Boundless, he may have believed, gives birth not only to our cosmos, but to others. We know that a number of pre-Socratic thinkers in the sixth and fifth centuries B.C. entertained this idea of a plurality of worlds, of *kosmoi*. Some thought of this plurality as exhibiting a sequential pattern, one cosmos at its birth succeeding the death of an earlier cosmos, and so on. Others regarded the plurality as not only sequential, but as allowing for the coexistence of many distinct finite worlds. If Anaximander himself subscribed to any of these views, he could be credited with anticipating a type of cosmological speculation that has obvious continuity with some proposals in recent cosmology.

Anaximander's tantalizingly brief yet suggestive appeal to the notions of cosmos and the Boundless (*Apeiron*) are central to cosmology. An examination of these concepts is relevant to the pursuit of cosmology wherever undertaken. For example, it is not too farfetched to see in the use made by contemporary cosmology of the ideas of elementary particle physics, in understanding the big bang origin of the universe, some family resemblance with Anaximander's notion of the Boundless. For some of these recent theories describe a pre-existent vacuum out of which the elementary particles are created that eventually form the matter and energy of the universe. Does this suggest that physics must inevitably fall back on some notion of an original indeterminate source to generate a structured cosmos? And is the concept of a process of coming into existence (what Anaximander called "separation") an idea that cosmology must appeal to? Is the process of creation out of a Boundless one that cosmology needs in order to make sense of the notion of a cosmos?

Heraclitus: Spokesman for Logos

Heraclitus, a native of Ephesus on the coast of Asia Minor, was in his prime at the beginning of the fifth century B.C. He thus belongs to the same general period in which the early Milesian cosmologists had taken their first steps and pointed the way to a scientific study of Nature. The fragmentary remains of Heraclitus's work suggest that he, too, was deeply interested in the main ideas of the leading Milesian philosophers and their proposals for obtaining a comprehensive theory of the cosmos and its varied processes. It is unlikely, however, that he himself took part as an active investigator in these many-sided scientific inquiries. The importance of Heraclitus lies elsewhere. His aphoristic, frequently enigmatic, yet carefully fashioned prose discloses another side to his role in the history of cosmology. If Anaximander was the prototype of the bold, creative scientist and cosmologist, then Heraclitus was the philosopher of the newer ways of thought for whom the existential overtones and bearings of the study of cosmology were of fundamental significance. The general tone of his work shows him to be primarily gripped by the importance of the new cosmologies in making possible the attainment of a basic wisdom about the status of human life in the cosmos. He was convinced they offered a new perspective that deserved to replace the older religious beliefs and myths. The new conceptions of the cosmos were pregnant with the intellectual and spiritual means for coming to terms with the limits of our human existence.

In conveying this fresh understanding and wisdom, his manner was that of a seer, an aloof and somewhat sardonic commentator. His primary interest was to rouse his fellow human beings to the importance of listening to *logos*—the rational and true account of the nature of things. It is the possession of this cosmic vision, of seeing beyond the relatively narrow range of one's daily preoccupations, that most people lack. And yet only if people have this vision and understanding can they be liberated from narrowness and blindness.

As is the case with the other pre-Socratic philosophers, all that remain of Heraclitus's writings are some fragmentary quotations and reports by ancient doxographers. Compounding this problem is the fact that Heraclitus framed his thought in an unusually compressed style, where words sometimes deliberately bear multiple senses and subtle, hidden allusions. It is no surprise, therefore, that he has the reputation of being obscure and enigmatic. Yet, as is often the case with those whose rich and many-layered thought is conveyed in this way, once the process of extraction, sifting, and analysis has done its work, what emerges justifies the expended effort.[4] In what follows, I shall select for special attention Heraclitus's treatment of the notion of *logos* and the illumination he claims it yields for recognizing, at its deepest level, the underlying unity of the life of the cosmos and human life.

Heraclitus's use of the term *logos* is a good example of the need to look for more than its ordinary, surface meaning. This is shown in the following group of statements, which may serve as a general introduction to his thought.

> Although this account (*logos*) holds forever, men ever fail to comprehend, both before hearing it and once they have heard (or "when they hear it for the first time"). Although all things come to pass in accordance with this account (*logos*), men are like the untried when they try such words and works as I set forth, distinguishing each according to its nature (*physis*) and telling how it is. But other men are oblivious of what they do awake, just as they are forgetful of what they do asleep. Not comprehending, they hear like the deaf. The saying bears witness to them: absent while present. Although the account (*logos*) is shared, most men live as though their thinking (*phronēsis*) were a private possession. Most men do not think things in the way that they encounter them, nor do they recognize what they experience, but believe their own opinions.[5]

---

[4] My account has benefited greatly from Charles H. Kahn's *The Art and Thought of Heraclitus* (New York: Cambridge University Press, 1979). All quotations are from this translation.

[5] Kahn, *Heraclitus*, I-IV.

In the very first sentence of the above, we meet with an apparent paradox in Heraclitus's use of the term *logos*. For on the one hand he uses it to refer to his own account, something that is obviously both personal and formulated at a certain time. Yet in the very next breath he describes this account as at once holding forever, and as that which men fail to understand even *before* hearing it! If this claim is not to be rejected as wholly incoherent, it is obvious that the term *logos* must have two distinct, even if related, meanings. In one of these meanings, Heraclitus uses the term *logos* in a standard way: it designates the use of language or speech. The account he is referring to is his own, one that he has formulated and is prepared to communicate. It is an account, to be sure, that Heraclitus would recommend men heed. He prizes it for its truth (its telling of how things are) and for its wisdom. Clearly, however, until Heraclitus communicates this account, no one can be blamed for not having listened, understood, or recognized its merits. Obviously, the only way of rendering the passage coherent is to recognize that Heraclitus is using the term *logos* in an additional sense. He is using it, in other words, to refer to something that is independent of any account—his or anyone else's. In short, the term *logos* must also be understood to refer to some independent, inherently objective state of affairs, some fact about the world itself, whether or not men recognize it and state it. In this latter sense, the *logos* is the rationally intelligible structure of the world: what *can* be understood but is not normally expressed or made explicit. For example, if men other than Heraclitus had discovered the objective truth, they could have known the *logos* even before Heraclitus's own account was given to them, since it was always "there" in the nature of things, awaiting discovery by whoever had enough wisdom and insight.

With a tone of both sadness and contempt, Heraclitus notes that most men are normally oblivious of this objective and eternal *logos*. In all likelihood they would even ignore or totally misunderstand what he, Heraclitus, is prepared to tell them. For most men's lives are spent in a kind of benighted ignorance and private dream world. They are constantly preoccupied with their own affairs, confident of their own opinions on this, that, or the other matter, but never lifting their minds to become aware of the *logos* of the world. Only if a person could awake to this knowledge could he be said to live in the real world—the world that is common to all enlightened men. For such men use reason (*nous*) and intelligence (*phronēsis*).

With the foregoing analysis of the double meaning of the term *logos*, we are able to grasp a fundamental theme in the thought of Heraclitus. That theme can be summed up as follows: When fully and properly employed, man's reason tells of things as they are. In one sense, *logos* is a rational telling, the giving of a true and wise account. At the same time, that *of* which the account is given is not itself a telling. It is, rather, the inherent, objective, intelligible structure of the world. It is the *logos* of things themselves. When the two meet and coalesce, there is a unity, a matching of language and subject matter. It is with *logos* in this full, double sense that Heraclitus is concerned.

We must now consider what, according to Heraclitus, is the content of the *logos*, the basic message it has for one who is enlightened. To search for this content is, for Heraclitus, the most important thing a person can do. Nor, despite the fact that all ordinary experience puts us in contact with the world, is this a guarantee that as a result one becomes aware of its underlying *logos*. Indeed, finding the *logos* is a matter of the greatest difficulty and demands the most persistent effort. It does not lie on the surface, accessible to everyone. Heraclitus puts this at one point by saying "I went in search of myself." Taken in one way, this seems incredibly naive, for what more obvious and easily accessible entity is there than one's self? What need is there to *search* for one's self? Of course, the self that Heraclitus would search for is that which comes with true self-knowledge, after much probing. "You will not find the limits of the soul (*psyche*)," he tells us, "by going, even if you travel over every way, so deep is its report (*logos*)." To have this self-knowledge requires seeing the relation of the self to the *logos* of the world.

Nor is this *logos* easily recognized. Like the Delphic oracle, Nature "neither declares nor conceals but gives a sign. . . . Nature loves to hide." There is a useful analogy that can be employed here in making clear Heraclitus's poetic way of expressing himself. Nature may be compared to someone who speaks (or writes) a language unfamiliar to us, or, if the language is familiar, someone whose deeper meanings and intentions are not available in the ordinary way. We hear the sounds or see the signs, but cannot make out what they say. It takes someone like Heraclitus, who thinks of himself as a spokesman (*prophētēs*) for the *logos*, to decipher and interpret what is said. What then, we ask Heraclitus, *is* being "said"? When pieced together, here are some of the answers Heraclitus gives, in words attributed to him:

It is wise, listening not to me but to the report (*logos*), to agree ⟨and say⟩ that all things are one. The ordering (*kosmos*), the same for all, no god nor man has made, but it ever was and is and will be: fire everliving, kindled in measures and in measures going out. All things are requital for fire, and fire for all things, as goods for gold and gold for goods. As they step into the same rivers, other and still other waters flow upon them. The name of the bow is life; its work is death. One must realize that war is shared and Conflict is Justice, and that all things come to pass (and are ordained?) in accordance with conflict. War is father of all and king of all; and some he has shown as gods, others men; some he has made slaves, others free. Death is all things we see awake; all we see asleep is sleep. Immortals ⟨are⟩ mortal, mortals immortal, living the others' death, dead in the others' life. The same . . . : living and dead, and the waking and the sleeping, and young and old. For these transposed are those, and those transposed again are these. The way up and down is one and the same.[6]

One important key to understanding statements such as the foregoing is to see them as connected with the main thrust of Milesian

---

[6] Kahn, *Heraclitus*, XXXVI, XXXVII, XL, L, LXXIX, LXXXII, LXXXIII, LXXXIX, XCII, XCIII, CIII.

cosmologies of the sort we encountered in Anaximander's pioneering views. For Heraclitus, as for Anaximander, the cosmos is an order, spread out in space and time, of natural forces, powers, and qualities engaged in ceaseless interactions. These interactions take the form of "aggressions" and "counter-aggressions." The world is the scene of a constant "war" in which no permanent victor emerges, but in the course of which, instead, a "harmony" or "justice" eventually prevails throughout various transformations. Unlike Parmenides, who focused in his ontology on the sheer fact of Being (*eon*) manifested by the cosmos, Heraclitus dwelled on the ever-present fact of *change* in the cosmos. He meditated on this omnipresent fact to the point where for him it was the basic *logos* of the cosmos. Unless one lets this fundamental fact seep into, permeate, and dominate one's consciousness, he claims, one cannot be said to understand the world. In one sense, of course, everyone to some extent has this awareness. For Heraclitus, however, we require more than an occasional or superficial awareness. If the term "obsession" is not too strong a word, one could say that Heraclitus was obsessed with this awareness. For him it marks the underlying order and unity of the world. Only from constantly being alert to this fact does genuine wisdom—a compound of understanding, resignation, and peace of mind—arise.

That all things manifest flux, change, transformation, coming-into-existence and going-out-of-existence is symbolized by Heraclitus's frequent use of the term "fire." Rather than identifying some particular element, force, or quality (chosen from among the four fundamental elements recognized by the ancients—earth, water, air, and fire) by means of which to explain and derive all the other elements, Heraclitus's appeal to fire had primarily a symbolic meaning. His stress on fire is not in the interest of giving a rival physical explanation, contending with those who would choose, for example, air (as Anaximenes did) or water (as Thales did). Instead, fire, for him, was a powerful emblem for the ever-changing character of all natural phenomena. He may, too, have extended this symbol of fire to describe not only changes *in* the cosmos, but to convey the hypothesis that the cosmos itself will eventually be destroyed "by fire." Whether he thought along these lines is not altogether clear, although it would be in perfect consonance with the main drift of his thought. What is not at all uncertain is that for Heraclitus the symbol of fire does powerfully remind us of the ever-changeful basic character of the world in which we live.

A final major point that needs to be made in trying to grasp Heraclitus's thought is that there is an underlying *unity* between the life of a human being and that of the cosmos. As products and exemplifications of the forces of Nature, human beings are all of a piece with other manifestations of the workings of these forces. Our birth and death, our mortality, is at bottom no different from that of any other entity or process. We cannot escape finitude and mortality, for it is the inescapable universal fact exhibited throughout the cosmos. When Heraclitus declares that "all things are one," he underlines the basic unity or common fate of all things. Every finite and mortal thing is the scene of the operation of pairs of opposites. Every pair of opposites—day and night, hot and cold, dry and wet, youth and old age, life and death—are so many examples of the war of opposites. Yet each pair of opposites belongs to a more inclusive unity, just as, taken collectively, individual unities form part of the whole that is the cosmos.

The world was not made for man any more than it was made for any other part of Nature. It was not made at all. There is no purpose or goal to the existence of the cosmos. All that stands out in stark, inescapable necessity about the cosmos is the orderly, impersonal changefulness that permeates it. Only by recognizing and accepting this fact—not superficially, but with all the candor and strength we can muster, Heraclitus seems to be saying—can we achieve enlightenment. We would then find a means of liberating ourselves from being totally engrossed in our private dream worlds of ultimately futile hopes and petty ambitions.

PARMENIDES: ONTOLOGIST OF BEING

Parmenides, to whom we turn next, offers profound illumination on the basic themes of cosmology. He lived toward the end of the sixth century B.C. and into the first part of the fifth century B.C. He undoubtedly shared in and absorbed the seminal inquiries into Nature that marked the work of Anaximander and other Milesian cosmologists. These new research interests had spread from their birthplace in Miletus, on the coast of Asia Minor, to other Greek colonies and eventually to Athens. Parmenides' work was carried on in Elea (Italy) on the Tyrrhenian Sea. Our knowledge of his thought, though once again hampered by having to contend with only fragmentary remains of his writings, is on slightly more secure ground, since some 161 lines of his *Poem* have been preserved. Here, too, the assessment and interpretation of his fundamental insights are not a matter of common agreement among scholars and commentators. Only by taking advantage of the best available scholarship can we venture, after a gap of some twenty-five hundred years and with full appreciation of the risks involved, to reconstruct the thought of one of the most profound and original of philosophers.

Aside from an important, relatively brief proem, the principal text of the *Poem* falls into two sections of unequal length. The first, and by far more significant, deals with Parmenides' conception of the Way of Truth and contains his central views on the nature of Being. It is with the distinctions and arguments he presents in this part of the *Poem* that we shall principally be concerned here. The second, much shorter section, consists of brief remarks on cosmogony. The latter section is commonly referred to as *Doxa*, the Way of Opinion. Whatever may have been the full details and extent of Parmenides' interest in, and contributions to, these protoscientific physical inquiries, we have no way of knowing. It is clear, however, that the bulk of his attention was devoted to the themes discussed in the Way of Truth. And it is for his contributions to this topic that his claim rests to be a thinker of first rank in the history of philosophy.

The term to describe the kind of topic that Parmenides discusses in the Way of Truth is "ontology." It is a term that was not coined until many centuries after the time of Parmenides. Ontology is the study of those concepts commonly conveyed by such expressions as "being," "reality," or "existence." For Parmenides, the study of being is fundamental; it occupies the center of all other inquiries. For example, it links in an important way with cosmology and other detailed inquiries into Nature. As we shall see shortly, it has important links, too, with what nowadays we identify as logic, methodology, and the theory of knowledge. According to Parmenides, unless one has a firm grasp of the truths of ontology concerning Being, all other inquiries lack a secure foundation.

A first step in understanding Parmenides' major thesis is to consider what, according to him, is a fundamental contrast between two ways or routes in the search for knowledge or an understanding of anything whatsoever.

> Come, mark my words: I shall tell you what are the only ways of search there are for knowing or understanding. The first way is *that it is and that it cannot not be*. This is the way of Conviction, for Conviction follows Truth. The next is *that it is not and that it is necessary that it not be*: [that is] a way of no information, a way from which no tidings come, for you cannot know *what is not*, nor can you point it out.[7]

This important passage calls attention to what, in Greek, is a fundamental presupposition in the use of the term *esti*. This expression corresponds to the use of the word "is" in English. Parmenides warns us that any rejection or disregard of the fundamental presupposition that underlies the meaningful use of *esti* leads to nonsense, to a fruitless way of thinking or inquiring.

The word *esti* in Greek can be used in at least three different ways. These are: (1) the *copulative-predicational use*; (2) the *existential* use; and (3) the *veridical* use. Parallel distinctions apply to the English word "is."[8]

Thus in the sentence "This table is brown," the word "is" functions copulatively; it is a signal that another expression is being

[7] Fragments 2.2, 2.3, 2.4, 2.5, 2.8; translation in Charles H. Kahn, "The Thesis of Parmenides," *Rev. of Metaphysics*, 22 (1969), 703, 707, 711, 713; cf. A.P.D. Mourelatos, *The Route of Parmenides* (New Haven: Yale University Press, 1970).

[8] Charles H. Kahn, *The Verb 'Be' in Ancient Greek* (Boston: Reidel, 1973).

used predicatively. In our example, "brown" is predicated of the object denoted by the nominative phrase "this table," where the latter serves as the grammatical subject of the sentence.

The second, existential use of *esti*—better conveyed in English by the phrase "there is" or "exists"—affirms that the object being referred to by the grammatical subject of the sentence does in fact exist.[9] There *is* such an object; it *exists*. In the sentence "The road between Athens and Thebes exists," the word "exists" has the force of affirming that the road is there, it can be found, it can be located, it is a part of the world, it is real.

The third, veridical use of *esti*, as also of "is" in English, has the force of affirming that the entire sentence in which it appears is true. We sometimes convey this use in English by italicizing the word "is" in writing, or giving it a special stress when uttered, as in the sentence "The kettle *is* boiling."

Given these different uses of the term *esti*, we may reconstruct the point Parmenides makes in the passage we have quoted, as follows: The most fundamental use of *esti* is the existential use. If one is going to search for knowledge of anything, Parmenides insists, it is necessary that there be something about which one can have such knowledge—that it exist or have being. If this be denied or disregarded—that is, if there is not something that has reality, being, or existence—then there is nothing about which a predication can be made. And if there is no predication, then *a fortiori* there cannot be either a true *or* a false statement or account. The existential sense of *esti*, accordingly, is a fundamental presupposi-

---

[9] The present use of the term "existential" should not be confused with the use of the same expression in connection with the condition of human existence as marked by its finitude and mortality. The latter use of the term derives from its prominence in the contemporary philosophy of existentialism, as found, for example, in the writings of Kierkegaard, Heidegger, Jaspers, Sartre, and others. The term "existential," when used in connection with an analysis of the varied uses of the term *esti* or "is," is a technical expression used by logicians, linguists, and others. It has to do with a special type or condition of the *meaning* of some *linguistic expression*. It is this latter use we are focusing on in the present discussion. It should be kept altogether separate from existentialists' use of "existential" to describe certain features of *human existence*.

tion, a methodological postulate that must be adopted in any search for knowledge or understanding. One cannot say anything about or inquire into what does not exist. This is a way of "no information," of "no tidings." Parmenides totally rejects any possible reference to, any thought or meaningful use of language about the nonexistent, about *nothing*. Such language or way of thinking is futile and meaningless.

According to Parmenides, the foregoing distinction and contrast between the two ways of searching for knowledge are the only two ways available. They are not only exclusive, they are exhaustive of the possibilities. Nor is there some third way that might be supposed to consist of a combination of these two ways. For if indeed, as Parmenides insists, the second way—that which would inquire into what does not exist—is untraversable, then of course any third way that would incorporate it would also be wholly futile and untraversable.

Having selected, then, the Way of Truth as the only way worth pursuing, and having established this point by stressing what is presupposed in the proper use of the term *esti*, Parmenides goes on, in the principal section of the *Poem* (fragment 8), to deal with the theme that is at the center of his philosophic interest. The term he uses to denote this topic is *eon*. We shall translate it as "Being." It is a nominative expression derived from the same verb root as the term *esti*. However, its use in Parmenides' account is not to be identified exclusively with what he has to say about *esti*. It is, rather, a special and important example, an application of the distinctions previously made. In his discussion of *eon*, Parmenides treats of that which underlies all dealings with, or references to, particular beings or existents. He is concerned with Being as such, with Ultimate Reality.[10]

Let us follow Parmenides now as he unfolds the various properties of Being, and gives his arguments to support the distinctions

---

[10] Cf. "Making Sense of Parmenides" in my book *Existence and Logic* (New York: New York University Press, 1974), 19-41.

he makes and the conclusions he arrives at. The first point that Parmenides makes is crucial and sets the stage for all that follows.

> Sole the account still remains of the route, that ____ is ____ [or "how ____ is"]; and on it there are very many signposts that what-is is ungenerable and imperishable. (B 8.1-3)[11]

When examined carefully, the foregoing passage incorporates the distinction between the use of the term *esti* and the use of the term *eon*. The first expression is here translated as "that ____ is ____" whereas the second, *eon*, is here translated as "what-is." In what follows, I shall use the expression "Being" as another way of translating *eon*. I shall use the capitalized expression "Being" in order to distinguish it from the use of the term "being" or "beings." The two are not the same. For if the expression "being" (or "existent") is employed as another way of indicating the existential use of *esti*, then what is to be said of Being could not be said of some particular being or existent. For example, while Being (what-is, *eon*) is ungenerated and imperishable, this surely is not the case with any ordinary being or existent—for example, this flower, that table.

Much of the standard, traditional interpretation of Parmenides' philosophy has been vitiated by permitting a basic confusion to be made between *esti* and *eon*. The result has been to attribute to Parmenides the outrageous view that there is no change, no motion, no coming-into-existence or going-out-of-existence, no plurality of things and events in the world. This absurd thesis need not be saddled on Parmenides. For once the distinction is recognized between Being (*eon*) and "that ____ is ____" (*esti*), what Parmenides wishes to affirm of Being—for example, that *it* is ungenerated and imperishable—need not be taken as applying to particular existents or beings. To attribute to Parmenides the view that denies the existence of plurality and change is to convict him of a flagrant rejection of the most ordinary experience, let alone of what is presupposed in any more sophisticated scientific investigation of the facts

[11] Cf. Mourelatos, *Route*, 94.

of nature. It not only makes a shambles of what ordinary people everywhere take for granted, it convicts Parmenides of a form of madness. It also makes totally incomprehensible the very fact of what not only other inquirers into natural phenomena presuppose in their descriptions (in meteorology, astronomy, and biology—to go no further), but the obvious and incontestable fact that Parmenides himself, in the *Doxa* section of his *Poem*, is engaged in the same type of scientific, physical, and cosmological inquiry. It assigns to Parmenides the most glaring inconsistency in his own thought.

What he has to say when he discusses ontology and the general notion of Being, on the one hand, and what he is engaged in trying to understand when he, and others, are engaged in trying to describe and explain ordinary natural phenomena and the structure of the cosmos, on the other, are two different matters. The theses Parmenides holds about Being do not in the least conflict with or make otiose the work of the scientist or the deliverances of everyday experience. These are two separate though related dimensions of what we can say about the world in which we live. If one accepts, with Parmenides, that Being is eternal, unchanging, indivisible, and totally unique, this in no way requires these metaphoric and negative terms of description, used in connection with Being, to hold also for the domain of ordinary experience or the phenomena investigated by the scientist. The two live side by side and are perfectly compatible with one another. Indeed, the realization of this fact shows unmistakably that Parmenides was a thinker who did not live or think on only one level or in one direction. And this, among other things, is what made him the great philosopher he was.

Once made, the fundamental distinction also allows us (as we shall see later) to meet the traditional criticism of Parmenides' philosophy of Being, that it is inconsistent with *any* attempt (including his own, in the Way of Opinion section of his *Poem*) to give an account of the genesis of the cosmos.

That what-is, *eon*, is ungenerated and imperishable is the cornerstone on which all other statements about Being rest, on which all deductions of its properties depend for their validity and truth. This central fact about Being may also be compared to the hub of a wheel from which all the spokes—all the truths and insights about the nature of Being—radiate. And for Parmenides it does not really matter where one starts, for in the end we come back to the same central point. Here, for example, in his own exposition, is the first proof he gives to support the claim that Being is ungenerated.

> For what birth will you quest of it? Having grown whither? from what? Nor will I allow you to say or to think "from what-is-not." For it is neither speakable nor thinkable that it is not [or "how it is not"]. Besides, what requirement should impel it, later or earlier [or "later rather than earlier"], having started from nothing, to grow? (B 8.6-10)[12]

Two main points are worth stressing in this argument. Notice that in deducing the fact that Being is ungenerated, Parmenides appeals to the fundamental point made in connection with *esti*, namely, that we cannot make any meaningful statement about what does not exist. This general point is applied to Non-Being as such, not to some more restricted inquiry or to ordinary experience. The linguistic opposite of "Being" is "Non-Being" or "Absolute Nothing." But the latter expressions have no referent. They do not and cannot refer (on pain of self-contradiction) to any reality. Since, therefore, the way to putative Non-Being is barred and is wholly untraversable, it makes no sense, Parmenides claims, to utter a statement in which one purports to describe the genesis or birth of Being. The generation of Being could only consist in a transition from Non-Being to Being, and such a transition is impossible. For in this description or explanation, one purports to refer to Non-Being. However, such a statement is devoid of meaning. It collapses before it can even get started. It is not a genuine statement, for it fails to refer to anything by the use of the expression "Non-Being." The statement lacks a subject. Since it lacks a

---

[12] Ibid., 98.

subject, it really does not make a predication either. One cannot even say the statement is false, for we are not given a complete statement to which an appraisal of truth or falsity can be applied.

The second point worth noticing in Parmenides' argument is that he appeals to the earliest formulation of what in later philosophy came to be known as the Principle of Sufficient Reason. Parmenides asks us to suppose—for the sake of argument, and contrary to his own fundamental claim that "Non-Being" lacks any referent—that there is something to which the term does refer. He then asks how *any* reason could be given or even be supposed to exist that would explain the coming-into-existence of Being. He denies there could be such a reason. The contrary-to-fact supposition, on which the (pseudo-)notion of the generation of Being rests, lacks an inner rationality. It is another justification for discarding the whole idea of the coming-into-being of Being itself.

The foregoing argument against the possibility of thinking of Being as that to which the concept of generation or birth is applicable is not followed at this point by a proof that Being is imperishable, that it is not capable of going out of existence. It is clear, however, that although Parmenides had earlier predicated imperishability of Being, he could easily supply the needed proof. For once again, to postulate going-out-of-existence to Being would require a transition from Being to Non-Being. And this supposition must also be rejected: it is incoherent, since it rests upon an appeal to the unacceptable notion of Non-Being.

With the foregoing attributes of ungenerability and imperishability firmly established as true of Being and as deriving from the elimination of the notion of Non-Being, Parmenides proceeds to deduce other equally necessary properties of Being. Thus Parmenides describes Being by a variety of terms—for example, "simple," "indivisible," "immobile," "complete," "unique," and a number of others. All these terms are either metaphoric or negative. While a term such as "immobile" is borrowed from the language used to describe a material entity (a body), it would be wholly mistaken to take this term in its literal meaning as applying to Being. For Being is not a body. Nor, like some material entity, is it physically divisible or decomposable into simpler elements or parts. Being has no parts at all, even conceptually, since it is not a material entity or any other type of entity. Its simplicity or "indivisibility" is a sign that it is not further analyzable into something more fundamental or elementary. Further, it is not capable of accretion or diminution. There is no more or less of Being, no quantitative dimension assignable to Being that would support such a description. Nor can the language of time, space, and motion be applied to Being. Thus Being is timeless, not in the sense that it endures forever, but rather in the sense that it is beyond time altogether. Similarly, Being is not spread out in space. It has no spatial extent or shape (not even that of a sphere). It follows that Being is wholly unique and cannot be compared to anything else. It is not subsumable under some wider or more inclusive category. As Parmenides remarks, "It lies by itself." Being, finally, is complete in the sense that it is not to be understood by reference to some end or goal. It is wholly self-contained and "inviolate." As Parmenides suggests, all these expressions are only "signposts." They provide clues in the way that metaphors do. They are not to be taken in their literal or ordinary meanings, for to do so would be to import what is inapplicable to that which is wholly unique. And, of course, insofar as some of these terms are also largely of a negative character—they tell us what Being is not—again they do not provide any positive characterization of Being. If, however, these signposts are successful, they lead, at the end of the road, to the "understanding," in the sense of a direct and immediate awareness of Being. And at that point, signposts are no longer needed. The metaphoric and negative terminology can be discarded as unnecessary and even as misleading. One is in the presence of Being itself.

We must recognize that despite all the subtle logical, methodological, and linguistic clues that Parmenides gives of the nature of Being, in the end what he is driving at cannot be put into complete sentences. The culminating insight into Being must remain a type of mystic vision. This vision is characteristically and notoriously evidenced by a pregnant silence, an inability to *say* what one sees. One is left at the end, at best, with a word—*eon*,

"Being," "Reality," "Existence," "what-exists"—or better still, with no words at all.

I have been expounding, thus far, some of the main doctrines of Parmenides concerning the central ontologic concept of Being. My exposition has stayed, as far as possible, fairly close to the text of the *Poem*. There still remain, however, a number of pressing questions we must consider. These will take us, admittedly, beyond the explicit text of Parmenides. Yet, it will be suggested, they make the enterprise of giving sense to the notion of Being more readily intelligible and accessible. The fundamental question I wish to consider is this. Is there anything beyond what Parmenides tells us about Being that relates it to ordinary experience or, indeed, to the concepts of cosmology and cosmogony? I wish to suggest there is, and that we can link the discussion of Being with what the pre-Socratic cosmologists (including Parmenides himself) were concerned with in their account of the structure or genesis of the cosmos. My main point is the following. What Parmenides is referring to, in describing Being, is not some particular *entity* that exists in the way an ordinary object or event does. Being is not an object or occurrence of any sort whatsoever. The use of the nominative expression "Being" tempts us, but also misleads us, into thinking that it does function referentially in a particular entity-designating way. But it does not. Or at least we get off on the wrong foot if we suppose that it does. We then get tangled in all sorts of spurious questions and are led to offer all sorts of dubious and highly implausible solutions.

One way of avoiding these pitfalls is to think of the term "Being," despite its nominative cast, as playing the role of a participle, and hence as containing verblike and adjectival associations. We could then say that what the term "Being" signifies is the given existence of the cosmos. We should have no awareness of Being if there were no cosmos. Without the prior understanding and application of the term "world" in its astronomic-cosmologic sense, the term *eon* would not have any foothold and relevance. *That* the world exists, not *what* it is, is what *eon* or Being has to do with. A first step in understanding the nature of Being is to see that it is manifested in the fact of the existence of the cosmos.

However, an awareness of Being does not tell us anything at all about the character of the cosmos. It does not have anything to do with *what* the cosmos is, as science might discover its properties. Whatever the cosmos is, whatever it contains, however it operates, whatever its temporal, spatial, or compositional structure may be thought or discovered to be, Being would be independent of and unaffected by these detailed, specific facts. Being holds for our cosmos or any other cosmos that exists "alongside" ours, or "before" it, or "after" it. It is the sheer fact of the existence of the cosmos that provides a principal route to the awareness of Being.

However, even if what we have said is a first step in grasping what Parmenides means by "Being," we have yet to grapple with the following question. Consider, for example, the view of Anaximander, according to which the cosmos came into existence out of the Boundless, the *Apeiron*. Or consider the views of other early cosmogonists—for example, Empedocles, Anaxagoras, Anaximenes, or Democritus—who had their own distinctive and rival theories about the origin of the cosmos. Or consider, finally, the views of Parmenides himself, as these can be gathered from the few brief remarks he makes on the topic of cosmogony. On his account, the cosmos, as a temporally and spatially finite order, had its beginning when Fire (Light) and Night (Darkness)—the primordial pair of contraries—made their first appearance. Parmenides does not venture to explain how this first pair arose, that is, the mechanism by which this took place. "Given" this beginning, it suffices for him to go on to describe the subsequent development of the cosmos. Following the primordial differentiation, a cosmos, in all its astronomic, meteorologic, and other modes of physical and biological detail, arose.

Let us consider, furthermore, what one is to make of a cosmogony such as Anaximander's that, *in addition* to the cosmos, posits the existence of the *Apeiron* or the Boundless. How are we to relate what I have said above of the participial or adjectival status of Being with respect to the cosmos when we entertain Anaximander's notion of the Boundless? Would Being, in Parmenides' use of this term, also apply to the Boundless that "lies beyond" the cosmos?

Parmenides could respond by claiming that everything he says about Being is perfectly compatible with such a notion. It in no way negates the ungenerated and imperishable character of Being. For he could respond to his would-be critic as follows: "When I say that Being is ungenerated and imperishable, I should extend this as far as is necessary in order to encompass all that has being. If the Boundless does exist from which the cosmos or other *kosmoi* arise, then not only does *eon* apply to the cosmos or to other *kosmoi*, it applies to and holds for the Boundless as well. However correlated or adjectivally associated with whatever exists, Being itself is still to be described in the way I have described it. Even if our cosmos was generated and will perish, this does not mean that Being was generated or will perish. The two dimensions are entirely distinct."

We must now turn, however, to another main question. We could ask: If Parmenides asserts, as he unmistakably does, that *eon* is ungenerated and imperishable, how is this to be reconciled with his own, or anyone else's, commitment to some form of cosmogony—to the belief that the cosmos had a genesis? Is this not a flagrant contradiction? The answer, I submit, comes from carefully distinguishing what Parmenides means by *eon* and how he understands "cosmos." The two are not identical. Parmenides, Anaximander, and other Greek cosmologists believed that the *cosmos* came into existence. It does not follow that if one subscribes to the view that the astronomical world came into existence or was formed at some time in the past, this also requires one to say that *Being* came into existence.

46

THREE

The Universe

THE UNIVERSE AS OBSERVABLE
AND INTELLIGIBLE

However fruitful and engaging our gleanings from these earliest ventures into cosmology may have been, they cannot suffice to meet the main task we have set for ourselves, which consists in the wish to explore the leading ideas of recent scientific cosmology and to examine some of their broad implications for our world view. Whatever the similarities or continuities of our own situation with the problems faced by thinkers in earlier epochs may be, we must do our own work afresh. Even if we succeed in identifying certain perennial themes and recurrent patterns of thought, science does not stand still. Therefore any serious interest in cosmology that is alive to the changing observational data and theories of science cannot afford to rest content with simply rehearsing the wisdom of the past. It must find its own answers as best it can by confronting these new results. Nor, of course, should we be naive enough to believe that having done this, we shall have settled matters once and for all. For there is no assurance that tomorrow the scientific picture will not change drastically. And in that case the work will have to be done all over again. But this is only to say that in cosmology, as in other areas of science, it would be futile to look for the "final answer," the "complete truth." For this is a mirage, a false ideal. At any given time—and the present time, including a recollection of the past, is all we ever do have—scientists can only make *comparative* evaluations of *available* options. There is no way of being assured that among these alternatives one will find *the* absolute truth. Indeed, to assume there is a unique and optimum way of rendering the world intelligible is itself a gratuitous belief for which no convincing arguments have ever been given. Nor need the abandonment of this too-tempting yet misleading goal of finding the absolutely *best* theory or formulation dampen the search for ever-*better* accounts.

In any case, it is with the current investigations of scientific cosmology that we must deal. These center on an evolutionary theory of the expanding universe. Evolutionary models of the expanding universe are the fruits of a complex series of research efforts carried out in recent decades in mathematical physics and observational astronomy. Prominent among these results are (1) the application of the basic ideas of the general theory of relativity to the subject matter of cosmology; (2) observational discoveries in astronomy relating to the spatial distribution and redshifts of the galaxies, as well as data concerning the isotropic 3-degree cosmic microwave background radiation; (3) the application of recent theories of particle physics to interpret conditions prevalent during very early stages in the development of the universe.

The first major step of cosmological model building in the modern period took place in 1917 with Einstein's application of the field equations of general relativity to the cosmological problem. He showed how to bring to bear the conceptual tools of relativity theory in order to describe the large-scale space-time structure of the universe. Along with Einstein's pioneering efforts, the work of the Russian mathematician Alexander Friedmann in the 1920s also marked an important milestone on the same path.

During this first phase of the development of relativistic cosmology, coordination of the theoretical concepts with empirical data centered on astronomical discoveries concerning the spatial distribution and redshifts of the galaxies. Galactic astronomy furnished the principal empirical illustrations and testing ground for the theories of relativistic cosmology. Hence discussions of the property of spatial homogeneity, the use of a scale factor to represent changes in the "size" of the universe over periods of cosmic time, efforts at determining the density distribution of matter in the universe, and calculation of the age of the universe based on an appeal to the Hubble constant or the deceleration factor in the expansion of the universe—all these discussions of the kinematics and dynamics of the universe were conducted on the assumption that the universe is essentially a universe of galaxies.

Beginning in the 1960s new discoveries provided fresh empirical facts and theoretical tools that made possible new approaches and insights pertaining to the problems of cosmology. These included (1) the discovery of the cosmic microwave background radiation that points to a hot big-bang stage in the development of the universe; and (2) the working-out of various theories of particle physics (quantum, gauge, Kaluza-Klein, etc.) that undertake to explain the emergence of material particles and their combinations or transformations in the course of the development of the universe, as well as the interconnections among the four fundamental forces of nature (strong, weak, electromagnetic, and gravitational). It was due to investigations such as these that the scope of cosmology in its description of the evolution of the universe was much broadened and enriched. In particular, these fresh insights stressed the way in which various temperature and energy conditions played their important role in the early stages of the development of the universe. In addition and parallel to these investigations into the early stages of the development of the universe, and exploiting the same fund of ideas, a number of recent theories have also aimed at forecasting the eventual fate of the universe.

A philosophical interest in recent cosmology is stimulated not only by reflecting on the distinctive claims of evolutionary cosmology and its account of the temporal structure of the universe as a whole, but on the scope and promise of cosmology as a scientific discipline in general. How much can be known about the universe as a whole, and what confidence can we place in any of its results?

One possible short way of describing the primary goal of cosmology is to say it seeks to make the universe intelligible. Phrased in this way, one set of philosophic questions arises from considering the key words in this short formula, namely, *the universe* and *intelligible*. How shall we understand them? To what does the expression "the universe" refer? If it has several different uses, what are they and how are they interrelated? If the universe can be made intelligible, how is this achieved and in what does it consist?

In characterizing what the universe is, it might seem adequate from one point of view to say it is the comprehensive whole that includes all physical objects, processes, and events within its scope. When approached from the side of language, the expression "the universe" could be regarded as a proper name that has this special object or entity as its referent. The expression "the universe" would then be classified as a singular referring expression rather than as a sortal (common) noun or general predicate, since it is used to refer to an individual object, not to a general property. Because of its great breadth, however, this way of describing the universe (and from a linguistic point of view, this way of categorizing the expression "the universe") is at best a schema that encompasses a great variety of more detailed and informative accounts. For this reason the foregoing formula is fairly useless except as it provides the occasion for raising questions about the use of such terms as "totality," "object," "process," and "event." While from a purely a priori perspective this might hold a certain amount of philosophic interest, the outcome is likely to have little value in illuminating the way in which the expression "the universe" functions in scientific cosmology at a particular stage of its inquiries—for example, at the present time. To approach an analysis of the expression "the universe" in a more fruitful way, it is well to begin by stressing the fact that, as with other expressions in our language, it cannot be understood in isolation. One application of the general principle of contextualism points to the need to examine the meaning of any phrase or subsentential unit of language as it performs its role in the context of inquiry and in the construction of more inclusive stretches of discourse.

When we take advantage of this principle with special reference to the inquiries of modern scientific cosmology, this yields two immediate fruits. In the first place, it is helpful to see how the expression "the universe" is embedded in the elaboration of a *cosmological model*. Second, the cosmological model itself needs to be examined in the wider historical context in which one can identify the proposal, testing, and assessment of various models of the universe at different stages of ongoing investigation. It follows that if one were to ask a cosmologist at the present stage of inquiry (or for that matter at any earlier stage) what he understands by the expression "the universe," his answer is likely to reflect his acceptance of a particular cosmological model.

Moreover, because any cosmological model contains diverse elements, principally of an observational and theoretical sort, it is likely that the term "universe" will be understood and used by our cosmologist in different ways, depending on which of these components is stressed. Of the two principal senses of the term "universe" that might receive this special emphasis, depending on whether it is the observational or the theoretical side of the model which is appealed to, one sense will be used in referring to the most inclusive domain of astronomical objects and physical processes about which observational data is provided by available instruments. The other sense will be used in referring to the universe as a whole—including the observable universe but extending beyond it—as this whole will be characterized by means of the theoretical concepts distinctive of the cosmological model under discussion.

The term *observable universe* is a convenient label for the large-scale spatio-temporal domain of astronomical and physical processes, objects, and phenomena about which observational data yield information. If there is no serious danger of misunderstanding, the cosmologist will frequently omit the qualifying adjective "observable": the context will make it clear that what he means is the observable region and not anything beyond. One major segment of a total cosmological model will thus consist of a body of observational data about the observable universe. It is normally the case that some of these data are reasonably well established and relatively fixed. Other parts, at varying distances from the settled core, are more fluid. The relatively unsettled parts undergo changes with improvements of instrumentation and the augmentation of reliable data. In general, then, any empirically oriented pursuit of cosmology includes a description of an observationally identifiable domain of objects, events, and processes. What this empirical core is—the starting point for all theoretical investigations—will vary with the amount and character of the accredited stabilized observational information accepted at a given stage of inquiry. For primitive man it sufficed to distinguish Earth and Sky, with the latter differentiated into the Sun, Moon, and stars. At a somewhat later (but still quite early) stage, a distinction was made within the realm of stars between the planets ("wanderers") and the fixed stars. If we skip over the intervening centuries, including the periods during which astronomy emerged in Western science with its successive contributions of observational information about what is to be found "in the sky" and come down to the present day, the stabilized empirical core of cosmologically relevant observational data about the observable universe would include, as a minimum, all that is known concerning the galaxies within the horizon of observability, the relative abundances of different elements, the baryon-photon density ratio, and data concerning the microwave background radiation.

Because any cosmological model will normally include an empirical core consisting of a description of the observable universe, the use of the expression "the universe" to designate that which is the referent of a total cosmological model is unlike the use of a singular referring expression to designate a purely fictional object. The explanation of its meaning must include as an essential component what can be identified observationally. Indeed, the empirical core of the universe includes all perceptually given material objects and events—of whatever type and magnitude—in space and time. It is these objects and events we normally call "real" as distinguished from those we call "fictional." And because the universe includes all these real (nonfictional) objects and events, it too is real in this sense.

Furthermore, insofar as "the universe" has as part of its meaning a genuine empirical core, it is to be contrasted with the use of a singular referring expression that suffers from failed reference, one that is vacuous because it cannot be correlated with an observationally identifiable object in space and time. In the case of a singular referring expression with failed reference, a name is introduced with the intention of designating some putatively real individual space-time object. However, no such object is ever confronted observationally. Such was the case, for example, with the use of the name "Vulcan" by some nineteenth century astronomers to designate the planet presumed to exist between the Sun and Mercury. No such planet was ever found. Unlike such a term, explanation of the meaning of the term "the universe" guarantees that it has an empirical core as part of its reference, however this may be specified at a particular stage of inquiry.

According to present-day understanding, various horizons limit the range of cosmologically relevant observational data and thereby set different types of bounds to the observable universe. Recognition of limitations in the spatial and temporal situation of the observer and in the storehouse of his instrumental resources justify the belief that if there were major changes in this situation or extensive additions to, and modifications in, types of available equipment, they would make possible the disclosure of objects and phenomena beyond those known at the present time. Similarly, taking into account the effect of the limiting velocity of light justifies an inferential leap to the existence of a domain of galaxies beyond the spatial bounds of the horizon set by that velocity. It follows from these and other examples that since the observable universe is limited in its scope, its contents do not exhaust all that exists on an astronomic or physical level. For this reason, the observable universe is incomplete when judged relatively to a theoretically envisaged inclusive domain of objects, processes, and phenomena.

It is the role of cosmological *theory* to produce a picture of the domain that is as comprehensive as possible from a physical point of view. Indeed, cosmological theory does not content itself simply with picturing a *more* extensive region of objects and phenomena. It undertakes to describe the *most* inclusive and complete system to which all other lesser regions and systems belong. The observable universe is part of this most inclusive whole. Accordingly, a common way of describing the purpose of a cosmological model is to say it gives an interpretation not only of the data concerning the observable region, but a picture of *the universe as a whole*. *A cosmological model goes beyond the observable universe to the universe as a maximally comprehensive ordered domain of processes and objects, to the extent that this can be made intelligible by means of physical theory.*

Expressions such as "the steady state universe," "the Einstein-de Sitter universe," and "the big bang universe," among others, refer to theoretical pictures of the universe as a whole. They designate what the universe is thought to be from the point of view of the distinctive conceptual resources of a particular cosmological model. For example, one or another evolutionary picture of the universe under current discussion provides a spatio-temporal framework of the widest scope within which all discriminated individual stages in the development of the universe can be included. Whereas the fund of observational data extends only to certain stages in the past, the theoretical picture goes beyond these limitations to the earliest and most remote stages, whether in the past or the future, that can be inferred on the basis of physical theory. Similarly, whereas observational data concerning the spatial extent of the observable domain of the galaxies is limited by the availability of instruments or other observational constraints, theory will undertake to give a picture of the universe as a maximally comprehensive domain of galaxies that extends beyond these observational limits. The intent behind the construction of any cosmological model, and so in particular of an evolutionary model, is to describe the properties of a maximally comprehensive intelligible domain. To say that this domain is maximally comprehensive is another way of saying that the universe is construed as an absolute whole: what a particular cosmological model regards as the universe is not part of some more inclusive domain. The intent is not to omit anything of a physical character from the scope of the model. By intent, therefore, the goal of a cosmological model is to regard the universe as a unique, all-inclusive physical whole.

To think of the universe as a maximally comprehensive domain that excludes no physical phenomena distinguishes the universe as an individual whole from all other individuals encountered in experience. For with respect to ordinary individuals we can either find or conceive of many individuals of the same kind. There are many persons, stars, galaxies, mountains, butterflies, and so on. However, there is only one universe. By definition, the universe is a unique, individual whole. Strictly speaking, therefore, there cannot be a plurality of universes (many universes, other universes, parallel universes). These phrases are all misuses of language. If one indulges in a mode of speech that allows more than one universe, this needs to be restated in such a way as to use some other term of which it makes sense to say there is a plurality. (For example, instead of referring to "island universes," as was the case when the existence of extra-galactic nebulae were discovered in the early part of this century, the term "island universe" was soon dropped altogether and was replaced by the term "galaxy".) By definition, the universe is the all-inclusive individual whole. Thus, as employed by some particular model, "the universe" may incorporate (along with many other examples, as part of what *it* designates as the all-inclusive whole) what some other cosmological model called "the universe." If this new cosmological model comes to be accepted, a new term for the maximally comprehensive domain referred to as "the universe" by older schemes will have to be found in order to avoid confusion with the altered and now preferred conception of "the universe."[1]

Since a major component of a fully developed cosmological model is of a primarily conceptual or theoretical character, a second major group of uses of the term "the universe" reflects this component and gives special emphasis to it. In offering his picture of the universe as a whole, the cosmologist appeals to laws, con-

[1] See Milton K. Munitz, "One Universe or Many?" *Journal of the History of Ideas* 12 (1951), 231-255.

cepts, and principles of interpretation that are intended to make this maximally comprehensive domain of physical processes and entities intelligible. To identify this sense of "the universe," we may group examples of its use under the general heading of *the intelligible universe*, in distinction from *the observable universe*.

Again, at a particular stage of inquiry, there are varying degrees of confidence or agreement by the community of experts with respect to different items in this component. At its core will be those conceptual elements attracting greatest confidence and agreement. Here are situated those well-tested physical laws or parts of a wider physical theory regarded as relevant to, and clarifying of, the problems at hand; standard mathematical techniques of representation and calculation; a fund of largely unquestioned conceptual resources of common sense and ordinary language; and a widely shared world view. Beyond this central core will be those conceptual or theoretical proposals that are still controversial, tentative, or in need of elaboration, testing, tightening, and adjustment to the demands of consistency with other parts of the body of commonly accepted knowledge.

Cosmological models differ from one another in how they describe the contents and structure of the unique maximally comprehensive domain. The Einstein static universe, a Friedmann universe, the big bang universe, and so on are distinguished from one another by the special conceptual tools each employs and the inferences each makes use of in offering its own special forms of explanation or prediction. In its own way, every cosmological model makes use of already established physical laws or principles, as well as its own freshly devised concepts or specially attractive analogies. Examples of theoretic concepts associated with particular cosmological models include the following: the concept of a scale factor or radius of space as a function of cosmic time $[R(t)]$ (as employed in schemes of relativistic models, Friedmann universes); the creation of matter and antimatter out of a pre-existent vacuum (in models that seek to explain the "origin" of the universe prior to the Planck time); the existence of a single unified force in the earliest stage of the universe before it underwent successive stages of symmetry breaking (as described by various supersymmetry and super-gravity theories); the notions of a Higgs field or a stage of super-cooling associated with an inflationary stage of the universe (according to inflationary models); the existence of parallel or other "universes" beyond our own (for example, in John Wheeler's conception of superspace); the use of spaces of greater dimensions than four in which to embed our four-dimensional space-time (for example, in recent theories of a Kaluza-Klein variety); and so on. As used in one or another cosmological model, none of these theoretic concepts reports on or describes some directly observable object, process, or phenomenon. On the basis of use of theoretic concepts such as those just mentioned, different cosmological models offer ways of interpreting available observational data and make predictions or retrodictions to early, present, or future stages in the evolution of the universe.

To say that the concept of the universe as a whole, as embodied and given specific form in any cosmological model, is a *theoretic concept* is to say something different from simply saying that any model is a *hypothesis*. As a hypothesis—that is, as a *proposal* for ordering the empirical material and rendering it intelligible—a cosmological model must submit to the ordinary criteria of scientific evaluation. The cosmological model that embodies the theoretic concept of the universe as a whole is open to adoption, modification, or rejection just as much as any other hypothesis adopted tentatively in the course of inquiry. The models in which this theoretic concept is embedded submit their distinctive interpretations to a process of appraisal on the grounds of consistency, systematic simplicity, mathematical elegance, comprehensive scope of explanatory power, and empirical test or corroboration. In short, as an integrated conceptual scheme, each cosmological model provides its own picture of the intelligible universe. It does so, incidentally, without requiring that every element of that scheme—every concept or mathematical tool made use of—be directly correlated with some observable object, process, or phenomenon. The point in calling the concept of the universe as a whole a theoretic concept is that even if a particular cosmological model comes to be accepted over its rivals, the notion that it embodies of the universe as a whole remains a theoretic human construct, an invented cognitive device.

When seen in this light, the concept of the universe as a whole is to be contrasted not only with ordinary empirically given objects, but even with the observable universe as a relative whole. As the referent of a comprehensive cosmological model, the universe as a unique absolute whole is not an observational datum. Thus one may ostensively explain the meaning of expressions such as "the Statue of Liberty," "the Moon," or "the Andromeda Galaxy" by employing various suitable perceptual faculties and instrumental resources. But one cannot give a satisfactory ostensive definition of "the universe as a whole." One cannot point to the universe as a whole, though one can perceptually identify various parts— even very extensive regions of the universe. However, the universe as a whole cannot be identified in the same way. One cannot pick out the universe as a whole and point to it by a gesture as one might in the case of a person, building, or particular astronomical object *within* the universe. In the case of bestowing a name upon an object given in perceptual experience, we should normally be given the object through direct observational confrontation, and then give a name to this object. The existence of the object is not in question: it would exist and could be examined even if a name had not be given to it. For example, if some strange marine creature were dredged up from the ocean's depths that had not be seen before or could not be readily classified, at least the creature can be examined and described; assigning a name or classificatory label can come later. After having agreed upon some referring device to identify it, one can then use it in statements that report various discovered or observed facts about the creature. This is the case with other countless standard, noncontroversial examples. However, when dealing with the universe as a whole, the situation is drastically different. We are not first observationally given an entity to which we assign the name "the universe."

Whatever else the universe may be said to be, it is at least that "entity" which is made up of the galaxies and clusters of galaxies among its major units and of the microwave background radiation. In this respect, there is an affinity between the use of the expression "the universe" as a referring device and a name such as "the Andromeda Galaxy." Both require, as part of the explanation of their respective meanings, reference to what is empirically identifiable. However, there are also important *dissimilarities* between the use of the term "the universe" and other singular referring devices for perceptually identifiable material objects. At best, the universe is "given" through the medium of a conceptual construction—through *understanding* a cosmological model. The latter is not the product of an exercise of any one or a combination of sensory organs. It is the outcome of employing man's creative intellectual powers. It is these intellectual faculties that help to conceive what cannot be identified primarily by observational means. The concept of the universe as a whole is a theoretical concept.

In stressing that the concept of the universe as a whole is a theoretical concept, it is important to guard against misunderstanding. The distinction between what is empirically given and what is conceived theoretically is not a distinction between types of cognitive experience that belong to two wholly distinct, watertight compartments. In all experience, whether of an ordinary or scientific sort, these two elements are co-present and intertwined in various ways. In the case of the science of cosmology, however, the way in which the empirical and the conceptual are interrelated is not of the sort one finds in simple examples of ordinary experience or even in many examples of other empirical sciences. As presented by a particular cosmological model, the concept of the universe as a whole is not arrived at by induction or by generalization from a sample of what is found in more direct observational experience of restricted regions of space and time. The construction of a cosmological model is not a matter of generalizing from a sample, even if the sample is as wide as the observable universe. While empirical elements are surely incorporated into, or serve as clues for, the final picture, there are also other elements in the construction of the model that are in no way empirically derived. An understanding of these more theoretical components requires an ability to follow the rules of an invented conceptual scheme. At the present stage of cosmological inquiry, a sophisticated cosmological model will typically exhibit a strong mathematical component and lean heavily on or extend and transform the accepted concepts, laws, and principles of classical Newtonian or relativistic mechanics and electromagnetic and thermodynamic theories, as well as the laws and theories of more recent quantum and particle physics.

The complex interaction of two broad layers—the observational and the conceptual—composes a total cosmological model. Each particular model has its own distinctive mixture of these components, a mixture that distinguishes it from rival contemporaneous or traditional models. When asked what they mean by "the universe," the answer different cosmologists or schools of cosmology will give reflects the way in which particular observational and conceptual ingredients are combined in their own preferred cosmological model.

"THE UNIVERSE AS A WHOLE": CONTRASTED PHILOSOPHIES

In describing the pursuit of cosmology as an ongoing effort to understand the structure of the universe as a whole, how shall we interpret the use of the expression "the universe as a whole"? There are basically two widely contrasted ways of responding to this question. When applied to the field of cosmology, they involve radically different philosophies of how to interpret what is commonly referred to as "the relation between thought and reality."

According to one interpretation, the expression "the universe as a whole" designates an entity that exists independently of, and antecedently to, all cosmological inquiry—an entity whose properties cosmology strives to disclose. The expression "the universe" is a name for this entity. This entity has its own inherent properties and intelligible structure. Those properties and that structure can be gradually discovered in a properly guided process of scientific research. Truth about the universe consists in a matching or correspondence between the statements made about the universe and the independent facts. Degrees of truth are correlated with the closeness of fit between language or thought on the one side and reality on the other. These degrees of fit range from partial correspondence to perfect correspondence. All cosmological theories have at least this much in common: in using the expression "the universe" as a name, they denote the same objectively existing entity. They differ from one another in the properties they ascribe to the universe, the predicates they use in describing it. Since different cosmological models make at least partially conflicting claims about the universe's structure, the process of scientific testing and evaluation is devoted to judging critically the relative merits of competing theories and to choosing the one that has the greatest strengths and fewest weaknesses. The outcome of this evaluation is an appraisal that assigns to the preferred theory the status of being a closer approximation to the truth—of being more probable—than its rivals. If the complete truth about the universe were ever to be known, it would consist in a perfect correspondence between the statements made in the ideal theory and the intelligible structure actually embodied in the universe in its independent existence.

According to the second interpretation of the concept of the universe as a whole, this concept functions only pragmatically. It is a useful human construct, introduced and employed in the course of cosmological inquiry. However, it need not be interpreted as presupposing the antecedent and independent existence of an entity to which that concept might be applied as a name or description. On this view, every cosmological model does indeed introduce and make use of the theoretical concept of the universe as a whole. It is introduced implicitly or explicitly wherever one engages in the articulation of a cosmological model. When so introduced, it means the maximally comprehensive domain of physical objects, processes, and phenomena as this is defined, described, and made intelligible by means of the conceptual resources employed in the given model. However, the expression "the universe as a whole" is not to be interpreted as referring to an entity possessed of a structure that pre-exists the conceptual characterization by a cosmological model. The concept of the universe as a whole comes into being only with the construction of the cosmological model itself. The intelligible structure that describes the universe as a whole is a human invention, a construct of creative imagination, language, and thought. The notion of the universe as a whole and the intelligible structure that describes its properties comprise an organizing schema by which to interpret observational data (the observable universe) and for making predictions and inferences to what lies beyond the observable region. It is not necessary to presuppose there is an object, entity, or totality that, antecedently to all inquiry, has a set of determinate properties and structure and that is the target of cosmological inquiry and knowledge. For no such object, entity, or totality is confronted by the cosmologist either at the outset of his inquiry or at any point during it. On the contrary, it is through the construction, testing, and evaluation of competing cosmological models that choices are effected by competent investigators about which model to adopt in order to give meaning and use to the term "the universe as a whole." The latter expression sums up the combination of items—observational data, descriptions, explanations, predictions, and retrodictions—that are set out in a particular cosmological model. The universe is what a cosmological model says it is. At a given stage of inquiry, the intelligible universe is that which is described by a particular cosmological model. In assigning at least partially different properties to the universe, competing cosmological models give separate definitions of "the universe." As a result, the universe as understood is always a conceptually bound universe. Though relative to its origins in the creative power of human imagination, thought, and language, the truth of a cosmological model is a matter of pragmatic justification, not of correspondence with antecedent fact. The testing and evaluation of the relative merits and weaknesses of competing models take place by appealing to commonly adopted scientific criteria of adequacy.

It would be a mistake to say that only the first or *realist* philosophy, sketched above, has a consistent or carefully worked out conception of intelligibility, truth, and objectivity, and that the second or *pragmatist* philosophy is lacking in or subverts these concepts.

On the contrary, each philosophy has its own interpretation of what objectivity, intelligibility, and truth amount to. In what follows, I shall explore a bit more fully the differences in the concept of intelligibility found in these two contrasted approaches, and undertake to show the advantages in adopting the guidelines of a pragmatist philosophy in interpreting the concept of the universe as a whole.

The history of the concept of an intelligible universe parallels major changes in technology, social structure, and dominant thought patterns of different periods of human culture. For example, in the early Babylonian cosmogonic myth *Enuma Elish*, the major regions of the world were established as a result of the authoritative decrees of a supremely powerful deity, Marduk, who, having slain the dragon Tiamat, carved up its carcass and allotted its various parts to subordinate gods.[2] The intelligibility of how things are ordered on a cosmic scale is here obviously analogized to the intelligibility inherent in the social structure of a domain that had been established through the arbitrary decisions of a powerful ruler.

Another stage in the development of the notion of intelligibility that has evident continuity with the foregoing is the one that stresses the practices of human crafts—for example, pottery, weaving, or carpentry. In this type of analogy, it is not a powerful ruler but a designing craftsman who, in following both inherited rules of his craft and the inspiration of his own individual imagination, is able to embody a pleasing or useful form in a finished product.

This analogy with the crafts for understanding the intelligibility of the cosmos at large was exploited by Plato. It is found in the dialogue *Timaeus*, where he gives (in the form of a myth—a "likely story") an account of his cosmogony. In this account, Plato makes use of the analogy of a craftsman (for example, a potter working in clay) who fashions a humanly useful work out of pre-existent, raw,

[2] Cf. Milton K. Munitz (ed.), *Theories of the Universe* (New York: Free Press, 1957), 8-20.

and "unordered" materials. Similarly, a Divine Craftsman (the Demiurge) imposes a rational order on raw, chaotic materials in creating a cosmos. Just as a human craftsman looks to some designful plan in molding his materials, so the Divine Craftsman looks to the domain of wholly intelligible perfect Forms as his ideals, paradigms, and guides in trying to embody these archetypes in the partly recalcitrant domain of pre-existent raw materials of sense. The outcome is the cosmos in the form of an organic being possessed of a body and a soul—a mixture of Reason and Necessity, a single, all-inclusive finite Cosmic Creature. In addition to exploiting this analogy from the side of the handicrafts (so prominent in his own culture), Plato was also strongly influenced by the Pythagoreans, who saw in numbers and geometric shapes the very elements out of which everything in the world could be constructed and rendered mathematically intelligible. Thus the intelligibility of the cosmos is not only the product of the beneficent plans of a designing Craftsman, but also that which belongs to numbers and geometric shapes. Once constructed by the Demiurge and confronted by us, the world can be properly understood to the extent that we are able to *discover* the teleological and quantitative properties that were put into the original material by a mathematical and benevolently purposeful Intelligence. We succeed in understanding the world as an ordered cosmos to the extent that our probing, finite human intellects are able to uncover and make clear to ourselves the rationally intelligible plan that was incorporated in it at its creation by the Demiurge, the Divine Craftsman.

Although there are, of course, well-known and important differences between the philosophies of Plato and Aristotle, it is not farfetched to see clear links with the views of his master Plato in Aristotle's conception of the intelligibility of the world. Aristotle surrendered the Platonic conception of a separate world of eternal Forms. Aristotle's God is no longer a Divine Craftsman. Furthermore, as a scientist having the orientation of a biologist rather than that of a mathematician, Aristotle gave a different emphasis to the functional teleological intelligibilities of substances in Nature. In

Aristotle's conception of Nature, the goals of things are not consciously planned by a Divine Craftsman. Instead, they are to be understood in terms of final causes, their naturally built-in functional ends. The world is constituted of substances, each class of which has its own essence. For Aristotle's biological orientation, "essence" is a matter of correct taxonomic classification, of setting out the genus and species of an individual substance. He gave primary attention to patterns of growth and development—to "natural" places and motions—rather than to mathematical ideas. Nevertheless, enough of the Platonic approach to intelligibility as an inherent feature of the world and its contents remains in Aristotle's philosophy to see in it a close relative of Plato's views.

Aristotle retains Plato's conception of the cosmos as an ordered whole having the form of a single all-inclusive organic unity. Any individual substance within the ordered world has its matter and form, its potentialities and actualities regulated by the inherent structures and essential confines of a genus-species-differentia hierarchy. So, too, the spatially finite cosmos on an astronomical level is intelligible in terms of the complex order of concentric spheres that stretches from the outermost heavens inward to the fixed central Earth. In this order, each broad domain is governed by its distinctive and appropriate natural motions.

For Aristotle, accordingly, the world is inherently intelligible. It is spread out not only before our eyes, but before *nous*, our intellectual capacity for rational understanding. The intelligible structure of the world is gradually discerned when the human faculty for rational understanding functions healthily and realizes its own proper intellectual virtues (strengths or excellences). Among the richly diversified domains of natural substances, the power of rational understanding belongs to man alone as a rational animal. In discovering facts about himself, including his cognitive powers, as well as about the powers of various other substances, man simply brings to the light of rational consciousness what already exists in a structured way prior to the act of conscious disclosure. As sophisticated exercises in rational inquiry, the sciences discover in detail the intelligible structure of the world. Under the guidance of logic and a disciplined method of inquiry, man's intellect, his *nous*, transforms the latent intelligibility of the world into a world understood. In short, for Aristotle knowledge is an uncovering of what is antecedently and independently there.

With the emergence of Christian theology, Creation is still dominated by the imagery of Craftsmanship, this time, however, interpreted without an appeal to the concept of a pre-existent material. God created the world *ex nihilo*. Cosmic creation becomes altogether a mystery, transcending any human analogy.

As modern science grew in prominence, with its emphasis on the discovery of laws of nature (themselves quantifiable and subject to mathematical operations of deduction and systematization), the conception of intelligibility as consisting in discoverable mathematical laws was joined, for many, with the traditional theistic view of God as the ultimate Creator, the unique and special Architect, Craftsman, and Governor. God is pictured as a Lawgiver who imposed a scientifically intelligible mathematico-physical order on the world at its genesis. Obvious descendants of this Platonically inspired view include, among many other examples, the growing emphasis in modern science, beginning in the seventeenth century, on the view of Nature as a vast, deterministically ordered machine, a world that operates according to discoverable, mathematically formulable physical laws; the view of eighteenth-century Deists who proclaimed that, at Creation, God wound up the universe like a clock and let it operate thereafter without interference and according to fixed mechanical laws; and the belief of James Jeans and other latter-day theistic Pythagoreans that "God is a mathematician."

From this realistic conception of the nature of intelligibility in some of its historical forebears and formulations, I turn next to a radically different view of the nature of intelligibility. The second broad type of philosophy mentioned earlier—a *pragmatist* orientation—stresses the creative role of the mind in achieving knowledge. It takes seriously the thesis that *what* we are said to know, whether through perception or conception, bears the marks of the way in which the knowing agent functions. What we know is a product to which the knowing agent makes a contribution that is distinctively his. The product of knowledge does not exist prior to or independently of that contribution. In coming to know reality, we inevitably *add* something that was not present until thought is exercised. Our knowledge, like a mirror, reflects at least in part something we put into it. This is a view to which Kant was a major contributor. According to Kant, intelligibility is that which has a human rather than a divine or natural source. The world becomes intelligible because *man*, not God, is the lawgiver.

The seeds for this radical shift in the conception of the relation between thought and reality were already sown by Descartes. He made a fundamental distinction between the mind of a knowing "subject" and its representations or ideas, on the one hand, and, on the other, the world as "object"—that which the mind purports to know by means of these mental contents. For Descartes, the basic question concerning knowledge has to do with the matter of its *certainty*. As a mathematician and physicist, Descartes was convinced that all genuine knowledge in any domain, scientific or otherwise, must adhere to a strictly deductive pattern of reasoning of the sort (he believed) one finds exemplified in well-established branches of mathematics. From absolutely unshakable, self-evident axiomatic premises, one proceeds by rigorous deductive steps to conclusions derived from these premises. The hallmark of all rationally secured knowledge is its certainty. As warranted by reason, all the truths it sanctions are indubitable. Inspired by this ideal, Descartes was principally concerned with finding secure *foundations* for any claims to knowledge. What kinds of evidential support can be found for the various cognitive claims we make? What intuitively true basic statements can be found that might serve to ground the entire superstructure of warranted claims to knowledge?

Kant, however, was not principally concerned with this question of the certainty of knowledge. For him, the central question of epistemology concerned the actual or possible *limits* of human knowledge. He undertook to show there are definite bounds to any actual or possible knowledge. These bounds are determined by the fixed a priori forms in the very operation of human cognitive faculties. In being a priori, these forms are not derived from or based on experience. Unlike what is a posteriori, that is, based on and derived from experience, a priori forms are universal: they hold without exception. They are necessary and permanently fixed for all human beings. They are not open to change, modification, or uncertainty. All human beings employ these forms by virtue of the unchanging and universal structure of the human mind. They are brought into operation in all acts of perception or conception. They are imposed on the raw data of sensory experience. Since all actual or possible experience lies within these limits and cannot transcend them, we can never know what reality may be "in itself," that is, apart from the mind's constructive activity. All we ever have is a knowledge of how the world *appears* to us, of *phenomena*, not of how things are in themselves, of *noumena*. What we know cannot be discussed apart from the a priori conditions involved in achieving knowledge. In its most basic characteristics—for example, as spatially and temporally ordered, as separated into substances, and explanatorily related by various causal laws—the constituents of the world, insofar as they are described and understood, are dependent on the forms of the mind for their specification. The *world*-as-known involves *human* conditions.

In the preface to the second edition of the *Critique of Pure Reason*, Kant says he sought to accomplish a second "Copernican revolution." Just as the original proposals of Copernicus revolutionized planetary astronomy by shifting from a geocentric to a heliocentric point of view, so Kant would accomplish a similar radical departure from earlier theories, this time with respect to the question of the relation of the knowing subject to the object known. Whereas classical theories of knowledge share the assumption that the attainment of knowledge consists in a conformity of man's ideas and beliefs to the independently existing properties of the object known, Kant's epistemological theory would reverse this demand. It asserts that in achieving knowledge, the object known must conform to the mind's own structuring a priori forms of perception and understanding.

Although since Kant's day much has been surrendered in his own formulation of this doctrine and insight, enough remains—for example, in the philosophy of pragmatism and the later philosophy of Wittgenstein—to continue this approach to the nature of intelligibility. Intelligibility is to be found within the limits of rules established by men in languages generally, and in conceptual systems or scientific theories in particular. It is through the creation of these rules that intelligibility is to be found. Once established and applied, the rules *confer* intelligibility on a subject matter given initially through observational experience.

A WITTGENSTEINIAN PERSPECTIVE

In the contemporary philosophic scene, the kinds of problems that Kant faced have been reformulated and restructured in ways that differ significantly from those he himself adopted. Thus the epistemological turn accomplished by Kant is transformed by Wittgenstein—a leading representative of twentieth-century analytic philosophy—into a linguistic matter. Kant's epistemological problems, stated in quasi-psychologistic terms concerning the powers and cognitive limits of the *mind*, are replaced by questions concerning the bounds of sense, the uses and cognitive limits of *linguistic expressions*. On this approach, language is not given special attention because it is viewed as a vehicle through which thought gets expressed. On the contrary, language is not secondary and ancillary, an external means for conveying something essentially mental and inner, namely thought, understanding, and inference. Rather, it is the other way around. The primary datum for analysis is language. Thus Wittgenstein stressed the importance of regarding any conceptual scheme, whatever its degree of sophistication, as essentially a use of language. Thought *is* language.

In analyzing the structure and operation of language in its various forms, Wittgenstein pointed to the need to make a fundamental distinction between two principal types of components. The first consists of what he called the *grammar* of the language—the rules that govern the use of expressions introduced and adopted in the language. The second consists of various *applications* of the grammar. A special example of one whole range of such applications is the making of *factual* statements.[3]

Following Wittgenstein, we shall understand by a *grammatical sentence* one that *states or explains the rule of use—the meaning—of some linguistic expression*. What falls under this heading, however, is richer and more diverse than what would ordinarily be so identified. As interpreted by Wittgenstein, grammar is a study of the specific character and modes of expression made use of in human thought. It has to do with the way we look at things. Since "thought" is a matter of the use of language, grammar deals with the multiform character of language. It describes the tool that is language. In particular, grammar concerns the meanings and uses of various sorts of linguistic expression. These meanings and uses are embodied in grammatical rules. To survey the complex web of these rules, to see them in their interrelations with one another, to note their similarities and differences, and to recognize the way they are embedded in "forms of life" (practices and modes of action)—all of this demands a never-ending process of analysis, a disentangling of confusions and careful attention to details. To make clear and illustrate the special character of these grammatical sentences in relation to, and in contrast with, other types of sentences is one of the special tasks and roles of philosophy.

When one approaches the concept of grammar in the above

[3] The chief works of Wittgenstein's later philosophy are *Philosophical Investigations*, 3d ed., trans. G.E.M. Anscombe (New York: Macmillan, 1968); *Remarks on the Foundations of Mathematics*, ed. G. H. von Wright, R. Rhees, and G.E.M. Anscombe; trans. G.E.M. Anscombe (rev. ed., Oxford: Blackwell, 1978); *On Certainty*, ed. G.E.M. Anscombe and G. H. von Wright; trans. G.E.M. Anscombe and D. Paul (Oxford: Blackwell, 1969). See also G. P. Baker and P.M.S. Hacker, *Wittgenstein: Understanding and Meaning*, vol. 1 (Chicago: Univ. of Chicago Press, 1980); idem, *Wittgenstein: Rules, Grammar and Necessity*, vol. 2 (Oxford: Blackwell, 1985); P.M.S. Hacker, *Insight and Illusion* (Oxford: Clarendon Press, 1972); M. K. Munitz, *Contemporary Analytic Philosophy* (New York: Macmillan, 1981), Chaps. 5, 6, 7.

sense, there are many examples of grammatical sentences that are not ordinarily recognized as such. Nevertheless, by probing one may discover that what appears at first glance to be a sentence of another type is, in fact, a grammatical sentence. The following are some of Wittgenstein's own examples of uncovered grammatical sentences: "Every rod has a length"; "I do not believe falsely"; "White is lighter than black"; "12 inches = 1 foot"; "The sum of the angles of a Euclidean triangle is 180 degrees." These are grammatical sentences, not in the trivial sense of conforming to the syntactic rules of the English language, but in the sense that they themselves *state* grammatical rules.

To recognize a grammatical rule, as distinguished from a factual or other type of sentence (which in outward appearance it may strongly resemble), is not a simple matter. It frequently calls for delicate and skillful analysis. Moreover, it has to be done piecemeal, since there are no guides that can be given in a wholesale way. In a stretch of discourse, say of science or philosophy, grammatical sentences may lie side by side with others of a wholly different type and not be easily recognized as such. Nor is the determination of whether a sentence is at bottom a grammatical rule always free of controversy. Take an example considered by Wittgenstein: "Machines cannot think." Is this a grammatical sentence or a factual one? Part of the answer depends on how we understand "machine" or "think." It also depends on whether we appeal to empirical data in order to help settle the issue. For insofar as we do, the sentence is *not* a grammatical one.

Grammatical sentences explain the rules of use of some linguistic expression. (In what follows, "linguistic expression" includes words, phrases, notational symbols, equations, graphs, entire sentences, and connected combinations of sentences or formulae, such as arguments or mathematical calculations.) Grammatical *rules of use* are to be distinguished from empirical, factual reports of *usage* and from *applications* of a rule of use. For example, a historical linguist or anthropologist who *reports* that such-and-such a group of people uses an expression in such-and-such a way is making a factual statement. He is *describing* an actual usage. His statement is either true or false. The fact that the subject matter to which his statement refers concerns language does not convert the statement into a grammatical sentence. A grammatical sentence *prescribes*, expresses, conveys, formulates, and explains a rule of use. It is neither true nor false, since it is not an empirical or factual statement. It is, rather, a stipulation, a convention, a form of representation, a way of looking at things—in short, a tool to be *applied*. Among its applications are factual or empirical statements. The following sentence is an example of a *grammatical rule of use*: "A hurricane is a violent cyclonic storm with winds moving at 73 or more miles per hour, originating in the tropics, especially in the West Indian region." It states the meaning of the term "hurricane." A particular *application* of the foregoing rule of use of the term "hurricane" would be found, for example, in the statement made by a Florida resident who says, on a particular occasion: "The hurricane we had last week did 50 million dollars worth of damage in our immediate vicinity." Again, if, on the basis of a statistical survey, one reports that in describing the actual weather, television reporters in the Eastern United States employ the term "hurricane" more frequently than the term "cyclone," such a report has to do with a prevalent *usage* of the term "hurricane." This statistical report is either true or false. It does not formulate a grammatical rule of use.

Grammatical rules are learned by acquiring competence in the performance of a *language-game* in which the use of an expression is illustrated, and in being able to *understand* how the linguistic expression is being used by others. That one understands a grammatical rule is exhibited in repeated performance, in behavior showing a pattern of correct application of the rule in question. Understanding is also shown in the way one goes about explaining the meaning of an expression—in the ability to state the rule, and through numerous examples to make clear what the rule is. Acquisition of competence in the use and understanding of a language consists in having been trained in and having adopted various rules, conventions, stipulations, and practices that govern the use of many different kinds of linguistic expressions. To learn the grammar of a language is to learn how to manipulate its symbols, to understand what someone else who already knows the language is saying, and to be able to communicate one's thoughts to others by means of the language. It is at bottom a training in understanding the *meaning* of the symbols and expressions in the language. To *understand* the grammar of a language is not yet, however, to *apply* it for one's special purposes in particular situations.

In his later works (principally in *Philosophical Investigations*), Wittgenstein stressed the fact that language is to be understood as playing very many different kinds of roles, fulfilling all sorts of needs and purposes in the different forms of life in which they are embedded. Among these, but by no means exhausting them, we may single out those language-games whose primary function is to serve as the means whereby man undertakes to describe, report on, provide information about, classify, and explain what he finds going on about him. Among the multitudinous purposes for which language is used by human beings may be singled out one whole segment that encompasses the uses of language for *cognitive* purposes. These include such special uses as describing the outcome of an experiment or field observations, writing history, formulating hypotheses, codifying the results of observations in the form of empirical laws, explaining an individual occurrence or certain regularities of observed phenomena, making predictions, and a host of related activities. Let us refer to these interests as *cognitive interests*, and let us refer to the various language uses that serve these cognitive interests as providing *means of representation* of their subject matter.

It is in connection with varied *applications* of the grammatical rules of language that questions can be raised about the warrantability, truth or falsity, justification, and grounds for the assertion of beliefs, predictions, criticisms, reports, hypotheses, and the like. Factual statements of one sort or another belong to these applications of grammatical sentences. Whereas grammatical sentences are neither true nor false, factual sentences, as applications of grammatical rules to particular circumstances, in order to accomplish one or another cognitive purpose, *can* be examined from the

73

point of view of their warrantability, justification, rational accept-ability—in short, their truth or falsity.

Let us collect the various subject matters—the various events and objects represented in language—and refer to them as belong-ing to or making up *the world*. One of the central contentions of Wittgenstein's later philosophy of language (as contrasted with his earlier philosophy of language expressed in his *Tractatus Logico-Philosophicus*) is that the character of the world is *constituted* by the very fact of the use of language.[4] The representative function of language is at the same time a constitutive function. The *appli-cation* of the various grammatical rules that differentiate languages from one another creates the form of the world. The detailed form of what it is to be an "object" or "fact," as constituents of the world, does not exist independently of language. How we describe an ob-ject or fact is assigned through the rules of use (the grammar) of some particular language-game. We cannot say anything about the world without, at the same time, recognizing the contribution made by language in structuring the world and giving it some form. In one respect, this is itself a grammatical proposition: it tells us something about how we are to understand the use of the term "the world." But it is also an existential statement, for in *using* the term "the world" we are applying it to make an assertion about what exists.

[4] When Wittgenstein, in the *Tractatus*, set about establishing the nature of the world that corresponds to what he regarded as the ideal language of logical atom-ism, he proposed a metaphysics incompatible with the dominantly Kantian orien-tation of his later philosophy. At best the metaphysics of the *Tractatus* might be linked with an "Aristotelian" view that argues for the correspondence or identity of structure between a purified language and the inherent intelligible structure of real-ity. I do not mean, of course, that the metaphysics of logical atomism is one that Aristotle would have accepted. I mean simply that the claim of identity of logical structure and the intelligible structure of reality is common both to the Aristotelian tradition and Wittgenstein's metaphysics in the *Tractatus*. However, it is only when one overcomes this kind of idolatry and realizes the relativity and constructive character of all language systems that one is turned in the direction of a broadly Kantian mode of thought. It is in this latter direction that Wittgenstein turned in his later philosophy.

A language is a mode of representation. It is comparable to a mode of projection in constructing a map. We cannot draw a map of a country without employing some mode of projection or other. The contours of the land are conveyed through some particular means of representation. There are no contours as such and independently of all modes of projection. However, having settled on some method of projection (some "language"), the particular form given to the contour of the land—say the coastline of a particular region or the elevation of a mountain—is not a matter for the method of projection to decide. To determine this, one needs to resort to observation, though the couching of the results of observation and the drawing of the map must fall back on some particular method of projection. Similarly, how the objects or facts of the world are to be described and explained requires some language or other, some set of grammatical rules by which they are to be represented. One can only refer to these objects or facts through some scheme of representation, which is essential to what is described or explained. According to Wittgenstein, it would be a serious mistake to believe that what the mode of representation is— what the grammatical rules of a language are—is somehow determined by the supposedly independently existing facts. There are no independently existing facts. For what it is to be a fact already requires some language or other to state what the fact is. We cannot, as it were, carry the language up to the facts as putatively independently existing entities, and examine them in order to see which language fits the facts best. For in examining the facts we are already employing some language and system of representation. The grammatical rules of a language are not determined by the world, since the world apart from men contains no grammatical rules. In creating languages, it is men who use their rules to determine how to represent the world. Wittgenstein argues it is a mistake to assume that experience *alone* can establish what the facts are.

A fundamental feature of Wittgenstein's later philosophy of language is its acknowledgment of the existence of many different languages, language-games, grammatical rules, and schemes of representation. Since he abandoned the view of the *Tractatus*—that there is one ideal language, composed of names, whose combination matches (is a picture of) the structure of the facts inherent in the world—it follows that with a multiplicity of actual languages, the world on its formal or structural side can be described in as many varied ways as the languages used to represent it. There is no unique essence or structure that is antecedently embodied in the world and that some ideal language would be uniquely competent to disclose. There is no uniquely preferable language that has absolute and permanent superiority to all actual or possible alternative schemes of representation.

The limits of thought and knowledge are the limits determined by the rules of grammar (the bounds of sense) belonging to the multiplicity of languages used to represent the world. We cannot in thought or by conceptual means pass beyond those limits. We cannot *say* anything about the world that exists independently of *all* languages. What has to be accepted as given, Wittgenstein maintains, is one or another network of forms of life and the language-games embedded in them.

For Wittgenstein, all grammatical rules are a priori in the sense that they are brought to our experience of the world as arbitrary inventions or constructions by men. In the Kantian way of expressing it, they are spontaneous creations of the human mind. There are, however, important differences in Wittgenstein's view of language-games and the transcendental machinery of the a priori forms in Kant. In place of Kant's insistence that the human mind is so constructed that the forms employed are *synthetic* a priori patterns imposed on the flux of experience, and the claim that these patterns are universal and necessary, that is, without exception for human perception and understanding, Wittgenstein regards the construction and use of languages in an altogether different light. There are countless different language-games, no uniquely correct or inevitable one. There is a multiplicity of ways in which our experience can be represented. In line with the foregoing, Wittgenstein would say that wherever someone claims to have established or discovered a necessary fact, he has covertly appealed to a grammatical proposition. There are "necessary facts," but only in the sense of their being arbitrary grammatical rules. A necessary proposition that purportedly represents an independently existing necessary fact is actually a way of stating a grammatical rule. It says something only about one's method of representation of the world.

An important example of the use of language for cognitive purposes is to be found in the formulation and use of *scientific theories*. A scientific theory consists fundamentally of two types of sentences. There are, first, those which, being grammatical, consist of various conceptual techniques of representation and calculation. Secondly, there are sentences that consist of the manifold applications of these conceptual tools. The latter make up the entire collection of factually descriptive and explanatory accounts of some subject matter—the various hypotheses, predictions, reports of observations— that are taken as confirmed, disconfirmed, or open to further testing. The grammar of a particular scientific theory includes both standard, commonly accepted items of linguistic or conceptual use, and, in addition, the distinctively new, creative ideas introduced by the inventor(s) of the theory. Thus, in addition to falling back on the standard rules of English or of Euclidean geometry, Newton introduced his innovative concepts of absolute space and time and of gravitational action-at-a-distance. Concepts distinctive of the radically different theory of Einsteinian relativity—for example, the curvature of space-time as a way of describing gravitation—are not present at all in the grammar of Newtonian theory. From the point of view of the latter, therefore, such concepts are not even possible, since they are not defined in terms of the basic grammar of Newtonian theory; they have no sense in that theory.

Within a scientific theory it is not always a simple matter to distinguish its grammatical components from its factual ones. Thus one commonly refers indiscriminately to the Law of Inertia, the force equation $F = ma$, the Law of the Pendulum, and Kepler's Laws for the orbits of the planets as "laws." Similarly, Einstein's field equations of relativity and Schwarzschild's solution to those equations are both referred to as being "theories." However, the equation $F = ma$ and Einstein's field equations are best regarded as basic grammatical rules. They should be distinguished from their applications that take the form of solutions, empirical laws, factual hypotheses, predictions, and the like. Such applications make use of the grammatical rules on which they rely for their own formulations.

Relativity theory, quantum theory, and other revolutionary conceptual innovations in modern physics represent what Thomas S. Kuhn calls "paradigm shifts." Paradigms consist in the adoption, training in, and acquisition of skill in the use of the grammar of some theory. A "revolution" marks the replacement of one set of "normal" grammatical rules, one conceptual scheme, by another.[5]

The choice from among different scientific theories (both their underlying grammar and the applications made of that grammar for descriptive, explanatory, and predictive purposes) is governed by pragmatic criteria. Theories are not to be judged by how well they correspond to a putatively independent, unique structure already embodied in some subject matter, nor in terms of how well they approximate to some supposedly ideal formulation that would totally and perfectly capture the supposedly real structure. Rather, theories are to be judged in terms of their relative or comparative effectiveness in rendering their subject matter intelligible. Theories are parts of a stream of human inquiry and have a position in the history of human creativity. Their role is not to uncover or lay bare some inherent structure in the world as it exists "in itself." Their role is to convert a world encountered in observational experience into an intelligible world.

The bounds of human thought are bounds that belong to the language-games human beings play, the conceptual schemes they devise. The bounds of a language scheme are not necessarily to be

[5] For a more detailed discussion, see T. S. Kuhn, *The Structure of Scientific Revolutions*, 2d ed. (Chicago: Univ. of Chicago Press, 1970); N. R. Hanson, *Patterns of Discovery* (Cambridge, Eng.: Cambridge Univ. Press, 1958); S. Toulmin, *Human Understanding*, vol. 1 (Oxford, 1972); W. H. Watson, *On Understanding Physics* (Cambridge, Eng.: Cambridge Univ. Press, 1938).

equated with what may be supposed to be the inherent bounds of a subject matter, and where the latter make it permanently impervious to further description or explanation. Conceptual bounds are due to man-made limitations that come with the use of some language scheme. The only way of escaping from these bounds is not to try—contradictorily and incoherently—to "conceive" what the world is "in itself" apart from human conceptualization. The only way of overcoming in thought the bounds of one scheme of language, one conceptual framework, is to fashion another and to see, pragmatically, whether it does any better—whether it answers more and different types of questions than the theories it replaces. Truth is thus not a matter of correspondence, of picturing some state of affairs already possessed of its own structure and properties. Truth is rather *warranted assertibility, rational acceptability*—the justification for the acceptance and use of one language scheme in preference to others. This justification is to be found in successful practice—in the number and character of the confirmed tests the preferred language scheme, theory, or conceptual framework can claim for itself in competition with its rivals.

The upshot of the foregoing analysis of the concept of intelligibility is the need to distinguish two broadly different ways of interpreting this concept and to avoid confusing them. On the realistic view, intelligibility is a property of some independently existing *subject matter*—the world as a whole or any part of it. If we use Aristotelian terminology, we could say that intelligibility is a potentiality in the form of a unique, essential structure, inherent in the subject matter to be understood, and awaiting discovery of that structure. When understood, the potentiality is transformed into an actuality. When the human power of rational understanding is exercised properly in accomplishing this transformation, the result is tantamount to disclosing the *truth* about the world. At that point, man's use of his intellectual and linguistic powers for saying how things are is optimally realized.

The other approach to intelligibility does not think of intelligibility as exclusively a property of some independently existing subject matter but rather as that which is to be found in connection

79

with the use of some linguistic rule or conceptual scheme. In Wittgensteinian terminology, what one understands is a rule of use—the grammar—of some linguistic expression. However, to say that one has such an understanding—that the rule is understood—is *not* tantamount to saying that some independently existing subject matter is thereby understood. Understanding a rule is not equivalent to knowing the truth (or falsity) of some account of a subject matter. In order to determine the truth or falsity of an account, one must *apply* the linguistic rules or conceptual scheme for purposes of description or explanation. Since there are many possible conceptual schemes, all of which are devised by human beings, there are many possible ways of conferring intelligibility on a subject matter. Therefore, in determining the truth or falsity of such application, one must evaluate a given scheme of description or explanation in comparison with the merits of other grammatical rules, other schemes of interpretation, similarly applied. Each grammar, conceptual scheme, theory, or model is intelligible insofar as *it* can be understood. If the subject matter to which a given set of rules is successfully applied is now itself said to be understood, this is a shorthand way of saying that the conceptual scheme expressed by these rules is to be preferred to other schemes. This use of the expression "a subject matter understood" is, however, to be distinguished from the meaning given to it on the basis of the first philosophy we examined earlier.

In applying the foregoing ideas to the field of cosmology, and in particular in favoring the second of the above approaches to the meaning of "intelligibility," one would say that the universe as a whole is described and made intelligible by a particular cosmological model. On the one hand, a cosmological model serves as a complex grammatical rule to define the use of the expression "the universe." As a grammatical rule, it is neither true nor false. It simply explains what we are to understand by the expression "the universe." However, a cosmological model can and does serve another role besides that of being a grammatical rule. It undertakes to describe and explain various observational data, events, processes, regularities, and objects. To say this subject matter is understood in the sense that the cosmological model's account is *true* is to enter a factual claim, to assert that one has a *satisfactory* cognitive grasp of this subject matter. This involves an *application* of the cosmological model as a grammatical rule. It is an application whose satisfactoriness or justification has to be assessed.

The next chapter will illustrate the main points of the foregoing general discussion of the scope of cosmology by examining some of the details of recent cosmological investigations. We shall first explore the principal ideas of classic relativistic cosmology, as inspired by Einstein's path-breaking proposals at the beginning of this century. We shall then survey some of the major lines of advance of more recent investigations in which the conceptual resources of quantum and particle physics have been brought to bear in grappling with the cosmological problem. Having accomplished this, we shall be in a better position to reflect on these ongoing achievements with an eye to assessing their deeper philosophical significance—how they might affect our conception of ultimate reality and the place of human existence in the wider scheme of things.

FOUR

The Beginning and End
of the Universe

THE EVOLVING UNIVERSE

As a first step in surveying the main features of current conceptions of the evolutionary universe, we shall briefly review the earlier contributions of Einstein and others to the development of models of relativistic cosmology. At the heart of the latter is the application of some of the main ideas of Einstein's general theory of relativity.

The classic Einsteinian general theory of relativity is essentially a theory of the gravitational field.[1] Instead of thinking, with New-

[1] The literature, of course, is vast. Among some basic references are A. Einstein, *The Meaning of Relativity* (Princeton, N.J.: Princeton University Press, 1955); A. Einstein, H. A. Weyl, and H. Minkowski, *The Principle of Relativity* (New York: Dover Publications, 1952); A. Pais, *"Subtle is the Lord": The Science and the Life of Albert Einstein* (New York: Oxford University Press, 1982); S. Weinberg, *Gravitation and Cosmology: Principles and Applications of the General Theory of Relativity* (New York: Wiley, 1972); C. W. Misner, K. S. Thorne, and J. A. Wheeler, *Gravitation* (San Francisco: W. H. Freeman, 1973); W. Rindler, *Essential Relativity: Special, General, and Cosmological*, rev. 2d ed. (New York: Springer-Verlag, 1977); Peter G. Bergmann, *The Riddle of Gravitation* (New York: Charles Scribner's Sons, 1968); Robert Geroch, *General Relativity from A to B* (Chicago: University of Chicago Press, 1978); Michael Friedman, *Foundations of Space-Time Theories: Relativistic Physics and Philosophy of Science* (Princeton, N.J.: Princeton University Press, 1983); John C. Graves, *The Conceptual Foundations of Contemporary Relativity Theory* (Cambridge, Mass.: MIT Press, 1971); Lawrence Sklar, *Space, Time, and Spacetime* (Berkeley: University of California Press, 1977).

ton, of gravitation as a force acting instantaneously and at any distance separating one body and another, Einstein proposed to think of gravitation as the effect exerted by the metric structure of a field acting locally on any body placed within the field.[2] At the heart of Einstein's new way of thinking are two ideas. First, gravitational phenomena are to be interpreted as due to the properties of a *field*. To describe this field, Einstein made use of the basic theoretical concept of space-time. Instead of being treated as separate and independent of one another (as they had been in Newtonian physics), space and time are bound together in a four-dimensional mathematical unity called "space-time." Secondly, the specific character of the gravitational field is conveyed by means of its *metrical* space-time structure. The phenomenon of gravitation is to be understood as the effect of the intrinsic curvature—a geometrical property—of space-time. It is the startling claim that gravitation is a matter of geometry and nothing else that made Einstein's theory the revolutionary proposal it was.

The geometry of space-time, whether of cosmological scope or as established for more limited regions, is determined by the concentrations and distributions of matter and energy. When applied to the problem of understanding the space-time geometric and physical structure of the universe as a whole, this approach gave birth to the discipline of relativistic cosmology. Our survey of some of the main features of this area of investigation is in the interest of seeing what specific forms this geometric conception of gravitation took when used to construct models of the universe as a whole. Our study will illustrate what it means to say that a theory of the universe represents a language-game with its own distinctive grammar.

The new ideas of the general theory of relativity required the use of special geometrical concepts developed largely since Newton's day. These included (1) the concepts of non-Euclidean geometry; (2) techniques developed by Carl Friedrich Gauss (1777-1855) and

---

[2] Metric structure, briefly, is the formula used to describe the infinitesimal squared distance between two points belonging to a manifold (a set of points).

Bernhard Riemann (1826-1866) for dealing with spaces of constant (uniform) curvature as well as with spaces of non-uniform (variable) curvature; and (3) ways of establishing precise conditions under which various types of coordinate systems and their associated metric coefficients may be used in spaces of different types of curvature.

In non-Euclidean geometries, instead of accepting the Euclidean parallel postulate, according to which (in one of its formulations) through any point outside a straight line there is one and only one parallel to that line, there are two rival but equally acceptable postulates that can be used in constructing a consistent scheme of geometry. According to one, through a given point outside a straight line there is more than one parallel (non-intersecting) line. This postulate belongs to the system of non-Euclidean geometry known as *hyperbolic geometry*. The other non-Euclidean geometry is *spherical geometry*. In this geometry, there are no parallel, non-intersecting lines.

Each Euclidean and non-Euclidean geometry describes a uniform geometric space. In a uniform geometry, all figures retain their form and properties whether undergoing displacements or rotations. Although all three geometries are uniform, the differences between non-Euclidean values and Euclidean ones become noticeable over very large distances, areas, and volumes. At small distances and in small regions of space, the values of non-Euclidean geometries are similar to Euclidean ones. Furthermore, the uniform spaces described by Euclidean and non-Euclidean geometries can be compared with respect to whether the space involved is "open" or "closed." In both Euclidean and hyperbolic geometries, straight lines can be extended indefinitely in either direction. Therefore both Euclidean and hyperbolic spaces are of infinite extent or "open." On the other hand, in a spherical space, straight lines (for example, the great circles on the surface of the Earth) are finite in length. Hence the space dealt with in spherical geometry is finite or "closed."

To understand the basic concept of curvature, consider the geometry of a two-dimensional surface. Thus the surface of the

Earth has the properties of spherical geometry, the flat surface of a table top has Euclidean properties, while the central region of a saddle-backed surface has the properties of hyperbolic geometry. Non-uniform surfaces have curvature properties that vary from one region to another. Let us confine our attention, for the moment, to a surface that is uniform. Its *curvature* is numerically equal to $1/R^2$. In this expression, R is the *radius of curvature*. A large radius of curvature results in a small curvature, and vice versa. In the case of a spherical surface, the expression "radius of curvature" has an obvious relation to the radius of the sphere and was derived from its use in this context. It need not, however, be so restricted. In dealing with uniform spaces of any of the three geometries, the expression "radius of curvature" is used in an extended technical sense. In the case of the surface of a sphere, the two radii of curvature, used to obtain the product R^2, are both on the same side of the surface. In a hyperbolic surface, the radii of curvature are on opposite sides of the surface. Hence, whereas the value of the curvature of a spherical surface is positive, the value for $1/R^2$ in the hyperbolic case is negative. Since the "radius" of a flat Euclidean surface is infinite, the curvature $(1/R^2)$ is zero.

Let the quantity k represent the curvature of a space, whatever the number of dimensions (two, three, or more) of the type of space involved may be—Euclidean, hyperbolic, or spherical. Then the geometries can be distinguished from one another by their curvatures. Thus for any uniform spherical space of any number of dimensions, the value of k at any point of the space is *positive*, for hyperbolic space it is *negative*, and for Euclidean space it is *zero*. These differences are normally represented by the numerical values $+1$, -1, and 0 for spherical, hyperbolic, and Euclidean spaces, respectively. The value $+1$, -1, or 0 is known as the *index of curvature* of a space. The curvature of a space is an *intrinsic* property of the space. This means it is not necessary to think of that space as embedded in a space of higher dimensions, in the way, for example, the two-dimensional surface of a sphere is embedded in a three-dimensional object. The curvature of the space can be determined by remaining entirely within the space of a given number of dimensions.

Distances and angle measures give important information that help determine the metric properties of a space. For example, formulae for angle sums of triangles or for the circumference and areas of circles distinguish the geometric properties belonging to different two-dimensional spaces (2-spaces) of different types of curvature, as do formulae for the properties of volumes (for example, cubes, cylinders, spheres, etc.) in different 3-spaces of different types of curvature, and so on.

An important discovery by Gauss allows for the expression of differences in curvature by means of a formula that states the *metric* properties of a space. This formula is an extension of the well-known Pythagorean formula in elementary geometry for the distance between two points: the square of the hypotenuse of a right-angled triangle is equal to the sum of the squares on the other two sides. Consider this distance in a two-dimensional space as expressed by means of rectangular Cartesian coordinates. Whatever the differences in rectangular systems of coordinate axes used, the value for the distance between two points will be the same. If coordinates other than rectangular ones are used, the same invariant value for the length will be found. Changes in types of coordinates can be accounted for without affecting the value of the length. In short, the metric value for a length is an intrinsic property of the space.

By way of example, consider the simple two-dimensional Euclidean case. In it, the Cartesian coordinates of a point are given by numbers along the x and y axes. Nearby points will have coordinates $x + dx$, $y + dy$—where dx and dy are called the "differentials of the coordinates." For a two-dimensional Euclidean space, the distance between two nearby points, dl, is given by the formula:

$$dl^2 = dx^2 + dy^2.$$

In three dimensions, it is

$$dl^2 = dx^2 + dy^2 + dz^2,$$

and so on.

In this scheme of coordinates, each of the *coefficients* of the *dx*, *dy*, *dz* components has the value 1. The coefficients for the distance between two points will be different for spaces of different intrinsic curvatures. These coefficients are known as *metric coefficients*. Since the metric of a space, as determined intrinsically, governs the distance between two nearby points and the angle measure between two lines, it gives all the necessary metric properties of that space.

Thus in the case of a four-dimensional space-time, the formula for the interval *ds* between two nearby points is given by

$$ds^2 = \sum_{\mu=1}^{4} \ \ \sum_{\nu=1}^{4} \ g_{\mu\nu} \, dx^\mu \, dx^\nu$$

where dx_μ, dx_ν take the values 1 to 4 to represent four different coordinates (one for time, the remaining three for space). This formula gives the *metric* of space-time. There are a total of ten *coefficients of the metric*, represented by the $g_{\mu\nu}$.

Instead of thinking of points as making up the distinctive elementary contents of a separate three-dimensional space, and instants as composing the basic contents of one-dimensional time, relativity theory recognizes only one category—*events*. Events are the fundamental constituents of a single four-dimensional reality. Each event requires for its location four items of information—three spatial and one temporal. For example, if one fastens on the entire history of a single material entity in space-time, it can be represented by a *world-line* that connects all the events that together constitute the identity of that entity. Similarly, any complex network of interactions among different entities can be represented by interconnecting world-lines. The totality of events explored by physics is the *manifold* or *world* of *space-time*. It is within the world of space-time that all physical objects are located and that processes transpire.

According to the theory of general relativity, gravitational interaction is to be interpreted as the result of the curvature of space-time. On this approach, the motions of free particles in a gravitational field are determined by the space-time curvature of the field. Furthermore, the theory explains what that curvature itself is due to. It shows the connection between the curvature or metric properties of space-time over extended regions, on the one hand, and the distribution of mass-energy (of matter and radiation) in that region, on the other. Roughly, the greater the amount of mass-energy, the more intense the degree of curvature or "warpage" of the field in its vicinity. Where, consequently, there is no matter or it is present in negligible amounts, space-time is flat—of zero curvature. On the other hand, where there are marked concentrations of mass-energy or of varying amounts in different regions, the curvature in those regions can be calculated. As thus determined, the gravitational field will, in turn, guide the space-time paths of free particles moving in the field. In short, there is an interdependence between matter and field that can be looked at in two ways. As John Wheeler phrases it, "Space acts on matter, telling it how to move. In turn, matter reacts back on space, telling it how to curve."[3] (In the context of general relativity, "matter" is understood, rather broadly, as whatever contributes to the mass-energy of a region and thereby determines its gravitational field.)

A simple two-dimensional analogy is useful. On a rubber sheet in which a heavy ball is placed, there will be a depression whose curvature is greatest where the ball is located and becomes less with increasing distance from this center. If one introduces lighter balls onto the sheet, while giving them some initial motion, their paths will be determined by the curvature of the sheet, with differences dependent on their distances from the heavy ball and its depression. The relations between the heavy and light balls in this simple model simulate the relations between the massive central Sun of our planetary system, the gravitational space-time field it determines, and the orbital paths of the planets in this curved gravitational field.

Through its *field equations*, the general theory of relativity offers a precise means for calculating these variations in curvature. Accordingly, the field equations may be thought of as embodying the essence of the theory. They make clear the connection between

[3] Misner, Thorne, and Wheeler, *Gravitation*, 5.

the density of mass-energy and the curvature. Schematically, the field equations have the general form,

$$\text{curvature of space-time} = \text{constant} \times \text{matter}.$$

An important technique of representation and calculation in relativity theory that stems from its basically geometric orientation consists in the use of *geodesics*. The basic idea of a geodesic is familiar from examples in elementary geometry, where one deals with purely spatial relations. Thus a straight line, defined as the *shortest distance* between two points, is an example of a geodesic. In a Euclidean space of two, three, or any number of dimensions, a straight line, as the shortest distance between two points, is uniquely distinguished from all other lines that might connect the same two points. Similarly, in a *curved* space, the shortest distance between two points will also be uniquely distinguished from all other lines connecting the same two points. This shortest line in curved space is a geodesic. A familiar example of a geodesic in curved space is a great circle on the two-dimensional curved surface of a sphere. Thus on the surface of the Earth the shortest distance between two points is illustrated by any of the meridians of longitude, the Equator, or any other great circle whose center coincides with the center of the Earth. Geodesics for curved spaces can be found in any space, whether hyperbolic or spherical, and of any number of dimensions. In every space, then, whatever its uniform curvature, whether Euclidean (having zero curvature) or non-Euclidean (having positive or negative curvatures), geodesics are the shortest lines connecting two points in that space.

In four-dimensional space-time, the "points" of this "space" are events. However, we can still use the language of geometry to describe this special type of "space." In the context of lines in space-time, the term "geodesic" is extended by partial analogy with spatial examples and generalized to include curves of intervals that have extremum values. By contrast with purely spatial distances between neighboring points, the numerical value for ds (the space-time interval between neighboring events) can be either positive, negative, or zero. That is, ds^2 can be greater or less than neighboring curves joining the same two points, or it can also have the value zero while neighboring lines have positive or negative values. In any case, whether the value of ds^2 is positive, negative, or zero, it will be an *extremum* as compared to all other neighboring lines.

In relativity theory, a distinction is made, on the one hand, between the geodesics of free material particles and, on the other, the geodesics of particles of light. The space-time interval for nearby events on the geodesic of a free material particle is said to be *timelike*; the numerical value of the squared length of this interval is *negative*. On the other hand, where the square of the interval between two nearby events is *positive*, the two events are said to have a *spacelike* separation. Finally, where the space-time interval has a squared numerical value of *zero*, the separation between the events is said to be *lightlike*. Thus, whereas the squared *distance* between two distinct points in a purely spatial manifold is always nonnegative, the squared *space-time interval* between two distinct point-events can be positive, negative, or zero.

The distinctions among timelike, lightlike, and spacelike intervals have a direct bearing on the nature of causal connections. Two causally related events cannot be connected by any process of transmission that exceeds the velocity of light. Consider two points p and q in space-time. Then if p and q are connected by a future-directed path that is either lightlike (null) or timelike, then a signal may be transmitted from p to q. Where two events are separated by a timelike interval, a causal signal traveling from one to the other will have a speed less than that of light, and two events with a lightlike separation will have a causal signal connecting them that travels with the velocity of light. On the other hand, if two events are separated by a spacelike interval, then no causal signal can travel from one to the other, since no signal can travel with a velocity greater than that of light.

These definitions lead to the introduction of the concept of *proper time*. Proper time is the time recorded by a clock attached to a free material particle. The ticks of a clock carried by such a free material particle define a time for each point-event of the particle's trajectory. Each tick represents the proper time of an event. Similarly, *proper distance* is the space-time interval between two events having a spacelike separation.

One way of summarizing these distinctions and their importance for the conceptual foundations of general relativity theory is this: When considered *locally*—that is to say, in infinitesimal regions of space-time—all geodesics are straight lines. These straight lines belong to a space-time that is flat. The space-time has zero curvature. It is flat in a manner comparable to—but not identical with—a Euclidean four-dimensional space. It is only when the geodesics of these particles are examined in extended regions of space-time that they appear curved. It is then recognized that the geodesics of material and light particles are subject to the influence of gravitational fields and are therefore curved. The geodesics of free particles in curved space-time will have extremum values: they will be the "shortest straight lines" in a broadened sense of "shortest" and "straight." The amount or degree to which geodesics deviate from purely local straightness is a measure of the curvature of the field.

The field equations state in general though precise quantitative terms the dependence of the curvature of space-time on the density and pressure of mass-energy in that region. In order to be of any service in dealing with some particular situation, however, the general equations need to be solved for a particular state of mass-energy. Major directions of application of the general theory of relativity, for which solutions of the field equations have been found, include the dynamics of planetary orbits and the behavior of light rays in the gravitational field of the Sun; the conditions for the gravitational collapse of certain types of stars into black holes; and the construction of various cosmological models of the space-time structure of the universe as a whole.

The earliest applications of the field equations, pioneered by Einstein and given an exact solution by Karl Schwarzschild in 1916, described the space-time in the external, static, and spherically symmetric gravitational field whose source is a single massive center of attraction. This is the situation in our solar system. In it, there is a single massive body—the Sun—whose mass determines the gravitational field in its vicinity. In this vicinity, particles that represent the planets and light move. The planets are treated as free material particles whose geodesic paths are determined solely by the space-time geometry surrounding the Sun. Similarly, the paths of light rays in the field of the Sun are correctly explained by the same geometrical facts. It was the confirmed predictions and logical explanations of these applications of the field equations that marked its first great successes. These predictions and explanations were three in number: the previously known (but hitherto unexplained) precession in the perihelion of Mercury; the gravitational red shift of radiation; and the bending of starlight as it grazes the Sun's disk.

Following the initial successes of relativity, Einstein turned, in 1917, to an application of those same general field equations to the space-time structure of the grandest physical system of all—the universe. In doing so, he opened up the field of inquiry that goes by the name of "relativistic cosmology."[4]

As with any other empirical science, cosmology involves a constant interplay between observational data and conceptual interpretation. Furnished with a steady stream of observational data by

[4] Cf. M. Berry, *Principles of Cosmology and Gravitation* (Cambridge, Eng.: Cambridge University Press, 1976); D. W. Sciama, *Modern Cosmology* (Cambridge, Eng.: Cambridge University Press, 1971); M. P. Ryan, Jr., and L. C. Shepley, *Homogeneous Relativistic Cosmologies* (Princeton, N.J.: Princeton University Press, 1975); E. R. Harrison, *Cosmology: The Science of the Universe* (Cambridge, Eng.: Cambridge University Press, 1981); O. Gingerich, ed., *Cosmology + 1* (San Francisco: W. H. Freeman, 1977); M. K. Munitz, ed., *Theories of the Universe: From Babylonian Myth to Modern Science* (New York: Macmillan, 1957); M. K. Munitz, *Space, Time, and Creation: Philosophical Aspects of Scientific Cosmology*, 2d ed. (New York: Dover Publications, 1981); J. D. North, *The Measure of the Universe: A History of Modern Cosmology* (Oxford: Oxford University Press, 1965); P.C.W. Davies, *Space and Time in the Modern Universe* (Cambridge, Eng.: Cambridge University Press, 1977); R. V. Wagoner and D. W. Goldsmith, *Cosmic Horizons* (San Francisco: W. H. Freeman, 1983); Ya. B. Zel'Dovich and I. D. Novikov, *The Structure and Evolution of the Universe* (Chicago: University of Chicago Press, 1983); J. Silk, *The Big Bang: The Creation and Evolution of the Universe* (San Francisco: Freeman, 1980).

the astronomer and the laboratory physicist, the cosmologist must construct a model of the universe that would make these observational findings intelligible from a theoretical point of view. In the construction of a cosmological model, one underlying and recurrent major concern of the cosmologist is to be able to give a coherent and empirically well-supported account of the spatio-temporal structure of the universe as a whole. One principal set of observational data that bears on this project has to do with the large-scale *spatially isotropic distribution* of the galaxies and their *red shifts*.

Stationed on Earth, astronomers receive information in the form of signals conveyed by electromagnetic radiation of various frequencies. The data are obtained by means of optical and radio telescopes, infrared detectors, radio antennae, and satellite-mounted telescopes. An Earth-bound astronomical observer occupies a fixed spatial position. He possesses only the possibility of rotational changes in that fixed position, changes in *direction* of observation. The general result of these observations is that in whatever direction one "looks," and apart from "local" irregularities, the large-scale observational picture of the universe is *isotropic*: it looks very much the same in all spatial directions. Beyond a distance of approximately 300 million light-years, the optically observable universe is everywhere the same. In short, space is uniformly populated out to the limits of observability. Radio telescopes reveal a similar isotropic distribution of radio sources.

The phenomenon of galactic *red shifts* is a further observational datum of great importance to contemporary cosmology. Like other sources of radiation, galaxies show distinctive patterns of lines in their spectra. When these patterns are compared to those obtained from standard laboratory samples of matter composed of atoms emitting the same type of radiation, significant differences are found in the relative position of their spectral lines. The line spectra of the galaxies are uniformly shifted toward the red end of the visible spectrum. This fact is linked in an important way with their relative distances. On the assumption that all galaxies, on the average, have the same *intrinsic luminosity*, the *apparent brightness* of a galaxy can be taken as a measure of its distance: the smaller the apparent brightness of a galaxy, the greater its distance from the observer. By 1929, on the basis of data he amassed, Hubble showed that the red shifts of galaxies increase with their distance. He established a positive linear correlation between the amount of red shift and the luminosity of the galaxy emitting the radiation. In other words, the greater the distance, the greater the red shift. This correlation is known as *Hubble's Law*. If the red shift is interpreted as indicating a recession velocity, the correlation can be expressed as a velocity-distance law. It states that the quantity of the red shift is equal to the distance of the galaxy from the observer multiplied by a constant, H. The red shift phenomenon is a major observational support for the belief that the universe is nonstatic—that on a grand scale it manifests a universal expansion.

In what follows, we shall briefly survey the main conceptual techniques used by the cosmologist to interpret the foregoing observational findings.

The principal method for interpreting the data of the isotropic spatial distribution of the galaxies makes use of the geometric concept of *spatial homogeneity*. Conceive of an observer who is able to roam freely—that is, to perform translations in space and who is not restricted, therefore, to a fixed position (as an Earth-bound observer is) to only rotational changes in the direction of observation. Assume further that such a free-roaming observer finds all fairly sizeable regions of space to be altogether similar in physical content and phenomena. To slightly vary our thought experiment, imagine a cubical box whose edges are each greater than 100 million light-years in length. Conceive that a box of these dimensions is constructible anywhere throughout the vast expanse of the observable universe. Let any one box encompass material that on the average is everywhere similar to that to be found in any other box. As envisaged in these thought-experiments, the universe would be said to be spatially homogeneous on a large scale.

The hypothesis that the actual universe is in fact spatially homogeneous is tantamount to saying that the universe satisfies the *Cosmological Principle*. This principle claims that all regions of

the universe are similar to one another at a particular temporal epoch in the development of the universe. Einstein expressed this
idea by saying "all places in the universe are alike." It embodies the
belief that it is unreasonable to suppose that, situated here on
Earth and in our own Galaxy, we occupy a privileged position in
the universe. It is thought more reasonable to assume that observers situated on any other galaxy throughout the universe would
also find their observational findings to be isotropic in character. It
can be shown mathematically that if such universally shared isotropic observations were to hold, the universe would be spatially
homogeneous. This hypothesis of spatial homogeneity carries forward to a maximum degree the revolution accomplished by Copernicus in removing the Earth from a central, uniquely privileged
spatial position in the universe. This concept is therefore also
sometimes referred to as the *Copernican Principle*. From the earliest stages of development of relativistic cosmology, accordingly,
the overwhelming majority of models that have been given serious
consideration are spatially homogeneous (uniform) models of the
universe.

Nevertheless, as we shall see later, while the choice of homogeneous cosmological models narrows the field considerably, it
still leaves a number of options open. Is the universe spatially open
or closed? Is its index of curvature $+1$, -1, or 0? How to choose
from among these available options is one of the chief problems
that continues to be faced in ongoing cosmological inquiry. In the
attempt to solve this problem, cosmologists look to the empirically
observed actual density of matter and energy in the universe to effect a choice. As yet, however, no sufficiently secure observational
data are available to ground such a choice. A further important
question is *why* the universe should be homogeneous at all.

In picturing the large-scale composition of the universe in accordance with the above guidelines, a typical first step is to
"smooth out" or idealize the matter content of the universe. The
universe is treated as having the character of a perfect fluid. The
internal complex structure of galaxies, clusters of galaxies, and
stars is disregarded. Instead, matter is regarded as "dust," as parti-

cles of a "gas" having everywhere a uniform density of mass-energy and a negligible pressure. To an observer located anywhere in the universe, observing such a uniform, smoothed-out density of matter, the particles in his neighborhood would have no average, mean motion. Individual, local velocities of galaxies would be small compared to the velocity of light. This supposition is supported by observation. The known individual velocities of galaxies show only relatively small deviations from the mean of their neighborhood.

Let us consider, next, the space-time *geometry* of this cosmic fluid. The geometric language employed for this purpose will deal both with its spatial properties—a three-dimensional segment of the four-dimensional manifold—as well as with the way this spatial segment fits into the broader picture of the temporal development of the universe.

In what follows, we shall frequently employ the expression *cosmic time* in describing the temporal behavior of the universe. It is important not to misconstrue this expression. It might be thought to reintroduce the equivalent of Newton's concept of absolute time. This would be a mistake, for we are approaching these questions from within the conceptual framework of general relativity. This theory puts its basic reliance on the concept of space-time, and this concept is at variance with the classical notions of absolute space and absolute time. One should not think, therefore, of what we are here calling "cosmic time" as in any way equivalent to Newton's concept of absolute time. For relativity theory, time is not an independent continuum whose properties can be determined apart from space. Therefore the assignment of a temporal structure to the universe as a physical system is intertwined with a determination of its spatial structure. Cosmic time is one dimension of the space-time structure of the universe as a whole.

Another preliminary, cautionary remark is worth making. In what follows, I shall sometimes make use of the expression "moving through space-time" in connection with the cosmological fluid. Once again, there is the danger that this kind of description may conjure up the image of space-time as an absolute "container" on the analogy of Newton's conceptions of space and time. However, this too, of course, would be wholly misleading. For whether used in connection with the universe or any lesser physical system, space-time is not to be thought of as comparable to a container. It is a set of relational properties of matter and energy; it has no independent existence of its own. Nevertheless, if used with caution, the imagery of the cosmological fluid "moving through" space-time is a simplifying device that is frequently helpful, although one should always be prepared to translate it into its proper relativistic and relational basis.

We turn now to examine, first, the way in which the language of geometry may be used to describe the three-dimensional, purely spatial segment of the four-dimensional space-time manifold of the universe. The three-dimensional spatial segment will be described by the geometry of a three-dimensional spacelike hypersurface. We may think of this hypersurface as defining *cosmic space*. (The intervals of spacelike lines on this purely spacelike hypersurface are to be distinguished from the intervals of the timelike lines of material particles and the lightlike lines of photons.) The spacelike hypersurface has the same properties everywhere. Any event located at a point of this spatial hypersurface will be surrounded by a region having the same density of the cosmological fluid as at any other point. As determined at any point of this hypersurface, the space-time curvature of the fluid will be the same as that at any other point of the hypersurface. Finally, since geometry recognizes three types of space of constant curvature—flat, spherical, and hyperbolic—the spatial curvature of the three-dimensional spacelike hypersurface will be one of these spaces of constant curvature.

Let us consider, next, the way in which the notion of *cosmic time* is introduced, and with it the method for representing the temporal development of the universe. If we imagine observers attached to various particles of the homogeneous and isotropic cosmological fluid, then all such observers will be at rest with respect to any given hypersurface, yet they will move through a sequence of such hypersurfaces as the fluid itself moves through space-time.

The paths of timelike geodesics of free material particles in the cosmological fluid are orthogonal to the three-dimensional spatial hypersurface. Each observer measures proper time by his own clock along his own timelike geodesic. The intervals of each timelike geodesic of a material particle, orthogonal to a given hypersurface, will measure proper time along its own individual world line. Let various observers set their individual clocks to a certain time when they observe the density of matter in their respective neighborhoods to have the same given value. Thus if the galaxies are uniformly distributed throughout space, then at a given moment of cosmic time the same density of galaxies will hold at any region of space. The homogeneity of the model assures the retention of the synchronized clocks (and so of the measures of cosmic time) with changes in density as the universe expands or contracts. (Any departures from the measurement of cosmic time—that is, any irregularities in timekeeping among different timekeepers—will be assigned to purely local or peculiar variations in velocity, and to local variations in gravitational fields associated with particular astronomical systems. These local variations and irregularities are disregarded in conceiving a wholly homogeneous universe.) Different moments of cosmic time are correlated with differences in the density distribution of the galaxies. All observers situated on particles of the cosmological fluid can thus employ a common set of synchronous temporal coordinates. By adding the same interval of some elapsed proper time to the coordinate time t_0 of our present, initial, arbitrary hypersurface, we arrive at different hypersurfaces, each of which is identified by its distinctive value of the cosmic time t. The cosmic time coordinate will be constant for each hypersurface but will change with changing hypersurfaces. Therefore, clocks attached to co-moving particles may be said to measure cosmic time t.

To further refine the foregoing ideas, we consider next the role of a *scale factor* in describing the space-time geometry of the evolving universe.

On a given hypersurface of spatial homogeneity at constant time t, the distance between any two nearby particles on the surface will have a fixed value. Consider the distance between the same two particles on a hypersurface at another time. Since we are considering different hypersurfaces, we must allow that the distance between neighboring world-lines is a function of the time, t. Let this function be designated as $R(t)$. The value of R may be a constant or it may change with changes in t. In the latter case, the distance separating two nearby geodesics of the cosmological fluid will either increase or decrease with a change of time. The role of R is that of a *scale factor*.

To illustrate the role of a scale factor, consider the readily visualizable case of a two-dimensional surface of a purely spatial three-dimensional sphere, where objects are confined to this two-dimensional surface. Let the mutual distances of these objects be fixed: the objects do not change their positions or their distances from one another on the surface. Let the entire sphere undergo a change only in size, as a function of change in the length of the radius of the sphere. Designate the radius by R. As R increases, the mutual distance between any two objects on the surface of the sphere will increase in a uniform way. If R were to decrease, the distances of objects on the surface would decrease, and if R were to remain constant, the distances would remain fixed. In this example, R is a *scale factor*. Thus, if R doubles, the distance between two points on the surface will also double inasmuch as it is the product of R and the fixed coordinate distance.

Since in cosmology one is concerned with the three-dimensional spatial segment of a four-dimensional space-time, the geometry of a three-dimensional hypersurface will be involved. Further, for homogeneous models the geometry of this three-dimensional hypersurface will be one of constant curvature. The term "radius of curvature" is appropriate and helpful for the case of spherical space. However, it can be misleading when used in connection with the other two cases. Thus to say the *size* of an expanding universe increases does not necessarily imply that the space of the universe is finite (spherical). It simply means that the distance between any two points increases with an increase in the scale factor.

It is also worth stressing that to say the universe is expanding does *not* mean it is expanding *into* a pre-existing space. There is no independent space apart from that of the universe. It is the space *of* the universe that is expanding. The expression only means that the scale factor *of* space is increasing with cosmic time. Moreover, this increasing scale factor of space can apply to a space that is infinite as well as to a space that is finite. Hence, if the space of the universe is Euclidean or hyperbolic, it too could expand—but not *into* another "infinite" pre-existing space. It would simply mean that the scale factor of the expanding infinite space is increasing. Thus the distance between any two points in infinite space would increase with an increase in scale factor. The foregoing remarks about expansion and scale factor would also apply, with suitable modifications, where space is decreasing. Once again, this would not involve a pre-existing space into which the universe contracts. An infinite space, too, could contract, but not into something "finite." It would simply mean the scale factor would decrease: for example, the distances between points would decrease proportionately to the decrease in scale factor. A space— whether finite or infinite—that contracted would have the scale factor decrease. And a scale factor could diminish to zero whether the space be finite or infinite: all distances, areas, and volumes would shrink to zero. Finally, the change in the cosmological scale factor, R, which affects the separation between all particles in the same way, is a function only of the cosmic time, t, that is, $R(t)$, and not of the spatial location of particles.

An immediate fruitful application of the foregoing concept of a scale factor is the interpretation of the Hubble Law of galactic red shifts. Hubble's Law states a positive linear correlation between the red shift of a galaxy and its distance from the observer. The red shift consists in an observed increase in wavelength of the received radiation as compared with the wavelength at the time of its emission. The red shift is the ratio

$$\frac{\lambda_o - \lambda}{\lambda}$$

where λ_o is the wavelength of the received radiation and λ is the wavelength of the same radiation at the time of its emission. Instead of regarding the cosmic galactic red shifts as a Doppler effect,

that is, as due to a recessional velocity of the emitting source
through space, one may better understand its nature as due to an
expansion *of* space. In that case, it may be interpreted as correlated
with a change in the scale factor R of space itself. The change of
wavelength from the time of emission to that of reception, represented by the ratio

$$\frac{\lambda_o - \lambda}{\lambda}$$

is correlated with a change in the scale factor of space. The latter
can be expressed by the ratio

$$\frac{R_o - R}{R}$$

where R_o is the value of the scale factor at the present time. Thus
when the emitted radiation had a wavelength λ, the scale factor of
the space of the universe was R. When that same radiation was received at a later cosmic time t_o, its observed wavelength was λ_o,
and at that time the scale factor was R_o. During that interval the
space of the universe stretched or expanded from R to R_o. The
Hubble Law holds because it is space that is expanding, rather than
because the galaxies are moving or changing their individual, peculiar, relative coordinate distances with respect to one another.
Accordingly, the Hubble red shift is to be identified as a *cosmic expansion red shift*, in order to distinguish it from a Doppler red shift,
where the latter is an ordinary, peculiar recessional velocity effect
of a galaxy moving through space as measured relative to the frame
of reference of another galaxy.[5]

We have been considering, thus far, a number of conceptual
tools of a primarily geometric character that are typically employed
in the construction of relativistic cosmological models. There is,
first of all, the general notion of *spatial homogeneity*. This concept
is of central importance in giving a geometric interpretation to the
observational data concerning the isotropic distribution of galaxies. A second conceptual technique has to do with the use of a *scale
factor*. The latter is of importance in interpreting Hubble's Law for

[5] For a more complete discussion of expansion red shifts, see Harrison, *Cosmology*, chap. 11.

the red shifts of galaxies. Together, these geometric concepts express the fact that the universe undergoes a process of cosmic evolution.

An important conceptual tool that collects and incorporates the foregoing ideas, in a way that is important for the construction of relativistic cosmological models, is a *space-time metric*. In order to see the importance of this concept, let us recall the broad pattern of ideas we discussed earlier in connection with the field equations of general relativity. We pointed out that the field equations provide a schema that enables the physicist to describe the pattern of motions in any physical system in which gravitational interaction is the dominant force at work. For Einsteinian relativity, this gravitational structure is equivalent to its four-dimensional geometric properties. In particular, the equations can be used to describe the large-scale properties of the universe, the most comprehensive physical system of all. This is the task and interest of relativistic cosmology. In order to yield solutions of the equations relevant to the problem of specifying the geometry of a relativistic cosmological model, it is necessary to provide two types of information. The field equations express a connection between the curvature of space-time and its mass-energy content. The equations show the interdependence between these two broad categories of information. In specifying the physical conditions, the right-hand side "tells the space-time how to curve," and in giving the metric and curvature properties of the space-time, the left-hand side "tells particles how to move."

In dealing with the space-time structure of the universe as a whole, when that structure is taken to exhibit the properties of a homogeneous system with a scale factor that is a function of time, certain conditions have to be met in specifying the formula for the metric of this system. H. P. Robertson, in 1935, and A. G. Walker, in 1936, gave a general formula that determines the metric properties of an entire class of homogeneous models of the universe. This class is referred to as *Robertson-Walker space-times*.

The metric formula can be stated in various ways, depending on what types of coordinates are used, and depending too on whether the plus or minus signs are assigned to the temporal or spatial segments. One version of the formula is the following:

$$ds^2 = -c^2 dt^2 + R^2(t) \frac{dr^2 + r^2\,(d\theta^2 + sin^2\,\theta\,d\phi^2)}{(1 + \tfrac{1}{4}\,kr^2)^2}$$

In the above formula, the quantity ds^2 represents the infinitesimal space-time interval between two nearby events. c is the velocity of light. The time coordinate t is the proper clock time established by any observer situated on any particle (galaxy) in the homogeneous space. Because of the homogeneous nature of space—the fact that there is no privileged observer, and that all observers occupy fixed co-moving coordinates—the proper time t assigned by one observer will be shared by all other observers. dt is the proper time marking the temporal interval between two nearby events as established by such observers. R is the scale factor. Thus R, as a function of cosmic time (t), determines the cosmic-temporal behavior *of* space. In the above formula, the quantity $R^2(t)$ therefore applies to the purely spatial segment of the formula, that which contains the three spatial coordinates r, θ, and ϕ. k is the sign of curvature. It can receive the values $+1$, -1, or 0, depending on whether the space is spherical, hyperbolic, or flat. r, θ, and ϕ represent three spatial coordinates used in a spherical system of coordinates. r is a radial coordinate, with θ and ϕ serving as angular coordinates. The coordinates r, θ, and ϕ are of the three-dimensional space. (It is important to distinguish r and R. Although r is a constant coordinate *in* space, R is a scale factor for the three-dimensional space as a whole.)

Our discussion of relativistic cosmological models up to this point has focused on two main theoretical ideas, that of *spatial homogeneity* and *cosmic time*. The principal mathematical tool for conveying the first idea is that of a three-dimensional spatial hypersurface of uniform curvature. To convey the second idea, use is made of a changing universal scale factor to describe the process of cosmic evolution in the form of a changing sequence of hypersurfaces. One way of summing up these ideas is to say that the sequence of changes in cosmic time of surfaces of homogeneous spatial curvature defines the broad *kinematic* space-time pattern of the universe.

However, this pattern is insufficient to describe the universe as a physical system. While the kinematics describes the spatio-temporal pattern of the universe, it leaves unspecified the details of its physical structure. To fill out these details, one must turn to other concepts and theories of physics—for example, to descriptions of the dynamics of the universe, its thermal history, and the role of elementary particles that underlie its material and energy content.

When approached from the point of view of Einstein's theory of gravitation, the description of the *dynamics* of the universe as a physical system involves an application of the field equations of general relativity. In their general form, those equations exhibit the interdependence of the space-time structure of a physical system and its mass-energy content. That content is described by its density and pressure. In the case of the universe whose dominant material content consists of the galaxies, the pressure is considered to be negligible since the system is treated as if it were a smoothed-out homogeneous system of dust or gas particles. In this system, the pressure is everywhere the same at any given time; there are no pressure gradients to influence a dynamic change by counteracting the force of gravitation. (In this respect, the universe is different from other physical systems, for example, stars. In the case of stars, thermonuclear pressure can wholly balance, or at any rate counteract, the gravitational forces during the course of the evolution of the star.) On a cosmological scale of distances, gravitational force is the dominant factor at work. The gravitational properties of the universe are entirely dependent on the density of its mass-energy. Since there are no counteracting forces operating on this scale, the universe is in a state of dynamic disequilibrium.

When Einstein in 1917 first came to apply his original field equations to the cosmologic problem, he took the dynamic instability of the universe to be a difficulty for cosmology. In common with the widely accepted view of the time, he assumed that the universe must be static—that it must exhibit neither contraction nor expansion. He therefore introduced the so-called cosmological constant Λ in order to counteract the gravitational force. This cosmological constant may be thought of as representing a force of repulsion acting at great distances. Along with the attractive force of gravitation that it counterbalances, it could maintain the universe in a state of dynamic equilibrium—static and unchanging. When the astronomical evidence presented by Hubble in 1929 showed the universe to be in fact undergoing an expansion, Einstein abandoned his static model. He expressed his regret at having introduced the cosmological constant at all, and went so far as to call it his "greatest blunder."

In the early 1920s Alexander Friedmann (1888-1925) showed that the field equations of the general theory of relativity allow a number of nonstatic cosmologic models to be constructed.[6] To see how this came about, let us recall the Robertson-Walker metric formula for homogeneous models of the universe. Beyond a conventional choice of coordinates, there are two fundamental quantities in this formula that require determination in order to specify the metrical structure of a cosmological model. These are: (1) the value of the curvature constant, k, and (2) the scale factor as a function of time, $R(t)$. The principal theoretical basis for determining these quantities is provided by the field equations of general relativity. These equations establish the links between the curvature and scale factor in the metric formula, on the one side, and the density of mass-energy, on the other. Establishing these links transforms the description of the universe from a purely kinematic system into a dynamic one.

This application of the field equations to cosmology was achieved in the pioneering studies of Alexander Friedmann in

---

[6] Alexander Friedmann, "Über die Krummung des Raumes," *Zeitschrift für Physik* 10 (1922), 377-386. This paper is translated as "On the Curvature of Space" by Brian Doyle, and appears in K. R. Lang and O. Gingerich, eds., *A Source Book in Astronomy and Astrophysics: 1900-1975* (Cambridge, Mass.: Harvard University Press, 1979), 838-843. A second paper by Friedmann, dealing with models of negative curvature, appeared in *Zeitschrift für Physik* 21 (1924), 326.

1922 and 1924. His derivation of an equation stating the general form for nonstatic models of the universe opened up a whole new approach to the subject. This equation is known as the *Friedmann equation*. It states the interconnection between the scale factor, the matter density, and space curvature.

In the version of this equation that follows, both the quantity representing pressure and the cosmological constant are omitted. The equation reads,

$$\dot{R}^2 = \frac{8\pi\, G\rho R^2 - k}{3}.$$

In the above, $\dot{R}$ is the rate of increase of the scale factor R with time; G is the gravitational constant; ρ is the matter density; and k is the curvature constant.

Another form in which the Friedmann equation can be written (once again omitting the cosmological constant) is

$$\ddot{R} = \frac{-4\pi G\rho R}{3}.$$

In the above, $\ddot{R}$ is the rate of change of $\dot{R}$, that is, the rate of change in the rate of change in R. An important fact about the foregoing equation is that $\ddot{R}$ is negative for all values of R. Using this fact, one may represent the various possibilities of $R(t)$, together with possible values for k, by means of a curve showing the relation between $R(t)$ and t. Since $\ddot{R}$ is negative for all values of R, the curve of $R(t)$ versus t will have a concave slope downward, indicating that $\dot{R}$ was greater in the past.

Confining our attention to those models for which the value of the cosmological constant (Λ) is zero, and taking into account the fact that the curvature index (k) may be 0, $+1$, or -1, we get the possibilities for a matter-dominated universe as shown in figure 1.

In this figure, t_0 represents the present moment of cosmic time. If we let the curve of R, as a function of t, be extended into the past where it intersects the t axis, this point, where $R = 0$, will be the point at which t will have the value zero. It is this point ($R = 0$, $t = 0$) that is frequently referred to as marking "the beginning of the universe." (In terms of how this is arrived at, it is clear that all

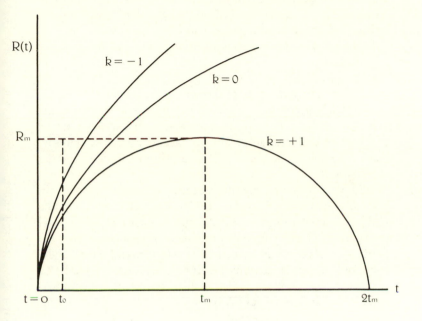

Figure 1. Friedmann models of the universe.

that "the beginning of the universe" can mean is "beginning of the expansion of the universe.") The "age of the universe" will then be defined as the time elapsed from $t = 0$ to t_0.

When $k = 0$, space is "flat" and open. In this case, the universe would continue its expansion into the infinite future. When $k = -1$, space is infinite, open, and hyperbolic. It undergoes a continuing expansion into the infinite future. When $k = +1$, space is spherical, closed, finite, and unbounded. In this last case, the scale factor R expands to a maximum R_m at t_m and then recontracts (collapses) in a "big crunch" to $R = 0$ at $2t_m$. These various theoretically possible models are known as *Friedmann models*.

In making a choice from among these models, a crucial item of information that is needed is a value for the average, smoothed-out mass-density of the universe, ρ. The mass density of the universe controls the gravitational forces present in the universe. Since the gravitational force is one of attraction, its effect is to slow down the expansion of the universe. The crucial question is what the rate of deceleration is. If one had a reasonably accurate measure of the average mass density, it would provide a measure of the rate of deceleration.

With respect to mass-density, an important measure is the *critical mass density*, ρ_c. By making use of the estimated value of the Hubble parameter for the present epoch of the universe, H_o, and the value of the gravitational constant, G, one obtains a formula for the critical density ρ_c. It is equal to $3H_o{}^2/8\pi G$. If one takes the commonly accepted value of the Hubble parameter (H) to be 15 kilometers per second per million light-years distance, the numerical value of the critical density is $\rho_c = 4.5 \times 10^{-30}$ grams per cubic centimeter.

Let the present mass-density of the universe, as determined by both observation and calculation, be designated as ρ_o. By knowing the relation between the present mass-density and the critical mass-density, one can determine whether the universe is spatially finite, closed, and therefore bound to undergo an eventual gravitational collapse through recontraction, or whether the universe is open and undergoing an expansion into the infinite future. If the present density of the universe is less than the critical density, the curvature is negative; and if it is equal to the critical density, the curvature is zero. In either case, the volume of the universe is infinite at any given moment of cosmic time. And in either case, the universe will expand forever. (For a space of zero curvature, the rate of expansion would approach zero in the infinite future as the scale factor (R) tends to infinity.) On the other hand, if the present density is greater than the critical density, the power of self-gravity is strong enough to bring the expansion of the universe to a stop. Such a universe has a positive spatial curvature and its volume is finite at any given epoch of cosmic time. It will reach a maximum degree of expansion after a finite time and will thereafter contract in a big crunch.

Because the question of the fate of the universe depends so closely on the determination of the mass-density, much effort is devoted in current research to obtaining a reliable measure of this quantity. The exact amount of the average mass-density is not known. Estimates for the average density of matter in all its forms lie between the values 5×10^{-29} to 3×10^{-31} grams per cubic centimeter. According to present estimates, the average density of matter due to the galaxies alone (ρ_{gal}), that is, to visible matter, is approximately 3×10^{-31} grams per cubic centimeter. Given the fact that the critical density, ρ_c, is approximately 4.5×10^{-30} grams per cubic centimeter, this would mean that the universe is infinite and will expand forever, since the actual density in this case would be less than the critical density. However, there may be various forms of invisible, dark matter—faint stars in galactic halos (nonluminous matter surrounding the luminous part of galaxies), an intergalactic gas of ionized hydrogen, black holes, massive neutrinos, and various exotic, quantum particles (for example, gravitinos, axions, etc.), whose existence is postulated in current theories of particle physics. Hence the total amount of matter in the universe may be considerably higher than the aforementioned figure—indeed, of the order of the critical density.

An Initial Cosmological Singularity

When the field equations of relativity are solved to represent the distinctive properties of the universe as a whole, it is commonly assumed that the universe is a physical system whose material content is distributed in a spatially uniform way. As we have seen, on the basis of this homogeneity one can define the concept of cosmic time. A universally agreed-upon scheme for measuring cosmic time can be adopted by all observers attached to the fundamental particles (galaxies) of the system. Changes in the universal cosmic scale factor (R) as a function of cosmic time (t) show whether the universe is expanding or contracting.

According to the field equations of relativity, the space-time curvature properties of a physical system are linked with the mass-energy density of matter (ρ) and pressure (p) in the system. Changes in the volume of the universe—and therefore in its density—are connected with changes in the scale factor. For example, an increase in R (expansion of the universe) makes for a decrease in density, and a decrease in R (contraction of the universe) results in an increase in density. It is assumed that whatever changes may occur in the density of the universe, from one stage of its development to another, will not violate the principle of the conservation of energy: the total amount of mass-energy would remain constant, whatever the number and character of local transformations of energy from one form to another.

In using the Friedmann equations to arrive at various models of the nonstatic universe, a common feature of such models is the fact that the curve for $R(t)$ points concave downward toward the t axis and intersects the t axis at $R(t) = 0$. The point of intersection of $R(t)$ with t is labeled $t = 0$. This means that the scale factor $R(t)$ must have had the value zero at some time in the finite past. This, in turn, means that when the scale factor or radius of curvature had the value zero, the curvature was infinite. Furthermore, when the scale factor was zero, the spatial volume of the universe, represented by the value R^3, was also zero. In describing the universe as shrinking to zero volume, one must avoid, of course, the mistake of picturing the universe as existing *in* space. Since space does not exist apart from the universe, it is the spatial structure *of* the universe that was of zero volume. Nor is this way of description confined to a finite space of positive curvature. Since the spatial curvature of the universe may belong to any of three different types—including two open infinite spaces (the Euclidean and hyperbolic)—*any* of these three spaces can undergo compression.

The density of a homogeneous material is mass per unit volume—for example, grams per cubic centimeter. Given both a zero volume and a conservation of the mass-energy of the universe, no finite value can be given to the ratio of the latter to the former (it is forbidden to divide by zero). This is normally expressed by saying that the density becomes *infinite*. It would be more accurate to say the standard meaning of "density" cannot be employed in this situation. The density cannot be assigned a finite measurable value, as is the case in all standard applications of the concept.

It is this condition—where the scale factor R is zero, the volume of the universe is zero, the curvature is infinite, t is zero, and the density is infinite—that marks the presence of an initial cosmological singularity. It is the presence of an *infinite density* that identifies the singularity as a *physical* singularity. (A physical—as distinguished from a "harmless" coordinate singularity—is present when a physical theory fails, by calculation or measurement, to assign normally finite, determinate values to various quantities within the range of the theory.) Because the laws of physics are inapplicable to this singularity, the situation marks a conceptual breakdown. It prevents the application of well-established physical laws at the point where the singularity occurs. To those for whom science cannot tolerate a conceptual breakdown, the problem is to find a way of eliminating the singularity. It is this type of abnormal physical singularity—in the form of an initial cosmological singularity at $t = 0$, $R = 0$—that is present in the use of relativity theory in Friedmann models.

In seeking to avoid this singularity, some cosmologists have suggested that one way to do so is to reject one of the crucial assumptions made in these models, namely, that of spatial homogeneity. This perfect symmetry, it has been argued, is highly unrealistic and artificial. The singularity would not obtain if the universe did not have ideally symmetric and homogeneous properties. The existence of sufficient inhomogeneity and irregularity would defocus the convergence—as all mass-energy is traced backward into the past. A singularity would thereby be avoided.

However, this "way out" has been proven to be incorrect.[7] The singularity cannot in fact be avoided in the way proposed. Even if the distribution of mass-energy had been irregular, there would be one or more singularities so long as the universe satisfied a physically reasonable equation of state—for example, provided the energy density of matter did not become negative or provided gravity was always attractive. These investigations show that by retrodicting to the past, the universe is seen as gravitationally collapsing in a time-reversed sense. The self-gravitation of the universe would be of such magnitude that singularities would develop in the very fabric of space-time. The properties of the space-time continuum presupposed by general relativity would no longer be present under these extreme conditions.

An important item in describing the properties of a space-time associated with a particular physical system is the behavior of world-lines and geodesic paths of free particles in the space-time. The distinctive character of the space-time is examined by means of the behavior of geodesics that traverse it. The relevant geodesics are the timelike geodesics of material particles and the null geodesics of particles of light (photons). Of special interest is the be-

---

[7] These investigations were carried out by Roger Penrose, Stephen Hawking, G.F.R. Ellis, and Robert Geroch, among others. Cf. R. Geroch, "What is a Singularity in General Relativity?" *Annals of Physics* 48 (1968), 526-540; R. Geroch and G. T. Horowitz, "Global Structure of Spacetimes," in S. W. Hawking and W. Israel, eds., *General Relativity* (Cambridge, Eng.: Cambridge University Press, 1979), 212-293; R. Penrose, "Gravitational Collapse and Space-time Singularities," *Phys. Rev. Lett.* 14 (1965), 57-59; S. Hawking, "The Occurrence of Singularities in Cosmology. III. Causality and Singularities," *Proc. Roy. Soc. Lond.* A, 300 (1967), 187-201; S. Hawking and R. Penrose, "The Singularities of Gravitational Collapse and Cosmology," *Proc. Roy. Soc. Lond.* A, 314 (1970), 529-548; S. Hawking and G.F.R. Ellis, *The Large-Scale Structure of Space-Time* (Cambridge, Eng.: Cambridge University. Press, 1973), chap. 10; D. Sciama, "Issues in Cosmology," in H. Woolf, ed., *Some Strangeness in the Proportion* (Reading, Mass.: Addison-Wesley Publishing Co., 1980), 387-404; F. J. Tipler, C.J.S. Clarke, and G.F.R. Ellis, "Singularities and Horizons—A Review Article," in A. Held, ed., *General Relativity and Gravitation* (New York: Plenum Press, 1980), 97-206; C. W. Misner, "Absolute Zero of Time," *Physical Review* 186 (1969), 1328-1333.

havior of geodesic paths in situations of extreme gravitational collapse. The Penrose-Hawking theorems prove that in the universe with its given mass-energy—and therefore undergoing gravitational collapse (in a time-reversed sense)—timelike and null geodesics cannot be extended indefinitely to arbitrarily large values of time. The geodesics reach an "edge" of space-time at singular points. A geodesic that reaches this edge must come to a stop. There are no further points of time to which it can be extended.

When a curve terminates after a finite proper length or after a finite proper time because it cannot be extended beyond that termination point, the space-time is said to be *incomplete* and to possess a singularity. To understand what this situation amounts to, consider, by way of example, the case of a freely falling material particle in a gravitational field. The geodesic path of this particle is timelike. Along its geodesic path the particle ticks off moments of local proper time as measured by the particle. In principle, the time coordinate can receive any arbitrary value from minus infinity to plus infinity—it can be extended indefinitely forward or backward to any arbitrary value—if the space-time manifold is differentiable, smooth, and complete. Another way of saying this is that a freely moving material particle or photon "cannot just disappear off the edge of the universe."[8]

In working with the concept of the manifold of space-time in its ordinary applications, the basic assumption is that it is free of inner contradictions. The standard assumption made by relativity theory is that the manifold of space-time is nonsingular and complete—that any non-spacelike geodesic can be extended to arbitrarily large values. However, the singularity theorems establish that under conditions of extreme gravitational collapse this completeness does not obtain—this standard presupposition breaks down and does not hold. *Time itself* "runs out." There are no further, indefinitely prolongable instants of time into which the timelike geodesic of a material particle *could* be extended. And this unusual situation is

[8] Hawking and Penrose, "Singularities of Gravitational Collapse and Cosmology," 539.

what is meant by saying that space-time itself exhibits a singularity.[9] The breakdown takes the form of showing that the manifold does not everywhere contain normal points of the continuum: there are also "singular points." These singular points are not constituent parts or elements of the space-time manifold.

In summary, as applied to cosmology, the theory of relativity rests on the conjoint appeal to the following assumptions: space-time is a continuum that has the mathematical properties of a differentiable manifold; the energy-density of the universe is a positive quantity; gravitation is an attractive force; there are no violations of causality. The Penrose-Hawking theorems demonstrate that these assumptions cannot be conjointly applied to the universe as a physical system when undergoing extreme gravitational collapse. Some of these assumptions must be surrendered. The theorems show that in conditions of extreme gravitational collapse there is a failure of an attempted application of the concept of space-time as ordinarily defined. The grammar (rule of use) of the standard concept of space-time cannot be applied under the conditions envisaged. The singularities established by the Penrose-Hawking theorems occur in the fabric of space-time itself: there are singular points that disrupt the otherwise smooth, differentiable, complete structure of space-time. These discontinuities in space-time render impossible the use of geodesics to represent the paths of material particles or particles of light at singular points. The geodesics break off at these points. Because of these singular points, space-time is not a complete and continuous manifold. Insofar as one relies on the theory of general relativity in its standard form, this situation violates an important condition for making the physical structure of the universe intelligible.

It is widely accepted by cosmologists that the occurrence of an initial cosmological singularity points to the need to find a more suitable theory. If found, this new theory would avoid the singu-

[9] S. Hawking and G.F.R. Ellis, "The Cosmic Black Body Radiation and the Existence of Singularities in Our Universe," *Astrophysical Journal* 152 (1968), 25; Hawking and Ellis, *Large-Scale Structure of Space-Time*, 357ff.

larity encountered by the classical theory of relativity. Since the standard theory meets its breakdown at the point where the concept of a complete manifold of space-time does not hold for situations of extreme gravitational collapse, what is called for is a more powerful theory—a new set of grammatical rules—that, when applied, can successfully describe and explain physical phenomena under these conditions of enormous density and temperature.

EXPLAINING THE ORIGIN OF THE UNIVERSE

It is characteristic of science generally, and of cosmology in particular, to be constantly on the lookout for ways of widening the scope of its understanding. What at one stage of inquiry may be taken as as an arbitrarily given datum—an initial condition—and so left unexplained, will provoke an attempt to move beyond these bounds and to extend the horizons of intelligibility. Scientists are reluctant to accept the unexplained as being permanently unexplainable. They look for some richer, more adequate theory by means of which to incorporate and explain what is left unexplained in a more restricted theory.

This is the situation one finds in cosmology with respect to the concept of the beginning of the universe. Our previous discussion gave examples of how the occasion for referring to "the beginning of the universe" arose from encountering a singularity in the use of a primarily geometro-dynamical approach to the space-time structure of the universe. This type of boundary was encountered both in the form of an infinite density and in the form of incomplete non-spacelike geodesics. The singularity occurs because of a breakdown in the use of the standard rules of relativity theory to describe the universe under conditions of (time-reversed) extreme gravitational collapse. These extreme conditions bring to light the inability of the standard rules of relativistic models to provide satisfactory descriptions and explanations of the physics involved. A conceptual boundary to the intelligible universe is reached at the point where the breakdown occurs.

However, rather than take the phrase "the beginning of the

universe" as marking a permanent block to further understanding, recent cosmology has sought to submit this initial condition to further analysis. Instead of taking it as unexplainable and unintelligible, it has sought to disentangle it into various substages and processes. If this could be accomplished, it might then be possible to identify and understand antecedent conditions, constituent elements, processes operating according to known laws, and immediate consequences—all of which are associated with what was hitherto lumped together under the umbrella term "the beginning of the universe."

The advances made in recent cosmology toward achieving this goal are largely due to the discovery of fresh observational data and the application of dramatic and rapidly accumulating insights in the field of elementary-particle physics. What follows is a brief summary of these major lines of advance.

In the earlier period of cosmological inquiry, the observational data of central interest were (1) the Hubble parameter, H, derived from data about the red shifts in the spectra of distant galaxies; (2) the isotropic spatial distribution of galaxies and radio sources; and (3) estimates of the mass-energy density in the observable universe. At the present stage of inquiry, some major observational data of interest are (1) the isotropy of the 3-degree Kelvin microwave background radiation; (2) the relative abundances of various elements in the universe; and (3) the ratio of the density of nucleons (protons and neutrons) to photon density. (This latter ratio is $10^{-9\pm1}$, thereby making photons by far the most abundant particles in the universe.)

Of these items, the data concerning the 3-degree microwave background radiation played a leading role in convincing most cosmologists of the need to abandon steady-state (continuous creation) theories and to adopt some form of evolutionary cosmology. This discovery was a principal empirical ground for inferring the occurrence of a primeval cosmic explosion—a hot big bang—as the earliest identifiable stage in the development of the universe. The microwave background radiation, now received, is to be explained as originating under special thermal and energy conditions that characterized the universe within a very short time after the big bang, but long before the emergence of galaxies.

There were earlier anticipations in theory of the phenomenon of microwave background radiation. In the 1940s, George Gamow and his co-workers Ralph Alpher and Robert Herman advanced the idea that the universe began in a highly superdense state at an enormously high temperature. They recognized the importance of distinguishing, in early stages of the universe, a radiation era that preceded and decoupled from a later matter era. In remarkable anticipation of later observations, they predicted the existence of microwave radiation at a temperature of about 5 degrees Kelvin—a prediction that is strikingly close to actually observed values. At the Bell laboratories, in 1965, Arno Penzias and Robert Wilson detected this phenomenon in the course of their search for an explanation of a persistent background noise in their radio antennae. They determined this ineliminable microwave radiation was isotropic and extragalactic in source. These initial findings were subsequently confirmed by observations carried out with the aid of radio antennae mounted on aircraft flying at high altitudes.

Received after an interval of billions of years, the microwave background radiation has a temperature now of approximately 3 degrees above absolute zero. This extremely low temperature represents the faint residual "glow" of a uniform gas of photons that has undergone cooling due to the spatial expansion of the universe since the epoch of its original emission. At the time of that emission, the temperature of the universe was approximately 10 billion degrees.

The spectrum of the received microwave background radiation corresponds to that emitted by a blackbody source in thermal equilibrium. The distribution of frequencies of the microwave background radiation corresponds to the Planck curve for a blackbody at 3 degrees Kelvin. The wavelength of blackbody radiation depends only on the temperature, in other words, on the average energy of the atoms of matter that closely interact with the radiation. In the case of blackbody radiation, this temperature is produced as the outcome of a complete interchange of temperature between the radiation and its surroundings. During a very early stage of the universe, shortly after the big bang, individual elementary particles (photons of various energies and wavelengths, as well as charged particles of matter—electrons, positrons, and protons) engaged in many interactions with one another in a very short time. As a result, an equilibrium of energy came to prevail among them. In particular, a state of uniform temperature was established in the gas of photons that subsequently decoupled from matter and emerged as the microwave radiation now observed.

The evidence furnished by the microwave background radiation is one important example, among others, of the need to have theories of the temporal development of the universe that recognize the central role of temperature and energy conditions in that development. It is, therefore, characteristic of recent particle theories, in their application to cosmology, to focus attention on the way temperature and energy conditions determine the relations among the elementary particles and the forces that govern their interactions, as these particles and forces come into operation at different stages in the development of the universe.[10] It is true, of course, that the

[10] For surveys of recent theories of particle physics, see *Particles and Fields: Readings from Scientific American*, with an Introduction by W. J. Kaufmann III (San Francisco: W. H. Freeman, 1980); J. C. Polkinghorne, *The Particle Play* (San Francisco: W. H. Freeman, 1981); P. Davies, *The Forces of Nature* (Cambridge, Eng.: Cambridge University Press, 1979); idem, *Superforce* (New York: Simon and Schuster, 1984); H. Pagels, *The Cosmic Code* (New York: Simon and Schuster, 1982); idem, *Perfect Symmetry* (New York: Simon and Schuster, 1985); J. E. Dodd, *The Ideas of Particle Physics* (Cambridge, Eng.: Cambridge University Press, 1984); Gerard 't Hooft, "Gauge Theories of the Forces between Elementary Particles," *Scientific American* (June 1980), 104-138; A. Zee, ed., *Unity of Forces in the Universe* (Singapore: World Scientific Pub. Co., 1982), vol. I; Steven Weinberg, "The Forces of Nature," *American Scientist* 65 (1977), 171-176; Howard Georgi and Sheldon Glashow, "Unified Theory of Elementary-particle Forces," *Physics Today* (September 1980), 30-39; David N. Schramm, "Particle Physics in the Very Early Universe," *Tenth Texas Symposium on Relativistic Astrophysics, Annals of the New York Academy of Sciences* 375 (1981), 54-68; idem, "Cosmology and GUTs: The Matter of the Universe," *Adv. Space. Res.* 3 (1984), 419-430; G. Steigman, "Cosmology Confronts Particle Physics," *Ann. Rev. Nucl. Sci.* 29 (1979), 313; H. R. Pagels, "Microcosmology: New Particles and Cosmology," *Annals of the New York*

geometric concepts of relativistic cosmology continue to play an important role in model construction. Thus the expansion of space bears an intimate and important relation to the cooling of the universe and thereby to the kinds of physical processes brought into play with lower temperatures. At the same time, these geometric concepts themselves need to be understood in the light of the thermal and temperature conditions present in the universe during its earliest stages of development. Indeed, the various laws and theories of particle physics have found—in the "laboratory" provided by the universe itself, especially in its earliest stages, rather than in man-made high-energy accelerators—a basis for applying its concepts and testing its predictions. Accordingly, as contrasted with the earlier emphasis by models of relativistic cosmology on the geometric concepts of spatial curvature and a changing scale factor in describing the temporal evolution of the universe, particle physics brings to the fore the concepts of temperature and energy—expressed in terms of millions of electron volts (MeV), billions of electron volts (GeV), or higher quantities. These concepts are, in turn, linked to the crucial ideas of symmetry and symmetry-breaking as found in current gauge theories of particle physics. These various concepts, and the laws that express their quantitative relations, are employed in explaining different types of physical interactions, transformations, and combinations of particles occurring at the several major stages in the development of the universe.

At the base of these theories are attempts to understand the nature and interconnections among four basic forces or interactions that dominate all physical phenomena: gravitational, electromagnetic, weak, and strong. Taken separately, these forces differ from one another in several ways. For example, both the gravitational

Academy of Sciences 422 (1984), 15-32; Frank Wilczek, "Foundations and Working Pictures in Microphysical Cosmology," *Physics Reports* (Review Section of *Physics Letters*) 104 (1984), 143-157; D. Sciama, "The Role of Particle Physics in Cosmology and Galactic Astronomy," in G. O. Abell and G. Chincarini, eds., *Early Evolution of the Universe and Its Present Structure* (1983), 493-506; E. W. Kolb et al., eds., *Inner Space/Outer Space: The Interface Between Cosmology and Particle Physics* (Chicago: University of Chicago Press, 1985).

and the electromagnetic forces have an infinite range, while both the strong and weak forces have extremely short ranges. The strong force binds protons and neutrons together in the nucleus of an atom; it has a range of 10^{-13} centimeter. The weak force governs the phenomenon of decay in atomic nuclei—for example, in radioactivity; it has a range of 10^{-15} centimeter. The strong and weak forces do not operate beyond their respective ranges. Within the atom the gravitational force is the weakest. However, on a cosmic scale it is the strongest—for example, it binds the planets to the Sun, the galaxies to one another.

Despite these differences of interaction-strength and ranges of operation among the fundamental forces, physicists have already made considerable progress in showing an underlying unity among them. Examples include an electroweak theory that accomplishes a unification of electric and weak forces, and grand unification theories (GUTs) that point to deep interrelations among strong, weak, and electromagnetic forces. Finally, recent work on supersymmetry theories is aimed at finding a satisfactory conceptual unification of all four fundamental forces, including the gravitational.

In all these theories, certain key ideas related to the notions of symmetry and symmetry-breaking play a central role. In its most general meaning, *symmetry* represents an *equivalence relation*. Where symmetry operations hold, the entity or system to which these apply shows a certain invariance and exhibits a particular type of conservation. Invariance in symmetry operations is associated with various types of conserved quantities—for example, energy, charge, mass, and spin—that belong to quantum particles (fields). A symmetry transformation leaves certain specified properties of a system unchanged. When stated in terms of specific physical laws, these invariances are conveyed in the mathematical language of group theory. One may think of *breaking* of symmetry—a separation and distinction among the forces in question—as due to conditions of lower energy and temperature. In effect, these lower energy conditions serve to cloak a more fundamental hidden pattern of symmetry. The latter would obtain and be explicit if the requisite additional energy were forthcoming—if the state of symmetry were to be restored.

Particle physicists refer to the different stages at which forces become differentiated from one another through spontaneous symmetry-breaking as examples of "freezing." There are, accordingly, several distinct levels or types of freezings. At the highest energy level, all four forces would be unified: there would be but one force, and a total or perfect symmetry of all forces would prevail. It is this condition that supersymmetry theories would describe. When this symmetry is broken, due to a drop in energy and temperature, the differentiation of forces described by grand unification theories takes place. At this stage, there are two main forces instead of one: on the one hand, the gravitational force, and on the other, the single force that combines the electroweak and strong forces. With a further drop in energy and temperature, the next freezing takes place in which three forces are present—namely, the electroweak, strong, and gravitational. Finally, at still lower energies and temperatures, the symmetry of the electroweak force is itself broken, and the familiar distinctions among the four forces emerge.

These investigations have the most profound bearing upon cosmology. The picture of successive freezings represent distinct plateaus of differentiation among forces at major stages in the evolution of the universe. The crucial facts that link theories of particle physics and cosmology are those connected with the successive drops in energy and temperature due to the expansion of the universe. Each major freezing represents a transition to a new physical level in which distinct forces (and the particles they involve) emerge from a relatively undifferentiated unity or matrix.

In recent physics, much progress has been made in understanding the physical processes at work not only in the early universe but also in the very early universe.[11] Until recently, the standard hot

---

[11] Cf. F. Trefil, *The Moment of Creation* (New York: Scribner's, 1983); G. W. Gibbons, S. W. Hawking, and S. T. Siklos, eds., *The Very Early Universe* (Cam-

big bang model of the expanding universe dominated cosmological thinking. It claimed that the universe began in a state of infinite density and temperature and subsequently expanded in a spatially uniform way. In support of this model, the direct observational evidence consisted of the microwave background radiation. Such evidence, however, reaches back not to the very beginning, as this is conceived by the theory, but only to the stage (several hundred thousand years after the big bang) at which matter decoupled from radiation and liberated that radiation. Further empirical evidence in support of the hot big bang model is of an indirect sort and consists in a broad agreement between the predictions of the theory and the actually observed relative abundances of light elements— for example, hydrogen, helium, deuterium, and lithium. The standard hot big bang model thus has much to contribute in helping to understand events on a cosmological scale in the "early universe," where the latter expression is used to designate occurrences that took place *after* about one second following the hot big bang. Nevertheless, the standard hot big bang model leaves unexplained the event labeled "the hot big bang" itself—an event to be accepted simply as an arbitrarily given initial condition.

Not content with these achievements, therefore, cosmologists have tried to extend their understanding beyond this point as well. They wish to understand the physical processes at work in the very early universe, that is, *within* one second after the "beginning." For example, they have sought to describe and explain the physical events that transpired as far back as 10^{-45} second after the big bang. One such recent advance consists in the use of the inflationary model of the universe to deal with certain properties of the universe left unaccounted for in the standard hot big bang model. In another direction of inquiry, some cosmologists have sought to probe the possible antecedent physical conditions prior to 10^{-43} second (the Planck time). Both types of theory try to understand what were the most fundamental processes at work during the ear-

bridge, Eng.: Cambridge University Press, 1983); E. W. Kolb and M. S. Turner, "The Early Universe," *Nature* 294 (1981), 521-526.

liest stages in the evolution of the universe. Both are examples of the introduction of novel conceptual tools—fresh grammatical rules in the Wittgensteinian sense—whose purpose is to escape the bounds of standard theories. The reasons for being dissatisfied with these bounds differ in each case, yet the pressure to overcome them is clearly common to both. I turn to a brief review of some of these recent exercises in concept formation and grammatical-rule construction.

Both the inflationary model and the standard big bang theory of the expanding universe are in basic agreement about the broad evolutionary pattern of the universe subsequent to 10^{-30} second after its initial intense thermal state. According to both theories, the universe began as a primordial fireball and—in the course of its expansion and cooling—gave rise to various physical, astronomical, and other phenomena. The inflationary model and the standard model diverge, however, in the account they give of what happened during the very short time when the universe was much less than a billionth of a second old. According to the inflationary model, in the extremely short time between 10^{-35} second and 10^{-32} second, the universe underwent enormously large inflation of its diameter by a factor of as much as 10^{50} beyond what had been previously assumed. During this period of very rapid and enormous inflation, the universe was in a supercooled state. While in this state, the physical conditions were prepared for a major phase transition that took place at the end of this brief period. Out of this phase transition emerged all the matter and energy that make up the observable universe.

A major incentive for developing the inflationary model was to deal with certain weaknesses and unresolved problems in the standard big bang theory. Two examples of these difficulties are "the horizon problem" and "the flatness problem."

The standard big bang theory assumes that, in starting as an intensely hot gas filling all of space, the universe expanded and cooled in a uniform way throughout its later history. However, when combined with the principle of the velocity of light, this assumption leads to the horizon problem. This problem consists in a failure on the part of the standard model to give a plausible explanation of how the conditions for the observed homogeneity of the universe could have been already prepared during the time that the universe expanded (at the presumed uniform rate) in its very early stages. Consider, for example, the isotropic distribution of the microwave background radiation. The conditions for its emission were already set in the uniform expansion of the primordial hot gas during the earliest moments after the big bang. However, it is difficult to reconcile this isotropy (and the homogeneity it implies) with the value for the velocity of light. The reasons for this inconsistency are as follows. No signal, information, or causal influence can travel faster than the velocity of light: the latter is a maximum for all transmissions of a radiational or material character. Anything that lies beyond the horizon of this velocity cannot have an effect upon what lies within the horizon. However, the microwave background radiation was emitted at a time when different, widely separated parts of the expanding universe were more than ninety times the horizon distance apart. Even under conditions of a very small universe—say at the end of the first 10^{-35} second—causal connections were limited to regions about 10^{-25} centimeter across. By virtue of the rate of expansion accepted by the standard theory, the universe had already expanded to a size that exceeded by far the horizon distance. Each region bounded by the horizon distance was only some 10^{-25} centimeter across; and there were as many as 10^{78} such regions that were causally isolated from one another. If causal influences had no time to travel from one widely separated part of the universe to another, and therefore no opportunity for a smoothing out of any possible temperature differences, how could they nevertheless have acquired the same temperature? It is unsatisfactory to have to accept this uniformity as an arbitrarily given initial condition, a mere coincidence.

Another problem relates to the question why the energy density of the universe is in fact so close to the critical density. This is referred to as the "flatness problem." If the density of the universe were much greater than the critical density, the universe would long ago have collapsed as a closed universe. But it obviously has not. On the other hand, if the density of the universe were much less than the critical density, then the matter in the universe would have scattered before there would be time for galaxies to form. But galaxies and all their manifold contents do exist. In short, there is apparently just enough repulsive force in the expansion of the universe to make the actual density very close to the critical density. Let Ω represent a dimensionless number for the ratio of the actual density to the critical density. Then, the value of Ω is close to 1 (the value lies somewhere between 0.1 and 2), and the spatial curvature of the universe is close to a Euclidean value. The universe is finely tuned to have a curvature in the neighborhood of zero—to be almost flat, to be on the borderline of being closed or open. Why is this so? This is the flatness problem.

The inflationary model of the expanding universe, originally proposed in 1981 by Alan Guth of the Massachusetts Institute of Technology (and subsequently improved by him, Andreas Albrecht, Paul Steinhardt, A. D. Linde, and others), offers answers to the foregoing questions and provides fresh insights about the structure of the universe, among them the claim that the observed universe is only a very small fraction of the universe as a whole.[12]

The basic idea of the inflationary model of the expanding universe is that at 10^{-35} second after the big bang the universe underwent a very rapid, exponentially increasing inflationary expansion involving a radical phase transition. It was the occurrence of this series of events that had profound cosmological consequences. An everyday, familiar example of phase transition is found in water as it changes, with a release of heat, from a liquid phase to the solid phase of ice, or, under heating, to the vapor phase of steam. Thus

[12] Alan H. Guth, "Speculations on the Origin of Matter, Energy, and Entropy in the Universe," in A. H. Guth, K. Huang, and R. L. Jaffe, eds., *Asymptotic Realms of Physics* (Cambridge, Mass.: MIT Press, 1983); A. H. Guth, "The New Inflationary Universe," *Annals of the New York Academy of Sciences* 422 (1984), 1-14; A. H. Guth and P. J. Steinhardt, "The Inflationary Universe," *Scientific American* (May 1984), 116-128; A. D. Linde, "The Inflationary Universe," *Rep. Prog. Phys.* 47 (1984), 925-986.

the change from a liquid to a solid phase is marked by the re-arrangement of the molecules in the liquid into a regular crystalline array. In the course of this changeover, a certain amount of energy—the latent heat—is removed. Under certain conditions, however, the liquid may remain in a liquid state as its temperature is lowered below its normal freezing point: the liquid enters a supercooled state. If suitable nuclei are then forthcoming for the formation of crystals, the liquid freezes and the latent heat, then released, will raise the temperature of the solid produced in the phase transition. It was this simple familiar thermodynamic model—with suitable subtle modifications—that underlies the main idea of the inflationary model. At 10^{-35} second, the universe, too, underwent its own, far more complicated and distinctive phase transition. According to Guth's original proposal, the symmetrical phase of matter and energy, as envisaged in grand unified theories, may have been prolonged in a supercooled state, at temperatures as low as 10^{22} degrees Kelvin. While in this supercooled symmetrical state, the universe rapidly underwent an accelerated inflationary expansion. This expansion, it can be shown, was due to the presence of a gravitational force that is connected with the existence of a negative pressure, and that is therefore effectively repulsive rather than attractive.[13]

At the end of this inflationary expansion era, the symmetry was broken and the universe entered an asymmetrical (broken-symmetry) phase. It was during this phase transition that an enormous amount of latent heat was released that reheated the regions affected to nearly 10^{27} degrees Kelvin. After that, the universe pursued a course of cooling and expansion similar to that described in the standard big bang theory. This phase transition involved the

[13] According to general relativity, the effect of gravity in a homogeneous medium is measured by the quantity $\rho + 3p/c^2$. Here ρ is the mass-energy density, p is the pressure exerted by the medium, and c is the constant for the velocity of light. In ordinary circumstances, pressure is positive, its role in gravity is minute, and it causes the matter which exerts it to expand. However, if there were a sufficiently large negative pressure, that is, if $\rho + 3p/c^2$ were negative, gravity would manifest a repulsive force.

passage from the grand unification (GUT) era, in which the strong force had been interchangeable with the electroweak force, to a new phase in which the strong force became separated from the electroweak force (the symmetry between leptons and quarks having been broken).

One of the important consequences of this inflationary exponential expansion of the universe is that it makes possible an altered conception of what the size of the domain of causal interaction was in the universe *before* the inflationary expansion, phase transition, or GUT freezing occurred. This was large enough for thermal equilibrium to have set in. In this pre-inflationary period, the universe was very much smaller than it had been thought to be according to the standard big bang theory. In this very much smaller universe, there was ample opportunity for different regions to be in causal contact with one another. It was possible for various parts of the universe to be in communication with one another without exceeding the velocity of light (the horizon distance). This meant that a uniformity of temperature, a frictional process of smoothing out of any initial differences, could be accomplished. Once the inflationary expansion set in, the thermal equilibrium had already been established. This equilibrium was preserved during the inflationary expansion and transmitted to later epochs after the brief inflationary phase ended and the universe returned to its normal rate of expansion. This uniformity could extend even beyond the size of the region of the universe observable at the present time. Thus the horizon problem is solved.

The flatness problem, as noted earlier, consists in the need to account for the fact that the energy density of the universe is close to the critical density, and hence that the curvature of the universe is close to the Euclidean value. In explaining this fact, the inflationary model of the universe makes use of a number of key concepts of particle physics. In focusing on the phase transition that marks the end of the grand unification era, a major outcome is the creation of matter in the form of baryons (a class of particles that includes the proton and neutron). It turns out that the actual mass density of baryons in the universe is believed to be close to that of the critical density. In deriving this quantity, the inflationary model shows that the phase transition involved the release of an enormous amount of latent energy. It was this release of energy, present in the form of what is known as the "Higgs field," that was converted into the form of baryonic matter. In order for this conversion to take place, it is necessary to conceive of the escape of the latent energy from a "false vacuum." (The original inflationary model and several improved versions of that model describe the false vacuum situation in different ways, in order to meet various problems. Each seeks to do justice and accommodate itself to available observational data.) Therefore, even if the universe before 10^{-35} second began with an expansion rate below the critical escape velocity, it follows that after the phase change and the inflationary expansion, the actual energy density was brought close to the critical density and the actual expansion velocity was brought close to the critical escape velocity. In the inflationary era, the energy density of the observable universe rapidly approaches the value of the critical density. Furthermore, since the value of Ω corresponds to a geometry whose metric is flat (Euclidean)—and it is around this value that present estimates of the ratio of energy density to critical density hover—it is possible to explain this fact. For with the rapid inflationary expansion of the universe, the ratio Ω is rapidly driven toward the value of $\Omega = 1$. This means that the observable universe will have a geometry that is flat for the same reason that a small patch on a curved surface approximates the geometry of a plane surface, as in the case of a balloon becoming flatter (in small regions of its surface) as it is inflated. It is in this way that the flatness problem is solved.

In taking advantage of recent theories of particle physics in order to give an account of the major stages in the evolution of the universe, cosmologists are able with reasonable confidence to trace back that evolution close to the point in the remote past that goes by the name of the "Planck time," that is, 10^{-43} second. Beyond that time (as well as below the Planck length-scale, 1.6×10^{-33} centimeter), the language of classical space-time geometry can no longer be applied in an unqualified way to guide calculations or describe possible measurements—in short, to give intelligible physical results. In order to overcome that barrier, it is necessary to fashion a more powerful conceptual scheme (apply a new set of grammatical rules). In current inquiry, there are a number of suggestions as to how this might be done, though there is no prevailing consensus. Nor, of course, can there be any direct confirming empirical evidence for any particular proposal insofar as it concerns the event referred to as "the origin of the universe."

Some cosmologists would, therefore, restrict the use of the phrase "origin of the universe" (if it is to be used at all) to the earliest stage that can be satisfactorily understood by present theories. They would point out that recent advances in physics—for example, grand unification and inflationary theories—have made possible the detailed description and understanding of events *following* the Planck time. On the basis of these theories, one can retrodict close to the Planck time, 10^{-43} second, but not beyond that. These cosmologists would argue, therefore, that the whole question of explaining the origin of the universe at $t = 0$, by relating it to "antecedent conditions," cannot be properly posed. It does not even make sense, on scientific grounds, to look for any explanations. There are neither securely established laws to guide this search, nor ways of observing and testing any inferences concerning what transpired "prior" to the Planck time. Though the terms "before," "prior," or "antecedent," as normally used, are parts of a reasonably well-defined temporal vocabulary (for example, of a relativistic theory of space-time or cosmic time), in the framing of the foregoing question about what happened "before" $t = 0$, by way of contrast, this question has no clear sense. It is a pseudo-question: it should be dissolved rather than inspire a search for an answer. These cosmologists might agree in spirit with St. Augustine's remark: "The world was made not in time but simultaneously with time. There was no time before the world." (When asked what God did before He created the world, St. Augustine replied that God was engaged in preparing Hell for those who ask such foolish questions!) In a similar vein, many cosmologists prefer to restrict the phrase "the origin of the universe" to describe the Planck time and what physically transpired immediately following it, and would dismiss all attempts to inquire into what happened "before."

On the other hand, although at the present state of knowledge any answers would admittedly be highly speculative and extremely tentative, some cosmologists would maintain that the question can be made meaningful and answerable. While conceding that, if one relies exclusively on classical relativistic theories of gravitation or even on recent grand unification theories (including the inflationary model), there is no adequate understanding of the event labeled "$t = 0$," these cosmologists propose to overcome this limitation. They would probe the events and physical conditions prior to the Planck time with the aid of fresh conceptual tools not envisaged either in classical theories of gravitation or, for that matter, in GUTs or the inflationary model. In this spirit, they are prepared to offer proposals that would explain the very origin of the universe in physical terms. A general label to encompass these investigations is "quantum cosmology."

In the formulation of these proposals, concepts of quantum gravity and the vacuum typically play a central role. The underlying idea is to explain the origin of the universe as due to a random, spontaneous, and wholly unpredictable fluctuation of the vacuum. In a special sense, therefore, these theories would give a new twist to, and a sophisticated version of, the belief that the universe arose out of nothing. Those who favor such ideas would dissolve the supposed absolute singularity and complete unintelligibility of the "moment of creation" at $t = 0$.

The earliest suggestion of this type of view appears in a brief paper by Edward P. Tryon, published in 1973. This initial effort has since been modified and improved by a number of others who seek to bring its ideas in line with developments in microphysics since 1973.[14] When considered on a cosmological scale, Tryon noticed

[14] Cf. E. P. Tryon, "Is the Universe a Vacuum Fluctuation?" *Nature* 246, (1973), 396-397; idem, "What Made the World?" *New Scientist* (8 March 1984),

that many standard conserved physical quantities add up to zero. (A quantity is said to be "conserved" when it retains the same net value throughout any physical process. Such conserved quantities are found on the level of ordinary physics—for example, in the case of energy, momentum, and electric charge—as well as in the domain of subatomic physics.) In order to lend credibility to the notion of the universe originating out of nothing, Tryon undertook to show that the universe has zero net values for all conserved quantities. Hence it would make sense to say that the universe, in containing such quantities, itself originated from nothing. In the process of emerging out of the vacuum, it does not violate any laws of conservation, since the vacuum state itself has zero energy.

On this approach, the very process of coming into existence of the universe may be understood as a vacuum fluctuation that resembles, in certain respects, processes of quantum fluctuation already made familiar in standard applications of quantum field theory to the domain of elementary particles. In those applications, quantum field theory successfully describes and explains the physical processes of creation, mutual interaction, and annihilation of various types of elementary particles. Also, of course, since it is a quantum theory, full use is made of the Uncertainty Relations. These uncertainties bear upon determining the position and momentum of particles, their energy-time relations, and the very number of particles present at any given time or place.

An important conceptual ingredient of such theories is that of the vacuum. From the point of view of a typical quantum field theory, even the most perfect vacuum, as a physical reality, is the scene of intense activity. Accordingly, the term "vacuum," in these contexts, has a special, radically different meaning from the one it has in popular usage or in traditional physics. A vacuum

14-16; R. Brout, F. Englert, and E. Gunzig, "The Creation of the Universe as a Quantum Phenomenon," *Annals of Physics* 115 (1978), 78-106; D. Atkatz and H. Pagels, "Origin of the Universe as a Quantum Tunneling Event," *Physical Review D* 25 (1982), 2065-2073; J. R. Gott III, "Creation of Open Universes from de Sitter Space," *Nature* 295 (1982), 304-307; A. D. Linde, "Quantum Creation of the Inflationary Universe," *Lettere Al Nuovo Cimento* 39 (1984), 401-405.

state is not an absolute void; it is not to be identified with wholly empty space. Any quantum field with which a vacuum state is associated may be thought of as made up of a large number of separate centers of oscillation and excitation. It consists of various harmonic oscillators, each of which possesses its own zero-point energy and zero-point motion. In the case of most fields, the energy is minimized when the value of the field is reduced to zero everywhere. Thus, the electron field has minimum energy when there are no real electrons present. A vacuum state is one in which any field has its lowest possible energy. Even in the absence of real particles, however, quantum theory allows for the possibility of the existence of a field and its fluctuations. The quantum-mechanical vacuum is not quiescent.

By contrast with the vacuum state, and as excitations of some field, real particles may be regarded as possessed of sufficient energy to make them real. They consist of multiple non-zero Planck units of quantum energy. On the other hand, those excitations or particles that fall below this level are only "virtual." For example, there are virtual photons, virtual electrons, virtual positrons, virtual protons and antiprotons, and so on. The virtual particles in the vacuum exist as pairs. Each pair consists of a particle and its antiparticle. (Some particles are their own antiparticles. For example, a photon—which is a particle of electromagnetic radiation—is its own antiparticle.) These particles and antiparticles are constantly being created and annihilated within the vacuum. At any given instant, there will be large numbers of pairs of particles and antiparticles having a momentary, transitory existence between their creation and annihilation. The spontaneous, temporary emergence of particles from a vacuum is called a "vacuum fluctuation." The average net effect of these individual occasions of creation and annihilation is zero. Nevertheless, the fluctuation from this average zero state is of great importance. Although on an overall basis fluctuations in the vacuum cancel one another, when taken over a very short period of time and over very short distances, they have a great impact on real particles. The effects of these vacuum fluctuations—the effects of the combined energy of these virtual particles, caught between their own creation and annihilation—make themselves felt and are observed within the world of real particles, even though the virtual particles are themselves unobserved and unobservable.

In applying the general idea of vacuum states and fluctuations associated with them to the problem of explaining the origin of the universe, one is dealing, of course, with a different type of problem from that ordinarily considered in some standard branch of quantum field theory. For in these standard contexts, one already "has" some actual set of real particles and fields, as these have emerged at a particular stage in the evolution of the universe. In the present case, however, the problem is to explain the origin of the universe, that is, how to describe the physical mechanisms by which any kind of real material and radiational particles or fields had come into existence at all. One way to think of the state of affairs being envisaged is that nothing we would normally think as comprising the real universe has yet come into existence. Nevertheless, with the aid of the concepts of fluctuations in vacuum quantum states and zero energies, one may conceive of them as constituting the state of nothing "pre-existing" the real physical universe. In the "pre"-universe state there were no real particles of matter or radiation, nor indeed any space or time (as conceived in classical theories) associated either with real particles or with their combinations in macroscopic bodies. All of the latter came into existence only with the appearance of real particles and fields of one sort or another.

One suggestion, made by R. Brout, F. Englert, and E. Gunzig, takes advantage of the ideas of quantum field theory and builds on Tryon's original proposal. They undertook to show that "the laws of quantum mechanics, formulated within the general relativistic framework, are perfectly consistent with the spontaneous creation of all the matter and radiation in the universe."[15] The basic idea is that the universe arose from local quantum fluctuations in the flat space-time metric of the vacuum. These fluctuations were of a

---

[15] Cf. Brout, Englert, and Gunzig, "Creation of the Universe."

spontaneous and unpredictable character. There is a probability, however small, that a quantum fluctuation involving a region of expanding space can acquire enough energy to keep expanding, instead of disappearing back into the vacuum. Since, according to relativity theory, gravity is associated with the metric structure of space-time, a quantum approach to gravity therefore also allows for spontaneous variations in the metric of the vacuum. Slight local variations in that metric—for example, occasions of slight local stretching or expansion of space—can be assumed to be constantly occurring. These variations in metric would, of course, be of sub-microscopic dimensions (that is, at or below the Planck length, 1.6×10^{-33} centimeter), and would in any case be wholly beyond any possibility of direct observation. The metric fluctuations of an unstable vacuum could result in a spontaneously broken symmetry whose manifestation took the form of a cosmologically relevant gravitational field. On the analysis proposed, the first matter nucleates around some space-time point in a region of the order of a Compton wavelength. This is a process comparable to the dynamical origin of the mass of elementary particles. The creation of particles of matter would lead to a further expansion of space. And this, in turn, would lead to further creation of matter, and so on. The matter content of the universe, as well as the character of its large-scale gravitational properties, was thus established by the sustained operation of what amounts to a feedback mechanism. On this approach, it is postulated that the cooperative process of creation of particles of matter, when it reached the degree of temperature and density referred to as the "fireball stage," ceased before reaching a singularity. By a slow buildup of matter, the universe reached the stage of the Planck time, but did not go through a big bang stage prior to that. Thereafter, the universe underwent a process of adiabatic expansion, and the present theory merges with other standard theories of the development of the universe.

Still another approach to quantum cosmology focuses on the notion of quantum tunneling.[16] This idea was employed, for ex-

---

[16] Cf. Atkatz and Pagels, "Origin of the Universe"; S. W. Hawking and I. G.

ample, by David Atkatz and Heinz Pagels. According to these authors, a paradigm for this process is found in the phenomenon of radioactive decay. In the latter situation, particles in the nucleus of an atom that might otherwise repel one another are kept bound together by short-range attractive nuclear forces. This forms a stable state in which the total energy is zero, since there is a balance between the forces that make for repulsion and those that make for binding. Nevertheless, when examined in the context of a vacuum state of zero energy, in which quantum and probability considerations are relevant, there is a finite probability that the particles bound within the nucleus will tunnel through the barrier that otherwise prevents their escape. In that case, the particles that have tunneled through the barrier will separate from one another. The result will be the emergence or "creation" of particles with mass out of the vacuum (zero energy state).

In applying some features of this model to the universe, the assumption is made that the universe pre-existed in a false vacuum state as a small empty sphere with no matter in it, and as a stable space-time state. The birth of the actual universe arose by a process of quantum-mechanical tunneling (barrier penetration). Like radioactive decay, the process of cosmic genesis is wholly a matter of finite probability (quantum mechanical amplitude). Having so emerged, the universe developed into the fireball stage. It was during this stage that particle creation occurred. The fireball subsequently underwent a process of expansion and cooling, during which particle creation ceased. The later stages of the expansion of the universe are marked by various evolutionary changes and transformations of the matter so created. In order for this scenario of cosmogenesis to work, however, it is necessary not only to assign to the universe throughout its evolution a homogeneous, isotropic, Robertson-Walker metric, and to treat the matter distribution of the universe as a perfect fluid, but in addition it is necessary to restrict such a model to one whose geometry is spatially compact

Moss, "Supercooled Phase Transitions in the Very Early Universe," *Phys. Letters*, 110 B (March 1982), 35-38.

and that holds for a finite three-space volume. The authors of this proposal recognize "that only a spatially compact universe can originate as a quantum tunneling event." In other words, the authors undertake to deal only with the genesis of a universe whose initial state exhibits the properties of a closed space. However, this scenario poses a difficulty that the authors themselves acknowledge. For if the actual closed universe arose by a process of quantum tunneling from a prior stable initial state, then the universe in its pre-creation state could not remain *indefinitely* long in that state, if indeed it is unstable with repect to quantum tunneling. The question thus arises how the universe, before it emerges at creation, got into that "earlier" state. How did *it* arise? They admit they have no answer to the question, "Where did *that* universe come from?"—that is, the one having a closed geometry and whose quantum genesis they do propose to explain.[17]

Further recent studies of quantum cosmology, having the same broad objectives as those illustrated above, have been conducted by Ya. B. Zeldovich, Stephen Hawking, Alexander Vilenkin, and others.[18]

If we are going to make sense of the foregoing proposals, it is clear that, in this context, "nothing" does not mean "absolute nothing." In discussions of quantum cosmology, the notion of

[17] Atkatz and Pagels, "Origin of the Universe," 2071, 2072.

[18] S. W. Hawking, "Quantum Cosmology," in B. S. DeWitt and R. Stora, eds., *Relativity, Groups and Topology*, II, Les Houches Session XL, 1983 (New York: Elsevier Scientific Publishers, 1984), 336-379; idem, "The Quantum Mechanics of the Universe," in *Proceedings, Geneva, Switzerland, CERN: Symposium on Large-Scale Structure of the Universe, Cosmology, and Fundamental Physics* (1984); J. B. Hartle and S. W. Hawking, "Wave Function of the Universe," *Physical Review D* 28 (1983), 2960-2975; S. W. Hawking, "The Quantum State of the Universe," *Nuclear Physics B* 239 (1984), 257-276; L. P. Grischuk and Ya. B. Zeldovich, "Complete Cosmological Theories," in M. J. Duff and C. J. Isham, *Quantum Structure of Space and Time* (Cambridge, Eng.: Cambridge University Press, 1982), 409-422; A. Vilenkin, "Creation of Universes from Nothing," *Phys. Letters* 117B (1982), 25-28; idem, "Birth of Inflationary Universes," *Physical Review D* 27 (1983), 2848-2855; idem, "Quantum Creation of Universes" *Physical Review D* 30 (1984), 509-511.

"nothing" needs to be contrasted with the existence of matter, energy, space, and time as these are conceived in a classical relativistic Einsteinian approach. Compared with these criteria for identifying what comprises the actual universe, the vacuum is indeed "nothing." But, clearly, if the vacuum can give birth to one universe—or perhaps several "universes"—by virtue of quantum processes of fluctuation and tunneling, the vacuum must have its own type of reality. In other words, the vacuum is not absolute nothing. If it were identified with, or referred to by this phrase, Parmenidean strictures would apply. Indeed, in "mining" the vacuum, these cosmologic theories might even be analogized, in certain respects, to the role Anaximander assigned to the *Apeiron* (the Boundless) in his own speculations concerning the birth of the cosmos.

From the vantage point of our own present philosophical interest in the pursuit of cosmology as a scientific discipline, it is sufficient to note the character of these investigations and that they should be carried forward at all. Rather than concern ourselves with examining further the technical and mathematical details of these activities, we shall want to set these activities themselves in the wider context of a philosophical interest in epistemology and ontology. They prompt us to ask what these efforts at understanding the genesis of the universe suggest with respect to the question of determining the scope and limits of cosmological knowledge, and with respect to the question concerning the relation of the universe as a physical structure to the broader ontological concept of existence. I will examine some aspects of these questions in chapters 5 and 6.

THE END OF THE UNIVERSE

The evolution of the universe consists of different temporal stages, each of which is marked by distinctive physical conditions and processes. Schematically, these stages may be broadly divided into a beginning, a middle, and an end. However, within this broad threefold division, a much greater amount of attention has recently been focused by cosmologists on the physical processes at work in the early stages of the development of the universe than on some of its other stages. These have been worked out in greater detail and have been better understood than, for example, the physical processes during the very late stages and end of the universe.

Evolutionary models of the universe describe various possible patterns of development in the light of accepted physical laws. In earlier, classic discussions of cosmology, these laws were principally the field equations of general relativity as applied to the cosmologic problem. On this approach, possible patterns of development of the universe were conveyed by the Friedmann models. Up to the middle decades of the present century, most discussions of the evolution of the universe were confined to an examination of these models. Thus earlier discussions of the ultimate fate of the universe devoted themselves to classifying and analyzing major examples of open and closed universes, and how these may be used to predict different types of ends to the universe. These options were examined in terms of various forms of expanding or contracting space, when these are linked to such factors as the critical mass-energy density, the Hubble parameter, and the deceleration factor. From this perspective, the primary concepts at work in describing the end of the universe were the geometry and dynamics of space-time.

These discussions have been of an exploratory nature and largely inconclusive—at least when compared with parallel, recent discussions of the origin of the universe. This situation can be attributed on the whole to the paucity of well-established observational data to help effect a choice from among available options. While the Friedmann models predict that the universe will come to a definite end in *some* form, the question what *particular* form the end of the universe will take is neither definitely predicted by theory nor supported by adequate and reliable observational data.

In recent decades, discussions of the future of the universe have been widened and deepened by taking into account the concepts and laws of elementary-particle physics. While the Friedmann models and the general principles of relativistic cosmology con-

tinue to be a mainstay and guide in virtually all ongoing investigations, accounts of the various possible forms that the future
course of the evolution of the universe might take are no longer
dependent exclusively on the guidance of the geometro-dynamic
concepts and laws of relativity physics. The formulation of, and increasing confidence in, these recent theories of microphysics have
made possible the description and explanation of physical processes under conditions of extremely high and extremely low temperatures and densities. These temperatures extend from 10^{32} degrees Kelvin to temperatures approaching absolute zero. And the
range of densities likewise extends from less than 10^{-300} gram to
10^{100} grams per cubic centimeter. These extreme physical conditions are to be found only at the opposite ends of the evolutionary
development of the universe—its earliest and latest stages—and
cannot be duplicated in the laboratory. Thus, while investigations
by physicists and cosmologists of the end of the universe still lag in
number and refinement of detail compared to investigations of the
origin of the universe, there has been a recent increase of attention
to this topic to redress the balance somewhat.[19]

The basic cleavage in options that bear on the question of the
end of the universe is between two types of models. On the one
hand, there are models according to which the universe will continue its present expansion into the infinite future, with ever-de-
creasing density and temperature. It will thus end in a whimper.
On the other hand, there are models according to which the present phase of expansion will come to an end after billions of years.
After that, the universe will begin to recontract and undergo a
gradual process of gravitational collapse. This will end, after several more billions of years, in a big crunch to match the big bang.

There is insufficiently accurate and detailed observational data

---

[19] Cf. J. N. Islam, *The Fate of the Universe* (Cambridge, Eng.: Cambridge,
Cambridge University Press, 1983); R. Gott III, J. E. Gunn, D. N. Schramm, and
B. M. Tinsley, "Will the Universe Expand Forever?" *Scientific American* (March
1976); F. J. Dyson, "Time Without End: Physics and Biology in an Open Uni-
verse," *Reviews of Modern Physics* 51 (1979), 447; M. J. Rees, "The Collapse of the
Universe: An Eschatological Study," *The Observatory* 89 (1969), 193.

at the present time to guide a firm choice between these principal options. A basic source of uncertainty concerns the lack of adequate information about the actual total quantity of the mass-energy content of the universe. This information is needed in order to determine whether the actual mass-energy density is below, at, or greater than the critical density. For if the actual mass-energy density is greater than the critical mass-energy density, the universe is closed and will eventually recontract. Otherwise it is open and so either has a Euclidean (flat) or a hyperbolic geometry. In either of the latter cases it will expand forever. One major source of uncertainty is connected with efforts to determine whether background neutrinos are massive. For neutrinos (or other particles) may have sufficient mass to just "close" the universe; they would contribute enough to the actual density to move it beyond the value of the critical density. However, a clear and firm decision is still not possible: it awaits further, more secure data. Meanwhile, all that can be done is to explore the possible options.

We begin by considering the fate of the universe on the assumption that it will continue to undergo an expansion into the infinite future.

The basic macroscopic constituents of the universe are galaxies and clusters of galaxies. The fate of a typical galaxy is bound up with that of its own major constituents, the stars. Astronomers classify stars into various species and types, depending on their masses, luminosities, and stages of evolutionary development. All stars consume fuel, mostly in the form of hydrogen. The mechanism of fuel consumption, as manifested by the star's radiation, is explained by well-established laws of nuclear physics. Since the amount of fuel available for nuclear burning or nucleosynthesis by any star is finite, it will be exhausted after a period of anywhere from a hundred to a thousand billion years, or perhaps as much as 10^{14} years. The universe will then be almost ten thousand times as old as it is now. Thereafter, the star will enter the last stages of its existence. More massive stars tend to burn up their fuel more rapidly, whereas less massive stars consume their fuel more slowly, many of them having a lifetime some hundreds of times longer than that of the Sun. Whatever the particular mass of a star, however, it will sooner or later use up its finite supply of fuel. It will end its life either as a white dwarf, a neutron star, or a black hole.

As the principal source of fuel, hydrogen is converted into helium. For example, as a typical star of relatively low mass, our own Sun will begin to exhaust its fuel supply after a period of approximately 5 billion years from now, that is, after a total lifetime of roughly 10 billion years. When a star such as our own Sun has converted most of its hydrogen supply into helium, at first it gradually expands and brightens into the type of star classified as a red giant. During this phase, our Sun will engulf Mercury, Venus, and the Earth. It will then begin to contract and slowly cool, eventually turning into a white dwarf. After a period of perhaps 100 billion years, it will finally turn into a condensed, burned-out blob of matter, for it is expected that a white dwarf will itself become in turn a yellow, brown, and eventually a black dwarf. The Earth, the life it supports, and all entities that depend on the Sun's radiation will have long ceased to exist. In general, stars less massive than 1.4 times the mass of the Sun undergo a process of fuel consumption and gravitational collapse in which they become white dwarfs.

In stars more massive than the Sun, gravitational collapse, accompanied by nuclear burning, will result in the production of elements heavier than carbon—for example, magnesium, silicon, sulfur, and iron. Some stars whose mass is greater than 1.4 the mass of the Sun may pass through a spectacular explosion as a supernova, where the remnant of this explosion takes the form of a neutron star. Among these are the rapidly rotating neutron stars, the pulsars. Some stars that are at least six times the mass of the Sun may blow themselves up in the violent burst of a supernova and end their lives as black holes. Very heavy elements, such as gold and uranium, are produced in these explosions and expelled into space.

Although there are important differences among the final states of stars that have become white dwarfs, neutron stars, and black holes, they are all identified by the fact that the matter of the star exists in a highly condensed form. Thus a typical neutron star is of the same order of mass as the Sun, but has a radius of only 10 to 20 kilometers. The density is so enormous that electrons are squeezed into the protons of the nuclei of atoms, turning them into neutrons, and the star becomes itself a single giant nucleus. A black hole, however, is the most condensed state of all.

A typical galaxy, which in its prime is a complex structure of matter and its multiple sources of stellar radiation, will eventually die and largely cease to radiate after the lapse of 1,000 billion (10^{12}) years. The galaxy will continue to exist, however, as a distinct unit by virtue of the mutual gravitational interaction that holds together its remnant material parts. These parts will consist of dead stars, various minor material fragments, and agglomerations such as planets, rocks, meteors, dust, or other bits that were too small in mass ever to become principal radiating sources.

This same evolutionary pattern will be repeated throughout the universe in all other galaxies. This fate awaits all galaxies in the course of a span of time of the order of 100,000 billion years since the big bang. Eventually all galaxies will die, because the "lights" that compose them and make them shine will go out, one by one. The stars that compose them will all have exhausted their fuel. The husks of dimming galaxies will continue to recede from one another in a universe increasingly cold and dark, for throughout all this the universe will be undergoing a continual drop in temperature as it expands. Nor will there be any rejuvenation of galaxies once dead, or a birth of new ones. For there will be no fresh supply of energy to start the process all over again, as long as the universe continues to expand into the infinite future.

A further process of change takes place in a galaxy even after its stars have ceased to radiate. In the course of anywhere from 10^{18} years to 10^{27} years, the galaxy will have lost as much as 99 percent of its stellar masses by a process of evaporation (much in the manner in which a liquid loses its molecules at its surface). This happens as a result of the collision of stars in the outer regions of the galaxy and their ejection from the galaxy. The force of gravitational collapse of the densely packed remaining stellar masses in the inner regions will cause them to be drawn inward by a process of mutual gravitational attraction, and thereby to collapse into a massive black hole. The stars that remain within the confines of the galaxy—where many such stars will themselves already have become black holes—will collide and coalesce in this dynamical process into the central region of a single, cannibal galactic black hole whose mass will be larger than a billion solar masses. A cluster of galaxies, too, will eventually suffer the same type of fate as an individual galaxy. It will become a supermassive black hole. This entire process may take anywhere from 10^{18} to 10^{27} years. There are upper limits, however, to the size and mass of black holes. They will not exceed a mass of 100 trillion times that of the Sun's mass.

In the increasingly dark, cold, and spatially open universe populated by stellar black holes, massive galactic and supermassive black holes formed by collapsing galaxies and clusters of galaxies, stray bits of matter, and by neutron or white dwarf stars that managed to escape and wander on their own, further physical processes take place that relentlessly drive the universe toward its end.

One of these processes is proton decay.[20] As a baryon, the proton is thought to be composed of three quarks (the fundamental constituents of nucleons)—carrying electric charges 2/3, $-1/3$, 2/3, to yield the number $+1$ for the proton. According to commonly accepted grand unification theories, under conditions of energy well above the order of 10^{15} GeV, quarks can be transformed into leptons such as electrons or positrons through the mediation of X bosons (exchange particles). While such loss of identity is highly improbable at lower energies and temperatures (because the X bosons necessary for the transformation to occur are very much less abundant at low temperatures), it is not impossible, and can be expected to take place from time to time. When this

---

[20] Cf. S. Weinberg, "The Decay of the Proton," *Scientific American* (June 1981); J. M. LoSecco, F. Reines, and D. Sinclair, "The Search for Proton Decay," *Scientific American* (June 1985); D. A. Dicus, J. R. Letaw, D. C. Teplitz, and V. L. Teplitz, "Effects of Proton Decay on the Cosmological Future," *Astrophysical Journal* 252 (1982), 1-9.

happens, the proton decays. Two of the quarks within the proton change into a positron and an antiquark. The third quark in the proton combines with the antiquark to form a pion (pi meson), thus bringing about the decay of the original proton.

The estimates of how long it would take a proton to decay vary somewhat from one theory to another. One such value gives the lifetime of a proton as about 10^{31} years, with a lower limit on the lifetime of the proton as 10^{29} or 10^{30} years. One way of expressing this is to say that in a collection of 10^{16} protons, there should be an instance of this decay once a year. (Given several thousand tons of matter—for example, water—it should be possible to detect instances of this decay rate. Indeed, several experiments are under way at the present time to see if this phenomenon can be detected observationally.) If the phenomenon of proton decay is experimentally confirmed, it would not only give added weight to grand unification theories, but have important implications for cosmology as well. It would mean that all matter in the universe made up of baryons is unstable and will eventually decay. Thus stars that have managed to escape capture by galactic black holes will succumb eventually to the process of proton decay after approximately 10^{30} years. It follows from the phenomenon of proton decay that after the passage of approximately 10^{32} years since the big bang, the universe will have lost all the matter composed of protons and neutrons. At that stage, the universe will be made up entirely of electrons, positrons, photons, and neutrinos, together with the black holes formed by the collapse of galaxies and clusters of galaxies.

But even this is not the whole story. There are other mechanisms and physical processes recognized by the physicist that affect all forms of matter and radiation that have managed to survive even proton decay. One of these is the process known as "Hawking radiation."[21] According to S. W. Hawking's analysis, first presented in 1974, black holes (that have been formed dynamically as a result of purely gravitational collapse) are able to lose mass, ra-

[21] Cf. S. W. Hawking, "The Quantum Mechanics of Black Holes," *Scientific American* (Jan. 1977), 34-40.

diate energy, and evaporate completely. This is a phenomenon whose occurrence can be understood in the light of the concepts and laws of quantum mechanics. The process of Hawking radiation from a black hole would account for the eventual dissolution and evaporation of the black hole itself.

As we have seen earlier, quantum theory maintains that the vacuum is filled with virtual pairs of particles and antiparticles. In making use of these ideas, Hawking argues that in the presence of a black hole, a vacuum fluctuation may occur in which one member of a particle/antiparticle pair may be able to escape the black hole, whereas the other falls into it. In other words, instead of annihilating each other, as they normally would, one member survives and remains as a real particle in the form of radiation. In this situation, this radiation would then appear to come from the black hole itself. It adds its energy to those particles already in the real domain. Since it is postulated that the total amount of energy must remain constant, with no energy created or destroyed, the other particle—having been swallowed by the black hole—must compensate for the positive energy taken away by its partner. This happens when the particle that falls into the black hole adds its negative energy to the black hole. This results in a *decrease* in the total mass of the black hole—in an amount that balances the release of energy in the form of radiation carried away by the particle that escaped. The entire process is referred to as one in which energy has "tunneled" through an energy barrier. Although this tunneling process could never occur according to classical physics, it is allowed by the rules of quantum mechanics. By repeated occurrences of this process, the black hole—whatever its initial mass—will eventually lose its mass and totally evaporate. A rule of black hole thermodynamics is that as the mass and size of the black hole decrease, the tunneling process becomes more frequent. The process of evaporation accelerates with decreasing mass. Sooner or later, therefore, all black holes—from the primordial mini-black holes present at the origin of the universe, to supermassive black holes formed by the collapse of clusters of galaxies—will radiate their energy away. The final stage of the evaporation of a black hole takes place rapidly. It may end in a tremendous explosion of radiation. The decay products will be mostly in the form of photons.

Primordial black holes have probably evaporated mostly over a period of time of approximately 15 billion years since the big bang. On the other hand, the process of evaporation of large black holes takes very much longer. Thus a black hole formed by a star of one solar mass would take about 10^{66} years to evaporate by the mechanism of Hawking radiation, while a black hole formed by the gravitational collapse of a single galaxy would take approximately 10^{90} to 10^{100} years to evaporate completely. Finally, a supermassive black hole formed as the outcome of the gravitational collapse of a large cluster of galaxies requires as much as 10^{108} years to evaporate by the process of Hawking radiation. The end stage of a radiating black hole, during the last second of its existence, is marked by a very bright burst of high-temperature radiation. Over a long period of time, these occasional, brief flareups of dying black holes, like fireflies on a dark moonless night, will briefly and intermittently illuminate an otherwise dark and cold universe. In short, all the galaxies in the universe that once existed will have completely disappeared after the lapse of the enormously long time of approximately 10^{100} years. All that will remain is a vast, cold, dark, extremely diffuse gas of such stable particles as electrons, positrons, photons, neutrinos, and gravitons. At this late stage, the universe will consist of a highly rarefied plasma of electron-positron pairs immersed in an ambient sea of radiation.

Recent investigations have sought to determine whether the surviving positron-electron pairs, as the sole remaining form of matter, will eventually annihilate one another, thereby leaving behind a radiation-dominated universe, or contrariwise, whether the expansion of the universe will prevent such annihilation and insure a continuation of stable particles of matter in the form of electrons and positrons.[22] One possibility is that a sufficient number of stray

[22] Cf. J. D. Barrow and F. J. Tipler, "Eternity is Unstable," *Nature* 276 (1978), 453-459; D. N. Page and M. R. McKee, "Matter Annihilation in the Late Universe," *Physical Review D* 24 (1981), 1458; idem, "Eternity Matters," *Nature* 291 (May 7, 1981).

electrons and positrons will survive—even with the evaporation of black holes, the annihilation of electron-positron pairs through random collisions, or the eventual disappearance of positronium atoms (formed by the union of electron-positron pairs). This will insure the existence of matter in sufficient quantity to exceed the amount of photon or background radiation whose energy has been decreased through red-shifting due to the expansion of the universe.

At the present stage of inquiry, the horizon of intelligibility—and predictability—with respect to the far future of an ever-expanding open universe (whether with the signature $k = -1$ or $k = 0$)—ends in uncertainty and lack of secure knowledge. The intelligible universe with respect to its distant future, as established by current cosmology, tapers off into the unkown.

We have been examining thus far the future prospects of the universe on the hypothesis that its geometry is described by one of the open models. The other main group of Friedmann models being given serious consideration in current cosmology is designated as "closed." According to the latter, the radius of space of the universe is finite and its geometry is of a spherical type. All currently accepted models of the universe are in agreement that the universe is undergoing an expansion and manifests an evolutionary development. However, unlike the case with open models, if the universe is to be described by a closed model, it will not expand forever: billions of years from now the expansion of the universe will cease. The universe will begin to recontract in accelerating fashion, undergo an overall compression, and terminate in a state of total gravitational collapse—a singular state of infinite density and temperature. Instead of ending in a whimper, the universe will end in a big crunch. All types of structure it had built up in its previous history will be totally destroyed in a devastating universal compression.

As an example of a closed universe, let us assume that the actual density is twice that of the critical density, and that the expansion rate of the universe, as given by the Hubble parameter, is 15 kilometers per second per million light years. Under these conditions, the universe will continue to expand for another 40 or 50 billion years beyond its present age. The expansion will then cease and the universe will begin slowly to recontract. It will take approximately another 50 billion years until it returns to the state in which it is now. Following that, it will take about 15 billion years to return to a singular state of density and temperature broadly comparable to that from which it initially started.

If one assumes that the actual density of the universe is twice that of the critical density, then (at the stage of maximum expansion) the universe will have become twice as large as it is now. Furthermore, the temperature of the microwave background radiation—which, at the present time, is approximately 3 degrees Kelvin—will have dropped to 1.5 degrees Kelvin. Beginning with the first stages of the recontraction of the universe, this turnaround will be followed by a sequence of physical and astronomic stages that largely duplicates—in reverse order—the various stages of evolution through which the universe had previously passed. The temperature of the microwave background radiation will gradually begin to rise. At the stage, for example, where the universe will have shrunk to one-hundredth of its present size, the temperature of the background radiation will have risen to about 300 degrees Kelvin. Moreover, since the galaxies will now be approaching one another rather than receding from one another, their spectra will begin to show blue shifts rather than red shifts. At first, only nearby galaxies will show blue shifts, while more distant ones will continue to show their customary red shifts. Gradually, however, all galaxies (including the most distant ones) will be blue-shifted in their spectra. At first—that is, roughly one billion years before the big crunch—large superclusters and clusters of galaxies will collide, overlap, and merge with one another with increasing frequency. Individual galaxies will similarly collide and merge about 100 million years before the end. Meanwhile, the temperature of the background radiation will have risen so high that not only, at first, will molecules in planets or interstellar space dissociate into their constituent atoms, but later, even atoms, in turn, will dissolve into nuclei and free electrons. At approximately 4,000 degrees Kelvin, electrons will be ejected from their atoms. At 10 million degrees, stars will have decomposed into their atomic nuclei, photon radiation, and free electrons. Stars will be vaporized. This will happen up to 1,000 years before the final stage of total collapse. The universe will have become—as it once was—a plasma of uniform density. When the temperature reaches 10 billion degrees, the density and temperature doubles in about a second. Even nuclei will have succumbed to further disintegration. Neutrons and protons will be torn loose from nuclei. At these temperatures and energies, collisions of photons will generate large numbers of electrons and positrons. Along with neutrinos and antineutrinos, these will reach a state of thermal equilibrium. The entire process will rapidly approach a final state of infinite density and temperature. After a period of approximately 100 billion years from its beginning, the imploding universe will have reached a fiery end to match its explosive beginning. It is an end totally different from the end foretold by a model of an ever-expanding, increasingly cold, totally dark, open universe.

This end, too, like its beginning, lies beyond present powers of understanding. If we follow the foregoing scenario, a number of questions immediately pose themselves. Will this universe, at its death, be followed by other universes? If so, is it part of an endless cyclic process of births and deaths of universes, not only in the future but in the past as well? To these questions there are no firm answers. According to many cosmologists, present theories do not suffice to understand the physics of the end of the universe any more than they are adequate to understand its very beginning. Once again, new conceptions of time, space, and matter will have to be constructed.

Cosmologists' inquiries into the beginning and end of the universe are clear examples of the kinds of topics that lead to the raising of questions of a more philosophical cast about the possible limits or horizons that stand in the way of satisfying the human ambition to understand the structure of the universe as a whole. It is to an examination of this general theme that we turn next.

FIVE

Cosmic Horizons

The Observable Universe and Its Horizons

The Greek word *horizon*, from which our English word derives, is based on a verb stem that means "to bound, divide, limit, confine, determine." In everyday language, the most common use of "horizon"—as the Oxford English Dictionary informs us—is to designate "the boundary line of that part of the earth's surface visible from a given point of view; the line at which the earth and sky appear to meet." A familiar example is the boundary line of earth and sky when seen at sea. By analogy with this paradigm case of a visual horizon, the term "horizon" may also be used to designate "the boundary or limit of any 'circle' or 'sphere' of view, thought, action; that which bounds one's mental vision or perception; the limit or range of one's knowledge, experience, or interest." What emerges from even a cursory examination of these ordinary uses, are two ideas: a horizon is a *boundary* of some sort, and it is *relative* to certain conditions.

Our present interest is in the character and significance of various types of horizons in the pursuit of cosmology. Here it becomes necessary to distinguish two major types of such horizons: (1) those that determine the bounds of the *observable universe*, and (2) those that determine the limits of the universe as a maximally comprehensive, intelligible domain—the *intelligible universe*. It is true that, as in any empirical science, the spheres of the observable and the conceptual do not exist in sharply separated compartments. On the contrary, at any given stage of cosmological inquiry, the universe-as-understood is guided and controlled by what is observed. Conversely, the character of the observable universe leans upon some preferred conceptual scheme. Despite these obvious interconnections, there is an important distinction between the observable universe and the intelligible universe, as well as important distinctions to be made with respect to the kinds of horizons that respectively limit each. The horizons that hold for the observable universe and the intelligible universe have different properties and different criteria of identification.

We must pose, therefore, the following questions: What determines a particular type of cosmological horizon? Is it fixed or moveable? How does the presence of a horizon affect the attainment of reliable knowledge of the universe? In what follows, we shall consider, first, these questions as they apply to the observable universe, and then, later, to the intelligible universe.

Let us first turn to the use of the term "observable" in expressions such as "observable universe" and "horizons of observability." In one direction, it refers to a property of the subject matter under investigation—the domain of objects, processes, and events—insofar as *it* can be observed. Reference to *its* observability calls attention to the fact that there are such-and-such properties of the domain of objects, processes, and events under investigation that allow it to be observed. Another direction of emphasis concerns the space-time condition and instrumental resources of the observer. "Observability" refers to the powers of the observer to determine certain properties of the subject matter being observed. These two directions of emphasis in the use of the term "observable universe," though distinguishable, are linked through a third aspect of the use of the term. This has to do with the intermediate messengers, the means for bringing information *from* the domain under investigation *to* the observer. Characterization of the observable universe and its horizons hinges upon these links, messengers, and means of connection between the subject matter and the observer. In light of the above, an adequate description of the

observable universe and its horizons must take note of the following major factors: (1) the situation of the observer; (2) available instrumentation; and (3) types of physical theory used in interpreting
the observable data, including the conception of the universe as a
maximally intelligible system to which the observable universe is
related.

Among the many uses of the expression "observable universe,"
there is one that is possible but nevertheless largely irrelevant and
inapplicable. It has the following characteristics. The denotation
of the term covers the same range of objects, events, and processes
as does the expression "the universe as a whole": the scope of the
observable universe is as wide as the universe as a whole. What distinguishes the two is simply that the referent of the term "universe
as a whole" is to be identified by means of observation. It designates the same subject matter as does the term "the universe as a
whole," only it is explored by observational means such as telescopes or other instrumental resources. On this view, a hypothetical observer who would investigate the observable universe would
not be physically limited or restricted in any way. He could freely
explore the entire universe both in space and in time. He could
observe whatever is transpiring in every region of space, however
small or large, and in every epoch or period of time, however short
or long, however recent or remote.[1] Such a hypothetical observer
would be equipped with the ideal instrumentation needed to carry
out a thorough observational inspection of the universe as a whole.

[1] Indeed, if one accepts a conception of the universe as a whole which allows
that, in addition to its space-time extent, it also includes the vacuum from which
the space-time universe emerged, then the "observable universe" would extend not
only to every part of the space-time domain but to the vacuum as well!

Further, there is much interest at the present time in "Kaluza-Klein" theories,
according to which the universe has more than three spatial dimensions. According
to one such widely discussed theory, there are *eleven* physical dimensions in all—a
total of ten spatial dimensions and one temporal dimension. Of these ten spatial
dimensions, however, seven are minuscule, compactified, and beyond all possibility of direct observation. Nevertheless, on the supposition regarding the meaning
to be assigned to the term "observable universe," there would be no limitations for
directly observing even these extra dimensions!

One way of summing up this meaning of "observable universe" is to say that what it designates has no horizons: there is nothing to limit its scope or range. In principle, one could obtain observational data about every detail, occurrence, and object in the universe as a whole—about its total content and structure. There are no limitations either in the situation of the observer or in his equipment that might not be overcome in practice. According to this conception, the observable universe is not a segment or partial domain of the universe as a whole; it is as wide as the universe as a whole itself.

The foregoing account of one possible meaning of the term "observable universe" cannot serve as a fruitful guide in our discussion. Even if this conception of the observable universe could be given unexceptionable clarity and total coherency (a generous and dubious supposition), it cannot be entertained as a serious option. There are several reasons for this inadequacy.

One main ground of objection is the fact that in positing wholly hypothetical observers, this conception of the observable universe ignores the actual limitations under which human observers must operate. Whatever the character of conditions of observability in everyday situations or in other sciences, there are special circumstances that make cosmology different in crucial respects. Unlike the paradigm situation of the observer on a ship at sea for whom the domain of observation and its horizon shifts with the movement of the ship, and unlike the situation envisaged in the previous description of the observable universe, all observations in cosmology are conducted from a *fixed* spatial position of the observer. Stationed on Earth, and confined to our Galaxy, he must depend on information brought *to* him by various messengers. To take one example of the consequences of this fact: The Earth-bound cosmologist has direct observational data about the *isotropic* distribution of the galaxies and the microwave background radiation. However, the claim or belief that there would be similar isotropic observations by all other observers at different spatial locations—the assumption of *homogeneity*, that is, the truth of the

Cosmological Principle—is a hypothesis that is not directly verifiable.[2]

Not only, however, is the cosmologist rooted in space, he is also rooted in time. Opportunities for observation are severely limited by the duration of an individual person's lifetime, as well as that of the whole scientific community. The time during which such information gathering has taken place or is likely to take place is minuscule compared to the large-scale space-time extent of the universe insofar as this is currently understood. In short, whether taken individually or collectively, the human observer occupies what is for all practical purposes a fixed point in space-time. There are no realistic opportunities for stretching the observer's opportunity for direct observation to match the entire space-time extent of the universe.

One upshot of all this is that what is asserted to hold of the observable universe is severely limited by the special conditions of the observer. There are, of course, mitigating circumstances that allow the fixed observer to overcome these limitations to some extent. Despite his own fixity, the human observer can and does receive news from elsewhere and elsewhen. Information is brought by various radiational messengers about constituent objects, events, and processes in the universe at distances of billions of light years, and from billions of years in the past. Even so, the special circumstance of the cosmologist is to be contrasted with observers in everyday situations or in other sciences. For others, the observable domain and its horizon shifts in traversing the domain under investigation. The possibility exists for obtaining information through a change of position in space and time that might correct information obtained from a fixed position. This opportunity is not available in practice to the cosmologist.

There is an obvious sense in which data about the observable universe is relative to the instrumental resources actually available

[2] Cf. G.F.R. Ellis, "Cosmology and Verifiability," *Quart. J. Royal Astron. Soc.* 16 (1975), 245-264; G.F.R. Ellis and E. R. Harrison, "Cosmological Principles I. Symmetry Principles," *Comments on Astrophysics and Space Physics* 6 (1974), 23-27.

at a given stage of inquiry. This type of observability is a function of the development of technology. It changes with the power of specific instruments—for example, the range of a 200-inch optical telescope as compared to that of a 100-inch telescope. It also changes with the invention of new types of instruments—for example, radio and X-ray telescopes, satellite-mounted instruments, and so on. While in earlier decades, astronomers relied exclusively on optical instruments—receiving information only from the visible part of the spectrum—the domain of the galaxies can now be explored by radio telescopes and other instruments at other wavelengths. It is only in recent decades that non-optical instruments— for example, X-ray and radio telescopes, infra-red detectors, and so on—have been added by astronomers to the number and variety of means for exploiting dimensions of the electromagnetic spectrum other than its visual part. In this sense of "observable," the extent of the observable universe is a function of existing instrumentation. While the range of the observable universe that can be explored changes with the increased power and sensitivity of instruments, at any given time that range is limited by the instruments actually available.

Specification of horizons of observability is not determined by pure observation. It is determined by some physical theory or cosmological model. Horizons of the observable universe—their number and character, their fixity or movability—depend on how theories accepted at a given point of scientific history specify them. This last point is of great importance in stressing the centrality of cosmological models. As made intelligible by a cosmological model, the conception of the universe as a whole controls what is reckoned as belonging to the observable universe and any horizon associated with the latter. Since concepts of the observable universe and its bounds are construed by physical theory, one may expect to find changes in their definition and characterization with changes in theory.

Taken in its most general sense, a cosmological horizon of the observable universe is a boundary between those objects or events that are observable and those that are not observable. However, there is no single way of drawing such boundaries. Depending on available instrumentation, conceptual constraints imposed by physical theory, the space-time situation of actual human observers, and the particular physical state the universe happens to be in as it undergoes its own evolutionary development, different types of cosmological horizon in the observable universe can be discriminated. It is clear from the foregoing, therefore, that the expression "observable universe" cannot be used in a wholesale and unanalyzed way. It must be relativized to the type of observational route employed. Probes into the depths of space and into the earliest periods in the evolution of the universe are limited, ultimately, by the kinds of observational tools, information, and theory relied on. As a result, there are several different types of horizon to the observable universe. In each case a specially tailored answer would have to be given in describing its special properties. Some are moveable, some are fixed; some are due to the situation of human observers at a particular point in the space-time history of the universe; some are due to the evolutionary properties of the universe; some are due to the limitations in man's technological inventiveness; some are due to the limiting velocity of light; some are due to the beginning or end of the universe as inferred by a particular cosmological model. In short, there is no wholesale way of describing all types of horizons by means of a single general formula. The characterization of cosmological horizons must be tackled, piecemeal, by distinguishing different senses of "horizon" and by noting the distinctive properties of each.

An illustration of this general point is to be found in the type of horizon whose special characteristic is determined by the fact that the velocity of light is a maximum. For example, this maximum velocity limits the amount of information available at a given moment to an observer of the realm of galaxies. In order to see this, it is helpful to begin by taking advantage of a distinction, originally due to E. A. Milne (1896-1950), between what he called a "world picture" and a "world map."

Let us imagine a superhuman observer—a god—who is not bound by the limitations of the maximum velocity of light. Such an observer could survey in a single instant the entire domain of galaxies that have already come into existence. His survey would not have to depend on the finite velocity of light. It would not betray any restriction in information of the kind that results from the delayed time it takes to bring information about the domain of galaxies to an ordinary human observer situated in the universe, and who is therefore bound by the mechanisms and processes of signal transmission. The entire domain of galaxies would be seen instantaneously by this privileged superhuman observer. His observational survey of all galaxies would yield what Milne calls a "world map."

Human observers do not possess a world map as the result of their observations. It is true they might reconstruct by means of theory and inference what the domain of galaxies was like at the time when the light was emitted by the galaxies. In that sense they, too, might have a world map. It would describe not what they actually observe, but what they infer. However, a superhuman, privileged observer would have a world map as the direct fruit of his observations without having to resort to the reconstruction or inferences of theory. A human observer must content himself with what Milne calls a "world picture." A world picture is a survey of those galaxies from which information has been received by a particular observer who depends on the transmission of signals emitted by galaxies or other luminous objects. That transmission takes time, since light travels at a finite velocity. Consequently, the picture an ordinary observer has of the galaxies is not of how they *are* at the moment of his reception of their light signals—for that would presuppose an instantaneous transmission—but instead of how they *were* when the signals were emitted at some point in their earlier history. A world picture is therefore different from a world map. All that astronomers ever obtain from direct observation are world pictures.

Let us now take advantage of the distinction between a world map and a world picture, and carry the analysis one step further. Consider a world picture of a collection of galaxies as established by the astronomer's recording instruments. How far can this world picture, in principle, extend? To what distance can it penetrate? What is the spatial range of the domain that might be explored by this means? Let us first consider answers to our questions for a static homogeneous universe. This type of universe is unlike ours in that it does not possess any overall evolutionary development, in the sense that its space does not expand or contract. We shall also assume that the space of this static universe is Euclidean. At a given moment in the experience of an observer in such a universe, the farthest distance to which his observations can extend is defined by the time it takes light, traveling at a fixed maximum velocity, to have arrived from a particular galaxy. Any galaxy that is at this maximum distance, or less, will be observable at that instant. Any other luminous object, if there is any, lying beyond that maximum distance, will not be observable by the given observer at that instant. For light will not have had time to travel that greater distance and still reach the observer. Of course, at any given time, the *actually* observed domain of the observable universe will depend on the range and sensitivity of available instruments. And this horizon of the actually observable universe, as a function of available *instrumentation*, is to be distinguished from—and is normally of *lesser* extent than—the horizon of the (in principle) observable domain, at a given moment of time, whose boundary is set by the *maximum velocity of light*. The latter boundary (on which we are now focusing our attention) would obtain for even the most advanced instrumentation that could detect objects at the limit of the observable domain.

Thus if all galaxies came into existence 14 billion years ago, then the farthest distance to which, in principle, observations of galaxies might now extend is 14 billion light-years. All galaxies that lie within the range of 14 billion light-years would be observable, whereas any luminous objects at a greater distance than 14 billion light-years would not be observable.

An observer attached to our Galaxy occupies the center of an observable region whose spatial extent is defined by the surface of a three-dimensional sphere. This sphere marks the spatial boundary of a domain from which the observer might obtain information. At the moment of observation, the spherical surface divides the entire domain of objects into two portions: those that fall within the bounds of the surface, and so constitute the observable universe, and those that lie outside. The observable region will not extend beyond the distance it takes light to reach the observer from the most distant galaxies or other luminous objects. All other objects beyond this range will be unobservable, since the light coming from them will not have had time to reach the observer at the moment of his observation. What holds for an observer attached to our Galaxy will also apply, of course, to observers on other galaxies. In a homogeneous universe, the same general results of observation obtained by observers in our Galaxy will also be found by other observers situated anywhere else. Each observer will be at the center of his own observable universe. The spherical surface that accomplishes this division is known as a *particle horizon*. (A "particle," in this context, means any material object—for example, a galaxy whose history in space-time is identified by a world-line that connects various events in the career of the particle.) Though fixed at a particular moment, the particle horizon is not immovable. With the passage of time for the observer, luminous objects that at a given moment lie in the unobservable region become observed: they move into the observable universe. With the advance of the observer's light-cone into the future, the spatial extent of his observable universe increases. At a later stage in the career of a particular observer—at a later point in his temporally ongoing world-line—information might become available from luminous objects that were previously unobservable. The spatial range of the observable universe (the particle horizon) expands with the advance of time. To illustrate this concept of a particle horizon and its change in spatial extent with the passage of time, let us revert to our previous simplifying assumption that all galaxies originated 14 billion years ago. As we saw, the farthest distance to which observations of galaxies might extend, at the moment labeled "now," is 14 billion light-years. It is the particle horizon for the observer at that moment. However, with the advance of time beyond "now" to later moments, the distance of the particle horizon changes correspondingly. Thus after the passage of one billion years, the distance to the particle horizon is in principle increased to 15 billion light-years.

So far, what we have described as holding for a particle horizon would apply to a static, Euclidean universe. In this, as in any other universe described in relativistic cosmology, the velocity of light serves to delimit the spatial range of galaxies observable at a given time by a centrally situated observer. However, further complications set in when we take into account, as we must, that the universe is not static but expanding. This means that the spatial boundary of the particle horizon changes not only with the advance of time for the observer, but with changes in the scale factor of the universe. Changes in scale factor do not apply to a static universe, but must be taken into account in the case of an expanding universe. This new factor introduces the question of the recession velocities of galaxies. Recall that Hubble's Law, when taken in a cosmological context, establishes a direct linear correlation between the recession velocity of galaxies and the distances of galaxies. The concept of the expansion of space is standardly interpreted in terms of the changing scale factor of expanding space. We must now take into account, therefore, the rate at which the boundary of the particle horizon changes according to the recession velocity of expanding space. In such a universe, the galaxies (regarded as particles) are taken to be at relative rest with respect to one another. They follow the average motion of matter through space-time. Their paths are represented by straight world-lines. In the case of expanding space, the scale factor increases with increasing values of cosmic time.

Next, consider a recession velocity of space that equals the velocity of light.[3] Since, according to Hubble's Law, the recession velocity increases with distance, let the recession velocity of ex-

---

[3] As conceived in models of relativistic cosmology, expanding space can expand with a speed equal to or greater than that of light. There is no objection to this: it does not come into conflict with the principles of the special theory of relativity. The latter forbids any *material body* to reach the velocity of light. However, space is not a material body.

panding space be taken at the velocity of light. At that velocity, the distance is *c/H*. This distance is known as the *Hubble length*. Let this Hubble length now serve as the radius of a sphere with the observer *O* at the center. The sphere, so identified, is known as the *Hubble sphere*. It is a sphere whose spherical surface is receding at the velocity of light. All galaxies within this sphere will (in principle) be observable by *O*, whereas all entities that lie beyond the Hubble sphere will be expanding at a velocity greater than that of light. Remembering that the galaxies are to be thought of as stationary with respect to one another in space, the term "recession velocities" of galaxies is a shorthand way of referring to the expansion of space. For the observer *O*, all galaxies within the Hubble sphere will be observable, and any objects beyond will not be observable. Insofar as the red shifts of galaxies are taken as a measure of their recession velocities, this means that those galaxies whose recession velocities are at the boundary of the Hubble sphere, or whose recession velocities are less than the velocity of light, will be observable. However, all galaxies, if any, whose recession velocities are greater than the velocity of light will lie beyond the bounds of the Hubble sphere and will not be observed. In this sense, the Hubble sphere represents, for expanding space, a particle horizon.

The upshot of all this is that the Hubble sphere defines the spatial bounds within which observational information is available about the domain of galaxies. Any galaxy or other object whose distance from the observer is greater than the Hubble length, and therefore whose recession velocity is greater than the speed of light (that is, belongs to that part of expanding space that is expanding at a speed greater than that of the speed of light) will not be observable by a particular observer at a particular moment on his world-line.

The Hubble sphere marks one type of horizon of the observable universe. The horizon exists not simply because of the finite velocity of light, but because the universe itself is expanding. And the recession of space at the velocity of light, in such an expanding universe, creates its own special form of particle horizon. The special details of the relation between a particle horizon and the expansion of space vary among different models, and cannot be summed up in a single formula. The intricacies of these relations lie beyond the scope of the present discussion.[4]

We turn, next, to consider the properties of another type of horizon in the evolving universe—an *event horizon*. An "event," in this context, is some momentary occurrence in space-time, as contrasted with an extended stretch of space-time holding for an enduring material particle. In the case of Friedmann models, an example of an event horizon is found where the spatial curvature is positive and where the universe recontracts to a singularity that marks its end. Another example of a cosmological event horizon is to be found in cosmological models with a positive repulsive Λ term, in which the universe expands so rapidly that regions of the universe exist from which light never reaches an observer. The event horizon marks the boundary of such regions. The event horizon is a boundary in an observer's light-cone that marks a division between events that lie within the observer's light-cone up to that point of time, and those events that lie outside the observer's light-cone and so would never be observed. In order to make this clear, we can make a threefold division among the class of events with respect to their observability. One includes the collection of events already observed by a particular observer, O, in his own past; a second group includes those events that might yet be observable by the same observer; and, finally, the third group includes those events that will never be observed by the same observer. The event horizon is to be distinguished, therefore, from a particle horizon.

Even if we confine ourselves to information brought by electromagnetic radiation, we have to make a further distinction in the use of the expression "observable universe," since there are two major types of information yielded by such energy. The first has to do with the domain of the galaxies and the second with the information yielded by the microwave background radiation. Inasmuch as the galaxies did not come into existence until some one

[4] Cf. E. R. Harrison, *Cosmology*, 376-380.

billion years after the big bang, this sense of "observable universe" is clearly narrower, from a temporal point of view, than that which extends to the universe during its earliest stages. The principal forms of electromagnetic energy used to explore the domain of galaxies belong to the visual and radio parts of the spectrum. Electromagnetic information about the pre-galactic domain of the observable universe is brought by the microwave background radiation. It is for this reason that the discovery of the microwave background radiation by Penzias and Wilson in 1965 was of great importance, for that type of radiation brought messages from a *pre-galactic* era.

The radiation era lasted from about the first second after the big bang into the next several hundred thousand years. During this period, radiation co-existed with a relatively small amount of matter in an expanding plasma in which no atoms were present. Because of the enormously high temperatures, densities, and energies of the particles present, matter could not only not clump into stars or galaxies, but could not even form stable atoms out of nuclei and electrons. Moreover, during this period, photons could not travel far in the universe without meeting and interacting with free electrons, thereby causing absorption or scattering. Photons were coupled to electrons, constantly interacting with them. This prevented photons from traveling as free particles. After approximately 500 thousand years, when the temperature had dropped sufficiently, electrons combined with nuclei to form light *atoms* of hydrogen. It was this process, and its continuation in the formation of relatively stable atoms such as helium and deuterium, that marked the separation of matter and radiation, whose beginning is known as the "decoupling era" because it demarcates the earlier radiation-dominated era from the later matter-dominated era. Whereas in the earlier era the energy of the universe consisted entirely of kinetic energy, in the matter-dominated phase the bulk of energy was located in the rest-masses of the nuclear particles that composed the matter of the universe.[5]

---

[5] According to the formula of special relativity, $E = mc^2$, the rest-mass of matter can be interchanged with pure energy. This formula makes it clear why, in the early

After the decoupling era had progressed to a point approximately one million years after the big bang, the universe became sufficiently transparent to the transmission of *free* photons. It was only when the temperature of the universe had dropped below 3,000 degrees Kelvin and the energies of interaction were correspondingly decreased that photons became free to move through space, relatively unimpeded by collisions with free electrons. The microwave radiation detected by Penzias and Wilson is the direct remnant and evidence of that epoch. The decoupling era thus has a special importance for the concept of horizons in the observable universe.

In light of the above, it helps to identify and locate the *photon horizon*.[6] This horizon constitutes the temporal divide between earlier epochs of the universe and later eras when photons were able to transmit direct information about the state of the universe at the time from which they derive. The photon horizon marks an information barrier. It limits direct observational information of the universe obtained by electromagnetic means to the time when free photon radiation was liberated to serve its role as a messenger. This horizon marks the limit of the observable universe insofar as this can be explored by electromagnetic energy. Whatever the degree of technological improvement in instruments for the detection of such radiation, the limits set by the photon horizon cannot be overcome. Because of it, it is impossible to obtain direct observational information by means of electromagnetic radiation concerning stages in the history of the universe *earlier* than the epoch marked by that horizon.

Can cosmology penetrate to depths of space and time beyond the photon horizon? The answer cannot be given as a simple "yes"

---

universe, enormous amounts of pure energy were required to create matter out of pure energy. And for the same reason, modern particle accelerators also require great amounts of energy to produce particles of matter. Of course, man-made accelerators will never be able to duplicate the enormous energy resources of the very early universe.

[6] Cf. R. V. Wagoner and D. W. Goldsmith, *Cosmic Horizons* (San Francisco: W. H. Freeman, 1982), 130.

or "no." It must be qualified to take into account the kinds of instrumentation and theory that may be forthcoming to accomplish such penetration. Some physical theory has already been worked out to describe the observable universe that would be open to exploration beyond the photon horizon *if* the instrumentation were available. Whereas the observable universe within the limits set by the photon horizon can be explored by now-available instrumentation, the wider range of the observable universe can only be entertained at the present time on the basis of theory, relatively primitive instrumentation, and observational data of a very limited and insecure character.

For example, one possible type of "telescope" would make use of neutrinos. Within approximately one second after the big bang—in addition to the interchange of photons and charged particles of matter (protons, positrons, electrons)—neutrinos and anti-neutrinos in equilibrium with matter were also present. When the temperature of the universe dropped below 10^{10} degrees Kelvin and the density likewise decreased (approximately a second or two after the big bang), neutrinos and anti-neutrinos became sufficiently decoupled from matter to allow them to become free particles. The universe became transparent to neutrinos. As a result of the cooling of the universe over the course of billions of years since then, the temperature of the neutrinos that permeate the universe now should be about 2 degrees Kelvin. A neutrino telescope, if available, would detect cosmic background neutrino radiation, and thus open another observational window on a very early stage in the history of the universe.

Another source of observational data that might some day be available to extend the range of the observable universe would consist in the detection of primordial gravitons (the theory-postulated elementary particles that are the carriers of the gravitational force). These particles would have their source in the very earliest stage of the evolution of the universe when the universe was in a state of extreme gravitational collapse (in a time-reversed sense). If detected, the gravitational radiation would disclose information about the universe in its earliest stage after gravitational force broke free ("froze") from the state in which all four fundamental forces were unified. However, the range of the observable universe, so explored, would have its own *gravitational horizon*.

Recent grand unification theories have suggested the existence of magnetic monopoles and free quarks. Magnetic monopoles carry an isolated magnetic charge, equivalent to that of a south or north pole, and free relic quarks are those relatively few quarks that have managed to escape from the interior of nucleons to which they are normally permanently confined. If observationally detected, both monopoles and free quarks would bring direct evidence of the state of the universe when it was 10^{-35} second old.

To sum up: Given the evolutionary development of the universe, the human situation at a particular moment in the space-time evolution of the universe, the fact that human observers are obliged to obtain such information as they can within their own backward light-cones, and the fact that the velocity of light is a maximum, what we call "the observable universe" is in fact a shorthand way of referring to various observable segments of the universe as a whole (where the latter is conceived by theory). Each observable segment is determined by a particular boundary or horizon.

One such boundary is the photon horizon. It is fixed and immovable, since according to current understanding it is set by the physical conditions of the universe as a whole at a particular stage of its own development. No improvement in human instrumentation can shift that horizon insofar as one depends on electromagnetic radiation. If suitable instruments were to become available to detect gravitational particles from the stage in the evolution of the universe that antedated the period of the photon horizon, or to also detect the existence of magnetic monopoles and relic free quarks, the range of the observable universe would be pushed back to the state of the universe at 10^{-35} second after the big bang. Given the Hubble Law correlating the red shifts of galaxies with their distances and the fact that the speed of light sets an upper limit to the transmission of all informational signals, a spatial bound exists to the observable domain of galaxies in the form of a particle horizon. While improved instrumentation may extend the range of galaxies observed up to the bounds of the particle horizon, that horizon is fixed at any given time. If it should turn out that the universe as a whole will come to a maximum extent of expansion and then re-contract to a singularity, then the observable universe will also have an event horizon. This horizon, too, would be fixed and im-movable, since it is dependent on the evolutionary development of the universe as a whole and is totally beyond human control. Given the space-time situation of human observers at this stage of the evolution of the universe as a whole, the horizons of the ob-servable regions of the universe are further determined for human observers by their backward light-cone, the spatial bounds of the particle horizon, and available instrumentation. For all practical purposes, the particle horizon and the backward light-cone are also fixed. Any shift in either would require the passage of significantly large stretches of time to enlarge the range of observability. More-over, it would require the continued existence of human investi-gators into a very long future, a condition which, to say the least, is surrounded by enormous uncertainty.

CONCEPTUAL HORIZONS AND THE KNOWN UNIVERSE

Just as there are different types of horizons in the observable uni-verse (due to limitations in the conditions of *observation*—for ex-ample, the space-time location of the observer, the use of available instrumentation, the decoupling era, the finite velocity of light, etc.), so, too, there are horizons in the intelligible universe. Un-like the case with the horizons of the observable universe, how-ever, the horizons of the intelligible universe are primarily linked to different types of boundary conditions present in the use of a *conceptual scheme*. Whereas a horizon of observability is primarily an *information barrier*, conceptual horizons in cosmology consist of bounds present in the use of the *language* employed by a cos-mological model to make the universe intelligible. Horizons of in-telligibility are inevitable and cannot be avoided, since they come in one form or another with the very use of the language rules of a particular cosmological model. To make explicit these conceptual bounds is the role of *grammatical sentences*, in the Wittgensteinian sense of "grammar." In any case, the criteria used for determining the character of horizons for the observable universe will not be the same as those that determine the character of conceptual horizons in the intelligible universe. The types of criteria for recognizing the latter depend on the kinds of bounds present in the use of language in a given model.

While they are all, at bottom, grammatical in character, the bounds of a model of the intelligible universe are themselves of different types. I shall distinguish two principal kinds. One type is normal and comes with the very use of one or another set of grammatical rules in describing or explaining various matters to which the rules are applied. The other type of bound arises where the normal rules encounter a breakdown when applied in special circumstances, and so lead to a singularity.

Some conceptual limitations of a model of the universe are due to the fact that only those matters are intelligible that lie within the bounds of its own grammatical rules. These include *definitional rules*. Among the latter are to be found those definitional rules that specify the meaning of expressions for standard concepts shared with other theories and models. For example, many models rely on the definitional rules for electric charge, mass density, spatial curvature, conservation of energy, scale factor, and so on. Along with definitional rules for individual concepts, a model's grammatical rules will also normally include various standard *rules of calculation and inference* of a mathematical or logical sort—for example, the rules of the differential calculus, non-Euclidean geometry, and so on. In addition, the grammatical rules of a particular model may include rules for specifying the meaning of concepts relatively distinctive to the model. Thus, as contrasted with older Friedmann relativistic models, an inflationary model may use novel concepts found in grand unification gauge symmetry theories. Other models may employ the novel ideas of "superspace" (Wheeler), or "a wave function (in the sense of quantum mechanics) for the universe as a whole" (Hawking), thereby setting them apart from models lacking or eschewing these concepts.

In short, the adoption of some combination of standard and special grammatical rules determines the normal conceptual bounds of a model. The model cannot be understood without identifying the particular fund of grammatical rules to which it appeals. Only those expressions and inferences are *meaningful* that are in accordance with the grammatical rules of a particular scheme, whether or not the hypotheses, predictions, explanations, or descriptions of empirical data offered by a particular model are confirmed and regarded as *true*. An expression not governed by any rule in a given model, while meaningless in that scheme, may, of course, be given a definite use in some other scheme. Thus the notion of "quark" (as referring to an elementary constituent of a neutron or proton) would be unintelligible in the context of classical atomic or nuclear physics—as, for example, formulated by Bohr, Schrödinger, or Heisenberg. However, it is given a definite meaning in contemporary quantum chromodynamics (theory of strong forces). Similarly, while meaningful in contemporary relativistic cosmology, the notion of the expansion of space is not meaningful in classical Newtonian physics or cosmology. Hence all questions of meaning are to be judged relative to the normal, established grammatical rules of a particular language scheme. Anything lying beyond those rules is meaningless from the vantage point of that language.

One could, of course, change the grammar of some language to make room for new grammatical rules and thereby transform the original language into a richer, perhaps more useful one. Thus the Weinberg-Salam theory of the electro-weak force is a richer theory than either quantum electrodynamics or the theory of the weak force, since it showed how to unify both. Again, by making use of a changing scale factor, the group of Friedmann relativistic models is richer, as a language, than the original Einstein static theory of the universe. To transcend the normal rules and limits of a language requires adopting new ones. Sometimes the changeover can be extremely radical and marks the occasion of a major scientific revolution—comparable in some ways to a religious conversion or the adoption of a totally new world picture. In these cases, an older, habitually used scheme is abandoned, perhaps in its entirety, in favor of a new scheme of thought. In other, less radical cases, there may be only a gradual enrichment of the language by the addition of new rules and concepts. Thus Einstein broadened the concept of relativity beyond its use in the special theory in order to account for the phenomenon of gravitation. In accomplishing transformations of a conceptual sort, whether radical or partial, it is, of course, necessary to insure that the new conceptual scheme, when taken in its entirety, is internally consistent. The added or changed concepts—their definitions, the new or different mathematical rules of calculation, and the principles that state the axioms of the new theory—must all be compatible with one another; they must not harbor any contradiction. To borrow a term from Leibniz, they must not only be, individually, logically possible, they must also be *compossible* when taken conjunctively.

I have described, thus far, general conditions that set the bounds of sense in the use of any language, and in particular the use of a cosmological model. These bounds are set by the rules of the language. The horizons of intelligibility are determined by these rules. However, there are other horizons that arise for different reasons from those that belong to the normal bounds just described. This special type of horizon consists in the presence of a singularity. In general, a singularity marks the point at which some law for describing the pattern among quantitatively expressed terms reaches a breakdown in its application. It marks a failure to yield a finite quantitative description of some phenomenon or state of a physical system, of the kind that would normally be available. Thus, if the solution of some physical law yields an infinite quantity for the variable representing a scalar quantity (say, temperature), instead of the finite values normally found, the derivation of the infinite value for the variable marks the presence of a singularity—the breakdown of the law at that point. Or consider the application of Maxwell's classic equations for the electromagnetic field that yield infinite values—and that are therefore undefined at those points. Another example, of greater relevance to our present interest, is found in those cosmological models that reach a singular point in the past of the universe, identified as its origin. Yet even here, the situation is somewhat different from singularities encountered, for example, in certain applications of Maxwell's equations. For whereas in Maxwell's theory there is a background metric within which the field quantities are specified, in the case of general relativity it is the metric itself that breaks down at the singular points. At those points, one is left with no conceptual tools based on the notion of space-time with which to operate.

In summary: a statement concerning a singularity (or other types of horizons of intelligibility in a cosmological model) says something about the model—about the language used in conceiving the universe. It concerns the range of the model's capacity—indeed its incapacity at certain points—to give an account of the universe as intelligible.

One immediate benefit and application of the foregoing approach to the notion of conceptual horizons in cosmological models is the way we may regard the introduction and use of the expression "the origin of the universe" in recent discussions—particularly popular expositions—of cosmology. This expression is commonly interpreted as referring to an actual ontological state of affairs, a fact about the universe as an independently existing entity that cosmology as a science has supposedly succeeded in bringing to light.[7]

As against this common interpretation, I wish to suggest that the cosmologist's use of the expression "the origin of the universe" is

---

[7] Here is a typical statement: "The existence of a past edge to time implies that in a very fundamental sense, the big bang represents the creation of the physical universe. It is not just the creation of matter, as so often envisaged in the past, but a creation of everything that is physically relevant, including space and time. . . . Its creation represents the instantaneous suspension of physical laws, the sudden, abrupt flash of lawlessness that allowed something to come out of nothing. It represents a true miracle—transcending physical principles." See P. Davies, *The Edge of Infinity* (New York: Simon and Schuster, 1981), 161.

best understood if taken as a description of the bounds of a conceptual scheme. It defines the horizon of the *intelligible universe*, that is, the universe as *conceived* in terms of a particular model or class of models. It should not be taken as referring to an inherent property of an objectively and independently existing entity—the universe "in itself."

As the foregoing discussion has stressed, any cosmological model has its own built-in limitations of one sort or another. It cannot answer certain pressing questions because it is not equipped to do so. Its laws and grammatical rules are incompetent to yield answers to the questions raised. At that point, the horizon of intelligibility—of description and explanation—consists in an inability to go ahead with the tools at hand. This in no way implies that this situation will remain a permanent block to further inquiry. It does not preclude the eventual discovery of other theories that would allow the horizons of older schemes to be overcome.

We see this process at work in recent developments in cosmology, both with respect to questions asked about the initial stages in the development of the universe and the efforts made to answer these questions. Take, for example, the following question: How is one to explain the existence and properties of leptons and quarks? Why are these particular elementary particles the ones that existed as part of the initial conditions at what some cosmological models would describe as the "origin of the universe"? Why did they come to possess the particular properties of charge and mass they are found to have? At the present stage of inquiry there are no wholly satisfactory answers to these questions, or at least no answers for which there is any broad consensus. The existence of leptons and quarks at the "origin of the universe" are the arbitrary "givens" from which some contemporary theories start, and on the basis of which they attempt to build up an intelligible universe. The answers to the previously mentioned questions lie outside the scope of these theories. They mark a horizon of intelligibility for those theories, but not for others—for example, not for cosmological models that appeal to the central ideas of supersymmetry and supergravity theories.

Also, of course, as we have seen, instead of accepting the view that the universe originated in a singular state of infinite temperature and density—a state that must be taken as an inexplicable initial condition—there are theories that would push back the boundaries of understanding by appealing to quantum laws that make use of the concept of fluctuations of a "pre-existent" vacuum.

Incidentally, to "push back" does not necessarily mean finding *earlier* moments of *time* at which to locate the "origin." For "time" itself is a concept whose grammar is specified in a particular theory. Not all cosmological models define "time" in the same way. Indeed, in "pushing back" the origin of the universe, that is, the horizon of cosmological intelligibility, some models do so by describing conditions in which neither space nor time, as commonly understood, are appropriate or relevant.

The foregoing examples of efforts to overcome the conceptual boundary—represented by some models as "the origin of the universe"—make clear a central point. Every cosmological model proposes its own account of how to define the range of the universe as a whole. Where employed, the stage identified as "the origin of the universe" marks one bound of the range of intelligibility for the universe as a whole recognized by the model in question. What is regarded as the universe as a whole for such models is one whose scope has, as its lower limit, the point referred to as the "origin" (or "moment of creation") of the universe. Insofar as another model seeks to overcome the boundary in question, it does so by proposing, in effect, another definition of "the universe as a whole." Thus if a cosmological model that appeals to the vacuum as the source from which the universe derives were accepted, it would actually be proposing a new definition of "the universe as a whole." For if the vacuum has its own type of physical reality and can be described by appropriate quantum or other laws of physics, then the vacuum state would have to be *included* in an enlarged conception of the universe as a whole. What, therefore, was regarded as "the universe as a whole" in more limited cosmological models is being challenged. If successful, the older use of the term "the universe as a whole" would have to be discarded and replaced by the newer conception. In this process of redefining the range of the universe as a whole and offering an enlarged or altered conceptual scheme for making this new scope of the universe intelligible, one consequence is that the concept of the origin of the universe, as employed in the discarded cosmological model, is now dissolved. It is replaced by a scheme that promises to link events in the evolutionary development of the universe by physical laws that may not have been known or used at all in older schemes.

This is not to overlook the fact, of course, that even if this shift in terminology and advance in understanding of the scope of the intelligible universe were accomplished, there would inevitably arise fresh horizons of intelligibility in the newer conceptions. Other types and examples of conceptual horizons would quickly become apparent. We saw an example of this in the work of Atkatz and Pagels. In proposing a quantum model of the vacuum out of which the universe (as described in some standard views) arose, their own account is unable to answer certain questions. They admit, for example, that since their quantum model can only explain the emergence of a spatially closed universe by a tunneling process from the pre-existent vacuum, this is a horizon of intelligibility they are unable to overcome. This type of situation—of encountering new types and examples of conceptual horizons—is endemic to *all* changes and advances in cosmological understanding. In short, all cosmological theories—well-tested or speculative, restricted or broad in scope—are conceptually bound. Each has its horizons, each its domain of competence. Hence, identifying a particular stage of the universe as the "origin of the universe" should be taken for what it is. It tells us something about the conceptual powers of a particular model or class of models.

In saying all this, I do not wish to deny that there is a perfectly legitimate sense in which one can say that current cosmology supports the idea that the universe, insofar as it can warrantedly be said to be known, *did have* a "beginning." But this is to say no more than that the known universe has undergone an evolutionary development and that according to one or another model describing this development, one can specify the special character of its "beginning." It does not follow, however, that an evolutionary development of the intelligible and known universe requires the earliest stages of that development to succeed a creation of the universe out of absolute nothing. The "origin," "beginning," or "creation" of the universe begins with the earliest physical state of the intelligible universe. This in no way excludes the possibility of linking the earliest stages with further preconditions of a physical sort, even though those preconditions may not yet be uniformly agreed on or satisfactorily understood. In any case, this earliest physical state is not to be identified with a singularity, since a singularity is not a state of the intelligible universe. It is a bound or horizon to that intelligibility. The initial cosmological singularity is a property of a cosmological model, a sign of the model's breakdown in making the universe intelligible, not a property of the universe it would describe.

In effect, every cosmological model constitutes a proposal to adopt its own grammar. However, the fact that a cosmological model may be thought of as being such a proposal does not thereby automatically guarantee its acceptability. There are rival proposals how to characterize the intelligible universe. There are as many versions of the intelligible universe (the universe as a whole)—as many "intelligible universes"—as there are cosmological models that differ in their respective grammars. The differences among competing models, moreover, are not merely notational differences such that one can translate from one into another and thereby show them to be equivalent in intellectual content. On the contrary, their grammars are at least in part incommensurable and mutually nontranslatable.

The process of scientific inquiry consists in the many-sided effort by a community of investigators (through discussion and empirical tests) to choose the model that has a greater number of merits and fewer weaknesses than any of its rivals. When a choice is made at a given stage of inquiry, even if only provisionally, and a broad consensus reached, the preferred cosmological model may be thought of as having been promoted from the status of being a proposal (a hypothesis) to being a confirmed and accepted account of what the universe is. From being simply one among other ways of rendering the universe intelligible, the process of confirmation and selection converts one of these schemes to the rank of being an account of *the known universe*. In addition, then, to the two previously distinguished senses of the expression "the universe"—that is, *the observable universe* and *the intelligible universe*—we may use the expression *the known universe* to identify what in fact the universe is thought to be at a particular stage of scientific inquiry, when the outcome of inquiry has reached a temporary halting place through a broad agreement among the experts. The intended referent of the expression "the known universe" includes the referent of the expression "the observable universe" within its scope. However, in order to identify the intended referent of "the known universe," one must understand the way a particular model characterizes the universe as a whole, and why that characterization is preferred to those offered by rival models. To mark this successful outcome of a process of search, evaluation, and choice, the qualifying adjectives "observable," "intelligible," and "known" will frequently be omitted altogether. It follows from the foregoing that we cannot explain the meaning of the expression "the universe" (when used in this way as a synonym for "the known universe") until we have specified a cosmological model that has the following characteristics: It has been submitted to a process of collecting observational data, identifying various types of objects and processes, applying accepted laws for describing, explaining, predicting, and retrodicting specific events and occurrences, performing calculations, and, finally, having its inferences tested. When all this is carried out and yields a reasonably satisfactory account preferred to its rivals, one can sum it up by saying that what is being described is *the universe*. The name "the universe" derives its meaning from this product of inquiry and cannot be given apart from it.

One of the immediate results of the foregoing analysis is that the expression "the universe" cannot be used as a name for an entity that purportedly exists "as such" or "in itself." By attaching a qualifying adjective such as "observable," "intelligible," or "known," to the term "the universe," it immediately becomes obvious that one must consider certain relevant conditions, procedures, and limitations relative to which the expression "the universe" is to be understood. The conditions and limitations are of an observational and conceptual nature, while the procedures of evaluation and choice among competing theories are guided by the commonly accepted standards of scientific method. The concept of "the universe" is *relative* to these conditions, limitations, and procedures. It has no absolute meaning independently of these. In short, the *known* universe is a product of a process of controlled and critical inquiry.

To say that the known universe is a human product is not to be confused with claiming for human beings some creative power for making the universe "in itself," as an independently existing entity or object. According to traditional cosmogonical accounts in myth and theology, the universe is made by a Supreme Being who has the requisite power to transform pre-existent materials or to create it *ex nihilo*. On such views, the term "the universe" ("the world" or some other equivalent) designates an entity to be distinguished from the creative agent that brings it into existence. Once made, this entity has its own structure and properties, whether these are recognized by human beings or not. Since, on the general view I am espousing in this book, I am proposing to avoid this use of the term "the universe" (to designate an object created, or otherwise existing and endowed with its own inherent properties), no such metaphysical claims are being made. Nor is it the case that in rejecting these traditional cosmogonic viewpoints, I am proposing to replace them by a philosophy that attributes cosmogonic power to man rather than to some divine agency. All that man's powers of inquiry and the use of language can bring into existence is a *knowledge product*—the *known universe*, not something designated as "the universe as such" or "in itself." To say the known universe is a knowledge product is to call special attention to the fact that the characterization of the universe as a whole is the outcome of a creative conceptual process, and that the choice of a particular account of the universe as a whole is the result of a process of human inquiry.

Complementary to and associated with traditional realistic metaphysical views concerning the universe (whether grounded in myth, theology, or a priori rational argument) are a number of characteristic views about the meanings of the terms "truth" and "objectivity." For such realistic philosophies, an account of any subject matter, and hence of the universe as a whole, is said to be true if it corresponds to the inherent structure and properties of the object under investigation. Truth is taken to consist of a disclosure—giving a faithful account—of what is already "there," "in fact," and "objectively." An obvious and pressing question is what becomes of "truth" and "objectivity" were we to adopt the approach to the nature of cosmology and to the meanings of the expression "the universe" I have been arguing for. Can the concepts of truth and objectivity still be retained in some form, given an appropriate set of meanings in the pragmatic, Wittgensteinian (modified Kantian) philosophy my discussion has sought to defend?

One important result of the notion of the intelligible universe is that we cannot coherently use this expression to refer to an entity to which we can have direct access in order to determine its properties and to see whether they are what some cosmological model says they are. The only access is *via* a cosmological model. The universe as a whole can be described only by means of the grammar of a cosmological model. The grammar is constitutive of the intelligible universe—the universe as a whole. The grammar is not applied to something that already has certain properties. The grammar is not external to that entity: it is internal to it. It constitutes what it is to be such-and-such an intelligible universe. Therefore, apart from that grammar (that model), there is no intelligible universe, no universe as a whole.

If the intelligible universe can only be thought of in connection with some conceptual scheme, and not as independent of it, then truth for cosmology can only be defined internally to the process of inquiry. If truth is not a matter of correspondence or matching with some antecedently existing subject matter (the universe in itself), then truth cannot be determined independently of a process of evaluation of the comparative merits of different cosmological models. In the course of this inquiry, some decision needs to be made about which scheme to adopt among competing accounts. Truth consists in warranted assertibility, the rationally justified preference for one account over others. Nor will the truth, in the sense of the warranted assertibility of some model, be described in terms of some degree of probability, if this is taken to mark some degree of approximation to the absolute truth. For, once again, this way of thinking is guided, at bottom, by a correspondence view of truth. It presumes that the absolute truth consists in a perfect match between an ideal theory (at which science is thought to aim) and what holds in fact. But if we surrender this conception of truth, then the conception of degrees of approximation to the truth (degrees of probability assigned to different accounts, when measured against this presumed ideal theory) goes by the board. All the cosmologist can achieve by way of truth, as a mark of his description of the known universe, is an appraisal of superiority—of *comparatively* greater merit—awarded to some particular cosmological model. The truth of a model is judged pragmatically, by how well it continues to exhibit its merits and proves successful in ongoing inquiry when judged in comparison with other accounts.

If the notion of truth needs to be redefined once we surrender a correspondence view, so, too, does the notion of objectivity. In traditional approaches, especially in modern epistemological philosophy, a distinction and contrast is made between what exists "in the mind of the subject" and what exists "objectively," that is, "externally" to the mind and its subjective ideas. The central problem faced by epistemologists, who are guided by this distinction between the subjective and the objective, is to decide which, if any, of the mind's ideas existing within the domain of the subjective, can be relied on to correspond to what exists independently of the mind—objectively. Once again, this entire way of thinking presupposes that it makes sense to think of reality as already possessed of some determinate set of properties, some determinate structure, and that it is the goal of the mind's quest for knowledge to uncover, to disclose, what those properties are and what that structure is "in itself."

But if we surrender this type of metaphysics, then we must also surrender the kind of epistemological nexus of problems built on this metaphysics—in particular, the distinction between the subjective and the objective, as defined in this approach. What, then, becomes of the notion of objectivity, once we abandon this way of thinking and adopt the pragmatic view sketched earlier? The answer is that objectivity is to be thought of as a property of the *known universe*. It belongs to the known universe, because the known universe is what is arrived at by a consensus of judgment on the part of a community of scientifically qualified investigators. What is objective, in this sense, can be contrasted with what is subjective. The latter term is now redefined to mean that which fails to earn the appraisal of acceptance, the award of being rationally and warrantedly assertible. The known universe is not "in the mind" nor is it "external" to the mind. It is neither. It is objective insofar as what it said to be known is to be contrasted with what is merely conjectured or imagined.

The known universe at one stage of inquiry will, accordingly, be different from what it is said to be at a different stage of inquiry. In this sense, the known universe undergoes change. Men live in differently construed known universes. There need not be—and there is not—only one known universe. Yet for all that, at any given stage of inquiry the known universe is objective at that stage.

SIX

The Boundless

ON TRANSCENDENCE

Let us assume that, at a particular stage of its inquiries, scientific cosmology were to reach a widely accepted description of the universe as a maximally comprehensive, intelligible domain, and that this description had received enough confirmation at that stage of inquiry to serve as an account of the known universe. Our previous discussion has sought to establish that even under these conditions there would still remain certain horizons of intelligibility and knowledge.

It is true that one can overcome the conceptual bounds (the grammar) of some particular account of the intelligible universe by moving into the conceptual framework of another cosmological model. This is illustrated in replacing a steady state model of the universe by an evolutionary one, or by moving forward from a relatively simple Friedmann model with its requirement of a singularity at the origin of the universe to a conception of the origin that brings to bear the conceptual resources of recent particle physics in understanding the processes at work surrounding the event called "the big bang." Advances in understanding are achieved by introducing different fundamental principles, useful analogies, or known laws that furnish a more satisfactory way of approaching the subject matter under investigation. In short, one can overcome the bounds of any particular account of the universe as a whole by changing to the conceptual framework of another model, another—at least in part different—account of the intelligible universe. It will be found, however, that the new model has its own conceptual bounds. However long continued, this process of pushing back conceptual horizons never has resulted in, and, it may be expected, never will eventuate in the possession of a model without any conceptual horizons whatsoever. Thus if one replaces a Friedmann version of the origin of the universe as a singularity by a model that describes and explains the origin in terms of particles manifesting a primordial unified force antedating any symmetry breaking, the existence of such unified particles at the origin will constitute another form of the given—a new and different horizon of intelligibility. If, in turn, even this horizon is pushed back by saying that the real particles of matter and energy present at the origin of the space-time universe arose by chance metrical fluctuations from the primordially structured vacuum, this new explanation will have only succeeded in establishing a new horizon. For how is one to explain the existence of the vacuum, its virtual particles, and any other properties it is believed to have? There seems to be no end to the prospect of asking these types of questions, whatever the advances made at each stage in removing the horizons of earlier, less adequate forms of making the universe intelligible. As long as cosmology continues to engage in the process of constructing, testing, and evaluating cosmological models—and it cannot do otherwise and still remain a form of scientific inquiry— there is no escape from the conceptual bounds of one model to another model that has no conceptual bounds of its own.

The same type of conclusion follows if we shift our discussion from the level of the intelligible universe to that of the known universe. Since an account of the known universe includes within itself a description of the observable universe and a conceptual scheme for rendering the universe as a whole intelligible, and since each of these has its own distinctive types of horizon, it follows that the account of the known universe will also be bound by virtue of these components. This will be the case with any account of the known universe at any stage of cosmological inquiry. For any description of the known universe there are domains beyond the limits of observability, questions left unanswered, problems left unsolved. No account of the known universe can claim finality or perfection for itself. Of course, this is not to say that some questions will not eventually be answered. Not everything which is unknown is unknowable. But even if certain questions that can be answered by the methods of science will be answered in the course of continued inquiry, there is no reason to believe that if one stops at any particular stage of inquiry, there will be no further questions, no fresh bounds and horizons connected with the use of a new account of the known universe. Cosmological inquiry is an indefinitely prolonged search for ever-better accounts of the known universe, a search that has no absolute terminus.

Let us agree, then, that the process of ongoing successful cosmological inquiry is marked by repeatedly overcoming the limits and horizons of less adequate views. Are we justified in saying that there are some horizons or limits to cosmic intelligibility and knowledge that will never be overcome, no matter how far pursued or how successful the process of increasing scientific understanding may be? Is there any warrant for pointing to what transcends all possible versions of the intelligible and known universe? If we answer these questions in the affirmative, what, if anything, can be said about this "beyond"? If we label this "beyond" *the Boundless,* shall we make use of this notion in the formulation of a sound philosophy?

I shall argue that we should make such use. There are various other expressions that one might use along with "the Boundless." Provided one has reached a point of awareness directed at what this term points to, other terms—if properly shielded from unwanted associations—can be added to the list, for example "Apeiron," "the Transcendent," "Being," "God," "Ein Sof," "the Infinite," "the One," "the Wholly Other," to mention but a few.

In a sense to be further explicated, the Boundless does not have to do with that which is within the range of observation, nor does it have to with that which is described by a cosmological model in the form of a maximally comprehensive, intelligible, ordered domain of objects and physical processes. The Boundless is neither observable, intelligible, nor known.

For the moment, let me add a few comments on the use of the term "transcendence." Like most other concepts of philosophic interest, the concept of transcendence collects a great variety of uses and illustrations, reflecting a rich historical accumulation and multiplicity of philosophic viewpoints. As a result, there is not a single concept so much as a family of related uses. Rather than engage, therefore, in a futile search for a definitional statement of its "essential" meaning, we do better to note briefly the different human situations (intellectual and other) that prompt the appeal to this concept.

There are two principal sources and occasions in the field of human experience for its use. One stems both from an acute sense of the apparently inescapable and unmodifiable limitations in the very nature of human existence, and at the same time the faith that nevertheless there are ways of overcoming these limitations. The other is associated with the purely metaphysical interest in formulating a theory of reality. Satisfaction of the latter type of interest takes the form of a world view according to which the domain of existents in space and time—of natural phenomena and objects—is not all there is. There is a reality that lies "beyond," is "outside," or is "wholly different from" objects in space and time. One immediate terminological way of linking these two contexts—the human-existential and the ontological—is to use the expression "transcending limits." To be sure, this blurs the distinction between what belongs to the character of human limitations and what marks an ontological boundary. At the same time, running together these disparate matters affords one the opportunity to look for possible analogies and interconnections between them.

In their original meanings, the terms "limit," "boundary," and "transcend" designated purely physical and spatial matters. The terms "bound" and "boundary," in English, derive from the old French term *bonde* and this in turn is related to the medieval Latin terms *bodena* or *butina*. It meant a frontier line that indicated a particular limit or extent of land, usually represented by a post, hedge, dyke, or wall of stone. Similarly, the term "limit," in English, derives from the Latin terms *limitem* or *limes*. In turn, these stood for a crossroad, byroad, or strip of unploughed land serving as a path through a field or vineyard. They were used, for example, to designate the open land along which a column of troops advanced into enemy territory. The Latin term *limes* also stood for a boundary between two fields or estates consisting of a stone or balk. In its original meaning, finally, the term "transcend" meant "to climb over or beyond, to surmount a physical obstacle or limit such as a wall or mountain." Of course, in ordinary speech and in philosophical discourse, all these terms have undergone analogical or metaphorical extensions. We continue to speak of "limits," "boundaries," and "transcendence" where nothing spatial or physical is involved at all. In the case of philosophic uses, it is especially important, therefore, to be on guard against the intrusion of unwanted or misleading analogies derived from originally literal, physical meanings.

Use of the concept of transcendence in religious, mystical, spiritual, and philosophic discourse can take two principal forms. Expressed in grammatical terms, there is, on the one hand, a name or noun—"the transcendent," or an adjective, "(such and such) is transcendent"—and, on the other hand, a verb, "to transcend," or a participle, "the (act of) transcending." Earlier, I distinguished two principal contexts in which the concept of transcendence is commonly employed: the human-existential and the metaphysical (ontological). Although there is no absolutely uniform, exclusive correlation of the grammatical form of the concept of transcendence as a name or as a verb with each of these principal contexts, there is a preponderance of use of the verb and participial forms in the human-existential context, and of the nominal and adjectival forms in the metaphysical context. It seems appropriate to speak of varied human efforts to transcend human limitations, and of acts or modes of transcending those limitations: the verb and participial forms of the concept of transcendence come to the fore. They call attention to what a human being does, either overtly or by the development of some inner attitude or belief, in attempting to overcome human existential limitations. By contrast, in the metaphysical context the primary concern is with that which "lies outside" or "beyond" some ontological boundary or limit. Here a nominal or adjectival form of the concept of transcendence seems more appropriate. One speaks of "the transcendent" or of "that which is transcendent." Although, to be sure, even in this latter context there is a human being who performs an act of transcending to some transcendent domain, entity, or aspect of reality, it is the ontological target of this act rather than the act of transcending that is of primary interest.

If we turn to the major examples of the concept of transcendence in a metaphysical context, we are struck by the manifold variety of these examples. The expression may be used to mark out some special entity, some class of entities, or some aspect of reality. There are at least three familiar and important examples of the concept of the transcendent in Western thought: Platonism, theism, and Kantian noumenalism. While each of these philosophies has its special motivations in arriving at its own conception of the transcendent, and while, too, there are important differences in what is said to be transcendent, there is nonetheless one common feature these philosophies share. They unite in the claim that the domain of space-time entities and phenomena does not exhaust reality. For Plato, the transcendent is identified with the entire class of Forms—those perfect, eternal, and intelligible entities that "lie outside" the domain of imperfect entities making up the sensible and material flux of existence. For the theist, the transcendent is identified with God, the Supreme Being who is wholly different from the spatio-temporal world of objects He created. For Kant, the world of objects in space and time, when seen in an epistemological perspective, is a domain of phenomena screening a transcendent noumenal reality. At bottom, each of these philosophies agrees that transcendent reality is wholly different from the objects and phenomena that belong to the world of space-time individuals.

Of the three philosophies mentioned—Platonism, theism, and

Kantian noumenalism—Platonism and Kantianism are technical philosophical positions that, for all their interest and historical importance, have engaged the attention of only a relatively small segment of the human species. The same cannot be said of theism. That philosophy has flourished over long stretches of human history, in the East as well as in the West, in versions that range from the most primitive to the most sophisticated. Its recurrent appeal and widespread adoption testify to its ability to meet certain fundamental and universally shared intellectual, spiritual, social, and emotional needs. These include: explaining the existence of the world as a whole; providing a ground plan for all of human history; giving a set of moral rules, injunctions, and goals that give order, direction, and purpose to an individual's life; providing a scheme of rewards and punishments—including, crucially, a belief in an afterlife; helping to establish a framework for sanctioning the performance of various rituals and ceremonies; offering an institutional framework that supports the arts, gives direction to the education of the young, and eases life's burdens through acts of charity and ministrations to the sick, the despairing, and the hungry.

As an ontology, theism rests upon a central belief in a Supreme Being who transcends the world. Confronted with the existence of the world, men seek for an explanation of its existence, just as they normally seek for explanations of some particular fact of a restricted character, for example, the occurrence of some event, the presence of some observed feature of an object, or the prevalence of a regularity in nature. The use of the term "Why" in posing the question, "Why does the world exist?" points to the presupposition that we can regard the existence of the world as something for which it makes sense to look for a reason, and that there must be a reason. No *part* of the world could serve in this capacity as a ground for the explanation of the existence of the world. For, in being only a part of the world, it is one of the items that, rather than able to provide an explanation, calls for one. Nor could the totality of entities in space and time provide this explanation. Therefore, the sought-for reason, it is argued, must exist "beyond" the world. It must be a power that, although not a part of the world, is the creative ground for the existence of the world and all that it contains. The Being possessed of this power is God.

Is the Boundless that transcends the horizons of the scientifically known or knowable universe to be conceived in these traditional theistic terms? This question surely needs to be faced in any attempt to come to terms with the results of recent cosmology. For does not the prominence and widespread adoption of an evolutionary cosmology, with its broad endorsement of the view that the universe had an origin and will have an end, make such a reexamination once more an urgent one? Should we not turn—or return—to a belief in God to fill out a sound conception of the Boundless? In an effort to meet this challenge, I propose, first, to review a major critique of traditional theism as given in Spinoza's philosophy. This philosophy not only offered formidable reasons for rejecting the traditional view of God as separate and distinct from Nature, but proposed in its place a reinterpretation of the concept of God according to which God and Nature are one and the same: God *is* Nature. In what follows, I shall give a number of reasons for rejecting certain fundamental features of Spinoza's reconstruction of the concept of God. I will do so, however, not in the interest of rehabilitating the traditional view of God, but in the interest, rather, of suggesting a view of the Boundless different from both traditional theistic and Spinozistic conceptions.

Spinoza on the Unity of God or Nature

Spinoza occupies an important position in that stage of the history of philosophy which marks the watershed between the periods customarily called "medieval" and "modern." Let us recall briefly the main doctrines of medieval religious philosophy in the West that served as the common core of Judaism, Christianity, and Islam. This religious philosophy, according to H. A. Wolfson, was

> . . . that system of thought which flourished between pagan Greek philosophy, which knew not of Scripture, and that body of philosophic writings which ever since the seventeenth

century has tried to free itself from the influence of Scripture. Medieval philosophy so defined was founded by Philo, who lived at the time of the rise of Christianity. Ostensibly Philo is only the interpreter of the Hebrew Scripture in terms of Greek philosophy. But actually he is more than that. He is the interpreter of Greek philosophy in terms of certain fundamental teachings of his Hebrew Scripture, whereby he revolutionized philosophy and remade it into what became the common philosophy of the three religions with cognate Scriptures, Judaism, Christianity, and Islam. This triple scriptural religious philosophy, which was built up by Philo, reigned supreme as a homogeneous, if not a thoroughly unified, system of thought until the seventeenth century, when it was pulled down by Spinoza.[1]

The common core of traditional theistic philosophy, as summed up by Wolfson, consisted of the following three principles.[2]

1. *The belief in God's infinite power and goodness.*

God is a being independent of the world and the source of its existence. God's being is eternal and necessary, whereas the existence of the world and the entire domain of entities in space and time is contingent. The world is dependent on God's will and infinite power of creation for its having come into existence and for its continued existence. In all His acts and judgments, God is completely free. He is guided by purposes of a wholly benevolent sort even though such purposes, in their detail and comprehensiveness, are not known by finite human intellects. God's purposes justify, ultimately, the choice of laws imposed on the world, the structure of human history as a whole, and the various rewards or punishments for individuals and groups.

2. *The doctrine of the unknowability and incomprehensibility of God's essence.*

---

[1] Harry A. Wolfson, *Religious Philosophy* (Cambridge, Mass.: Harvard University Press, 1961), Preface.

[2] Ibid., 2-11.

That God exists is accepted as axiomatic by all varieties of theism. To say that God is incomprehensible is to say that in some fundamental way we do not know *what* God is. Notions of mystery, total otherness, unnameability, absolute uniqueness, simplicity, and unknowability are some of the typical ways in which this doctrine was described in traditional theology.

3. *Revelation is a means of disclosure to men of certain truths.*

For Philo, revelation takes two forms. One is the historical revelation in which God gave the Law to Moses at Mount Sinai, and through him to all men. It is embodied in the Holy Scriptures. Secondly, revelation is given to certain chosen individuals to whom the meaning of the initially revealed Law is made progressively clear. The several religious traditions give different accounts of when, how, and to whom these final or progressive revelations are given. All would agree, however, that such revelations are the basic source of truth and that they are not to be equated with or replaced by knowledge that men might attain by the use of their own unaided reason.

Stated negatively, Spinoza's philosophy consists in a rejection of each of the above doctrines of traditional theism. However, an understanding of Spinoza's principal positive philosophic motivations would disclose that these motivations were, in a deeper sense, genuinely religious. He was concerned, as were traditional religions, with becoming aware of and appropriately responsive to the ultimate source of our being. This theme is what his major work, the *Ethics*, is all about. Spinoza was perfectly willing to call this ultimate reality "God," and the goal of man's life "salvation" or "spiritual freedom." His disagreements with traditional religion derived from his having made a painstaking philosophic analysis of these concepts, and from his proposal to redefine these terms.

I have used the expression "ultimate source of our being" to characterize the direction in which Spinoza's philosophy coincides with that of traditional religion. If there is an ultimate reality, what is it? It was an interest in finding an answer to this kind of metaphysical or ontologic question that Spinoza shared with traditional religion. In one of its important dimensions, traditional religion had its own replies to these metaphysical questions. They belong to theology. As a philosopher, Spinoza was not prepared to accept the methodologic or epistemologic basis that guided and sanctioned its answers to these questions. For in all theologies, of whatever stripe, there is a fundamental reliance on revelation, faith, mystical vision, or an uncritical use of imagination—whatever the appeal, occasionally and secondarily, to argument and reason. Spinoza found those primary nonrational methods or sources of belief unsatisfactory. He would put his own entire and exclusive confidence in the use of man's reason.

The attempt to work out the details of the structure of the world in an astronomic or cosmologic sense were not at the heart of either traditional theology or, for that matter, Spinoza's philosophy. In both, there were, to be sure, some ventures in this direction. In describing the nature and order of the astronomic universe, medieval theology relied for the most part on Ptolemaic astronomy and Aristotelian physics. And Spinoza, as the beneficiary of scientific results achieved since the days of Copernicus and especially with the great advances initiated by Descartes, also incorporated these modern views in his own conception of the physical universe. But this is not where his strength lies, nor is there, comparatively speaking, much attention given to these matters in his writings. His interest lies elsewhere. For what Spinoza wishes to ask, at bottom, is how the world in the astronomic, cosmologic sense—whatever its detailed structure is said to be—is related to God (ultimate reality). And to this question Spinoza has a definite and, for his time, revolutionary answer. For, he maintains, far from being distinct realities, God, Nature, and the cosmos are one and the same. He would show by rational argument that one cannot accept the traditional claim that *only* God, as traditionally conceived in theistic religion, is the ultimate reality, with the world assigned a derivative, contingent status as the created handiwork of God. For Spinoza there is no distinction between God and the cosmos. There is only one ultimate reality, and we can assign whatever names we choose to label this one ultimate reality. Spinoza calls it "God," "Nature," "Substance," or also (sometimes) "the

Universe." What is important, for our own present purposes, is to explore this ontologic side of Spinoza's thought as it bears on our overall interest in the philosophic dimensions of cosmology.

Spinoza's ontology takes for its first axiom the statement, "Everything which is, is either in itself or in another."[3] And the definition of substance reads, "By substance, I understand that which is in itself and is conceived through itself; in other words, that, the conception of which does not need the conception of another thing from which it must be formed."[4] If substance is that which is in itself, and if everything is either in itself or in another, it is evident that one of the key ideas is conveyed by the expression "in itself." What is *conceived* through itself presupposes that we know what it means to say that something *is* "in itself." What, then, does this latter phrase mean?

In trying to make this clear, we must narrow our sights and concentrate on the word "in." This little word, however, cloaks a complex variety of uses, a mass of intertwining conceptual roots. Let us begin by noting that "in" is obviously some kind of relational expression. Put the matter of *relata* in formal terms, for the moment, and say A is *in* B. What are the senses of "in," and what kinds of substitutions can we make for A and B that go along with different senses of "in"? Moreover, what does it mean to say, with Spinoza, that A is "in itself," that A is *in* A? Despite the façade of a supposedly luminous and universally intelligible, "geometrical," deductive format and method, the challenge to understand Spinoza's language is not only complicated by a certain internal variability and complexity of usage in his own writings, but by the fact that his language is rooted in a rich historical heritage of ancient and medieval ideas. In fact, in order to understand the phrase "in itself," it is to Aristotle to whom we must turn first, since Spinoza's use of this expression is indirectly influenced by Aristotle's discus-

---

[3] Spinoza, *Ethics*, Part I, Axiom I, trans. W. H. White, revised by A. H. Stirling, 4th ed. (London: Milford, 1929); cf. *The Collected Works of Spinoza*, vol. 1, ed. and trans. Edwin Curley (Princeton, N.J.: Princeton University Press, 1985).

[4] Spinoza, *Ethics*, Part I, Definition 3.

sion of the term "in," as filtered through Avicenna, Maimonides, and other medieval thinkers.

Aristotle lists the following senses in which one thing is said to be "in" another:

1. The sense in which a physical part is *in* a physical whole to which it belongs, as the finger is *in* the hand.

2. The sense in which a whole is *in* the parts that make it up, "for there is no whole over and above the parts."

3. The sense in which a species is *in* its genus, as "man" is *in* "animal."

4. The sense in which a genus is *in* any of its species and more generally, any feature of a species is *in* the definition of the species.

5. The sense in which form is *in* matter, in the way, for example, "health is *in* the hot and the cold."

6. The sense in which events center *in* their primary motive agent, as, for example, "the affairs of Greece center *in* the king."

7. The sense in which the existence of a thing centers *in* its final cause, its end, or that for the sake of which it exists or was made.

8. The strictest sense of all is that in which a thing is said to be *in* a place.[5]

In this list of eight different senses of "in," it is possible to discern four distinct groups:

1. That which has to do with a *spatial* relation. This (in [8] above) Aristotle recognizes as the "strictest sense of all." A is said to be *in* B where A is one thing and B is another thing or a place. For Aristotle, "place" is to be thought of as what is occupied by some body. A thing located in some body is also, by virtue of this fact, located in some place. We may designate A as the contained and B as the container. If this is "the strictest sense of all," then it marks the literal or paradigm use of "in." The other senses are metaphoric extensions of this primary sense.

2. That which has to do with the *part-whole* relation—whether

---

[5] Aristotle, *Physics*, 210a, 15ff., trans. R. P. Hardie and R. K. Gaye, in *The Works of Aristotle*, vol. 2, ed. W. D. Ross (Oxford: Clarendon Press, 1930).

that of a part to the whole or its converse, the relation of a whole to its part.

3. That which has to do with the *genus-species* relation, where A is the genus and B the species, or where A is the species and B the genus.

4. That which has to do with a *causal* relation, in one or another of Aristotle's distinctions among different kinds of causes: material, formal, efficient, or final. Thus A may be the formal cause (form), B the matter; or A may be the efficient cause ("motive agent"), B the effect; or, given A, some particular thing or event, B, is its final cause, its good or goal (*telos*).

Let us consider what lies behind Spinoza's description of Substance as that which is "in itself," as distinguished from, yet related to, that which is "in another." By adopting the Aristotelian distinctions among the several meanings of "in," we may identify three principal ways in which Spinoza interpreted the term "Substance." One model exploits the part-whole and spatial meanings of "in," a second rests on the distinction between a genus and species, and a third appeals to and develops the efficient-cause concept. The first route leads to the view that Substance is an absolute all-inclusive *Individual Whole*, containing all particular entities that exist within it as its parts, as its modes. The second route leads to the view of Substance as a *Summum Genus*, in terms of which everything else is to be conceived by being subsumed as a species or individual instance. However, the *Summum Genus* is not to be conceived in terms of anything higher or more fundamental. The third route leads to the view that Substance is the *Creative Source*, the sole ultimate efficient cause for the modes that are its effects or products. We shall examine, in turn, the considerations that led Spinoza to adopt each of these models for Substance (God or Nature).

Let us try to reconstruct what Spinoza had in mind when he thought of Substance as an absolute all-inclusive Individual Whole, and how he may have reached this conception by falling back on two of the senses of "in"—the spatial and the part-whole. Both these senses may be joined. A concrete object is *in* another, in the sense in which a physical entity is said to be a part of a physical whole (as a finger is in a hand), or in the sense in which an object is in a place insofar as it is in another body (as wine is in a jug). In the sense in which a particular physical object is in another object, as part to a more inclusive whole, or as occupant to occupier, we can readily see how Spinoza would ask himself the following question: When we apply these combined senses of "in" to what is traditionally called a substance, in the sense in which Aristotle spoke of primary substances—for example, this man, that statue—do we not find that the result is something that is *in* something else? Not only is the finger in the hand or the wine in the jug, but the hand is in the individual man, and the jug is in the cabinet or in the room. And so on. Once started, we are driven to extend the range of spatial inclusiveness or the nesting of objects within more and more inclusive physical wholes. In this way, all particular objects are *in* something else. Spinoza will therefore come to think of what are traditionally called "substances" as *modes*, as fragmentary parts or contents of a more inclusive whole. Moreover, Spinoza would surely have asked himself whether there is any way in which, by thinking of parts as nested within wholes—and these latter within still more inclusive wholes—we should come to the end of this nesting process. And we may suppose Spinoza to have reached an affirmative answer to this question. There must be, he would say, some Whole that is *not in* anything else, that is not itself part of some still more inclusive whole. He writes: "Nature is infinite and all is contained therein."[6] What is lacking, at this point in Spinoza's account, is any adequate analysis of the various possible meanings of the term "infinite." Is this to be understood, for example, in a purely quantitative sense? Are there various nonquantitative uses of the term "infinite" that are more appropriate? Is the infinite actual or potential? If there are different types or orders of infinity, how are these related to one another? Admittedly these questions are among the most vexing in the field

[6] Spinoza, *Short Treatise on God, Man, and His Well-Being*, trans. A. Wolf (reprinted; New York: Russell and Russell, 1963), 32.

of philosophy. While some progress in dealing with these questions has been made since Spinoza's day, they still remain for the most part a tangled mass of obscurity and controversy.

Can we say, moreover, that what is not in something else—since it is an all-inclusive container or all-inclusive whole—is *in itself*? If we take the senses of "in" we have been considering, can anything be said to be *in* itself? Is not the term "in" applicable only to a part or to an occupant? And if we wish to say that there is some Individual Whole that is not part of some wider whole nor a spatial occupant of another body or system, would it not be a violation of the use of "in," in these meanings, to say that the Individual Whole is in itself? Is not this a misuse of language? Aristotle had discussed this very question in his *Physics* and indicated his objections to speaking this way. And Plato, too, before him, in examining dialectically the concept of the One in his dialogue the *Parmenides*, had pointed out similar difficulties. Let us recall Aristotle's objections, before considering what Spinoza might have said by way of rejoinder and in defense of his using the phrase "in itself" in connection with Substance. Consider the case of the wine in the jar. The jar is the container, the wine the contained. Aristotle points out that if it were possible for a thing to be in itself, this could mean that the container would be the contained, and the contained would be the container: the jar would be the wine and the wine the jar. However, this is absurd. The jar and the wine are different. Bodies occupy different places, not the same place. To deny this—to claim that two different bodies could occupy the same place—goes hand in hand with making the absurd assumption that the container could be in itself, that is, identical with the contained.[7]

Confronted with this type of argument, we can imagine Spinoza readily agreeing with it. In characterizing Substance as that which is in itself, he would say, it is not necessary to assert that it is both container and contained, or that it is both whole and part. Rather, the phrase "in itself" has essentially a negative import. It signifies

[7] Aristotle, *Physics*, 210b, 8-22.

that what is said to be "in itself" means that it *is not* in something else. To be "in itself" means "*not* to be spatially or physically *in* anything else." Spinoza, then, uses the term "Substance" (and also frequently the term "Nature" and less frequently the term "Universe") to mean the all-inclusive Individual Whole that is in itself—where this latter phrase is to be understood as having a negative import. Unlike its parts, Substance is not within anything else.

With respect to the detailed causal laws that interconnect all the parts of this all-inclusive Individual Whole (*totius Naturae ordo et cohaerentia*), Spinoza recognized that we have no complete knowledge, although science progressively discovers such interconnections. He offers the analogy of a small worm that lives in the blood and

> . . . whose sight is keen enough to distinguish the particles of blood, lymph, etc., and his reason to observe how each part on collision with another either rebounds, or communicates a part of its own motion, etc. That worm would live in this blood as we live in this part of the universe, and he would consider each particle of blood to be a whole, and not a part. And he could not know how all the parts are controlled by the universal nature of blood, and are forced, as the universal nature of blood demands, to adapt themselves to one another, so as to harmonize with one another in a certain way. . . . But, since there are very many other causes which in a certain way control the laws of the nature of blood, and are in turn controlled by the blood, hence it comes about that other motions and other changes take place in the blood, which result not only from the mere relation of the motion of its parts to one another, but from the relation of the motion of the blood and also of the external causes to one another: in this way, the blood has the character of a part and not of a whole. I have only spoken of whole and part.

Spinoza then applies this analogy of the worm in the blood to man's situation in Nature:

Now, all the bodies of Nature can and should be conceived in the same way as we have here conceived the blood: for all bodies are surrounded by others, and are mutually determined to exist and to act in a definite and determined manner, while there is preserved in all together, that is, in the whole Universe, the same proportion of motion and rest. Hence it follows that every body, in so far as it exists modified in a certain way, must be considered to be a part of the whole Universe, to be in accord with the whole of it, and to be connected with the other parts. And since the nature of the Universe is not limited, like the nature of the blood, but absolutely infinite, its parts are controlled by the nature of this infinite power in infinite ways, are compelled to suffer infinite changes. . . . Since it is of the nature of substance to be infinite, it follows that each part belongs to the nature of corporeal substance, and can neither exist nor be conceived without it.[8]

It is clear from the foregoing that Spinoza conceived of Substance, Nature, or the Universe as an all-inclusive physical whole. When considered under the attribute of Extension, he took this corporeal whole to be quantitatively infinite. In addition to being conceived under the attribute of Extension, this same whole can be conceived under the attribute of Thought. According to his metaphysics, Substance has an infinite number of attributes, but only those of Extension and Thought are known to us. Nature can be conceived in either or both of these parallel ways. Not only, therefore, can all the parts of Nature be considered under the attribute of Extension, and so as bodies, they can in each case also be considered under the attribute of Thought, and so as possessed of "minds" or in terms of the "ideas" that correspond to their bodies. It is only of the parts of Nature qua bodies, under the attribute of Extension, however, that we can speak of them as literally *in* Nature, that is, as located. Minds or ideas are "in" Nature only in

---

[8] Spinoza, *Letters*, XXXII, in A. Wolf, ed. and trans., *The Correspondence of Spinoza* (London: Allen and Unwin, 1928), 210-212.

a modified, stretched use of "in," since they cannot be physically located in space. Yet since, for him, anything that is a body and so locatable in the Universe has a "mind" or exemplifies an intelligible "idea" that is associated with it, one can refer to these minds or ideas as being "in" Nature, in this derivative sense.

I turn next to the second model of Substance used by Spinoza—that according to which Substance is a *Summum Genus*. As noted earlier, according to the Aristotelian classification a second group of meanings of "in" is that which rests on the distinction between a genus and its species. The definition of a species includes reference to the genus in terms of which it is conceived and "in" which it is. Reference to the genus is part of the essence, the defining essential traits or characteristics in terms of which a species is understood. Similarly, on this traditional Aristotelian approach, to conceive or understand an individual entity means to subsume it under the species to which it belongs, and thus indirectly, by means of its species, under the genus of which it is also an individual instance.

Spinoza's treatment of the nature of scientific knowledge was strongly influenced by the growing emphasis in seventeenth-century science on the notion of laws of nature. These laws can be couched in the language of causality, in the sense of regular lawful connection between (efficient) causes and their discoverable effects. Scientific knowledge consists in setting out the causes of things. For Spinoza, Nature as a Whole is not a mere aggregate of parts. The phrase "mere aggregate" suggests that there are no principles of unity or order that interrelate the various components that make up the Whole. And this Spinoza would surely deny. Patches of unity and order have already been discovered and increasingly brought to light with the advances of science. Spinoza's rationalist faith is that these successes are to be taken as encouraging the belief that all of Nature is orderly and intelligible. It is far from being a mere aggregate of disconnected parts. At any given time, actual scientific knowledge is, of course, limited. It is only a fragment of what a complete system of knowledge would be. The deductively arranged systems of knowledge are partial systems, not yet unified and integrated into a single, all-inclusive, deductively organized system of knowledge. If ever realized, that single system, Spinoza believed, would rest upon a set of absolutely fundamental principles or axioms, the knowledge of which would yield an explanation of everything in the entire Universe. That there is a single ultimate scheme of unified and complete knowledge, toward which science moves as its final goal, is the faith of the scientist as Spinoza construes it. One would then be able to deduce from these ultimate principles all those features, as well as the very existence of the parts of the Individual Whole. The statement of this goal is what Spinoza designates by the expression *scientia intuitiva*, and thereby his own rationalist faith that Nature is through and through a rational Whole. At the same time, he also adapted to this way of thinking the traditional Aristotelian and medieval conception of knowledge as largely taxonomic or classificatory in nature, rather than as consisting of a discovery of laws of nature. For the classificatory conception, the guiding distinctions are those having to do with the relations of genus, species, differentia, and individual instance.

Despite this merging of two rather different orientations, Spinoza's basic distinction between what is conceived through itself and what is conceived through another is unaffected. Indeed, it is somewhat more helpful to examine Spinoza's main point within the framework of distinctions that stresses the genus-species relation. Spinoza falls back on this way of describing what it means to conceive of something, as this was widely accepted and employed in medieval philosophy. He adapts this way of thinking to his own philosophic outlook and uses it to describe the nature of Substance and its relation to its modes. As is the case with any genus, Substance too is a genus in terms of which what is subsumed under it is conceived. Unlike ordinary genera, however, Substance is "conceived through itself." With an ordinary genus, for example, "animal"—of which "rational" is a species (and to which individual men belong as instances)—one can subsume (conceive) the genus in terms of a wider, more inclusive genus. As a genus, "animal" can be subsumed under the wider genus "living thing," while "living thing" is conceived (subsumed) in terms of still wider genera, and so on. However, when one considers Substance as a genus, this process of subsumption (and therefore "conceiving the essence of") under a wider, more inclusive genus is no longer possible. There is no more fundamental genus than Substance. It is, therefore, "to be conceived in itself" and not in terms of another. In short, Substance is a *Summum Genus*. Once again, when Spinoza describes (but not *defines*) "Substance," he says that Substance is "conceived through itself." This phrase is to be understood as having a negative import. It signifies that since Substance is a *Summum Genus*, it cannot be conceived in terms of anything else. While modes can be conceived positively in terms of other things, Substance can only be "conceived" negatively. This is another way of saying that, strictly speaking, Substance cannot be conceived at all. And this can be interpreted as saying that, for Spinoza, Substance (God or Nature) is indefinable and therefore unknowable. We do not know, and cannot know, what the *essence* of Substance (God or Nature) is. Traditional theology had also spoken of God's unknowability, our inability to know the essence of God. We pointed out earlier, however, that among other central doctrines of traditional theism, Spinoza rejected this thesis of theism. Does this not suggest that far from being in conflict with traditional theism, Spinoza is here agreeing with, rather than rejecting, this aspect of its doctrines? There is no inconsistency here, however. For the traditional emphasis on God's unknowability was primarily a way of stressing the unavoidable limits of human knowledge. God is a mystery for man. While God does have an essence, it is unknowable to man. However, this is not what Spinoza means by unknowability; he has no room in his philosophy for the notion of mystery. Far from being unknowable, as men progressively uncover the causal structure of events, Nature or God becomes knowable by science. Nor is there any limit to this process. In principle, Nature is intelligible or rational through and through. When Spinoza stresses the unknowability of God, he is not referring to any inherent limitation to the goal of complete scientific understanding. He is referring, rather, to the fact that, considered as a *Summum Genus*, Nature or God is not further *definable*. To say that God is not definable does not mean that Nature is not knowable in its internal causal structure.

A third, major, complementary model that Spinoza relies on is the notion that Substance (Nature or God) is an absolute, free *Creative Power*. The distinction between a supreme, active, Creative Power and the passive products of the operation of this Power is a distinction obviously associated with Spinoza's transmutation of traditional theism's conception of a transcendent Creator who brings the World into existence. In traditional theism, God as Creator is an Immaterial Being distinct from the World. Spinoza rejected this conception of God as a distinct, immaterial Creator of Nature. He rejected the conception of God as supernatural. Spinoza rejects theism's conception of God's creative power as a bringing into existence of the world *ex nihilo*, and so as consisting in a special mysterious form of making. He rejects the conception of creation as involving a final cause (*telos*), the intent on the part of the Creator to realize in His creatures a benevolent Design, to achieve an ultimate good. All such beliefs are examples of anthropomorphism. In them, we see man creating God in man's image, not the reverse. This conception of creation relies on human making, art, and craftsmanship as models by which to try to understand the genesis of the world. It assumes that God is possessed of conscious will and benevolent purposes. For Spinoza, this way of thinking is an elaborate exercise in mythmaking, an exercise in imagination—and belongs to what he thinks of as the lowest or "first" grade of knowledge. It is to be sharply contrasted with the method of pursuing knowledge in science. The latter exhibits what he calls the "second" and "third" grades of knowledge. Scientific ways of finding causal intelligibility in Nature dispense with anthropomorphic categories and analogies. They treat Nature as operating impersonally, without design or purpose, and only according to strictly necessary causal laws. These laws link events with one another regardless of how their outcome is judged from the point of their benefit to man.

It is clear, nevertheless, that Spinoza retained enough of the traditional conception of God as a Creator in order to draw a distinction between God and the aggregate totality of modes, the passive products of God's creative agency. In giving an account of his own conception of God, he says, for example: "God is not only the cause of the commencement of the existence of things, but also of their continuance in existence, or, in other words (to use scholastic phraseology) God is the *causa essendi rerum.*"[9] For Spinoza, in other words, God continues to be thought of on the theistic model as an Individual Creator and Cause of the existence of particular entities. He discarded the Biblical conception of a personal God operating by purpose and design. For Spinoza, God is a Creative Agent operating entirely by causal necessity. And "cause" is to be understood in the sense of "efficient cause," not in the sense of "final cause." God is an Infinite Being that is *causa sui*, self-caused, and so to be contrasted with the modes. Once again, the notion of *causa sui*, a being that is self-caused, is to be taken as having only a negative import. God is *unlike* other beings: for whereas all other beings or entities are causally dependent on still other things, God is not causally dependent on anything else. There are various locutions Spinoza uses to describe the role of God as Creative Power vis-à-vis the modes. These include *activity*, as contrasted with *passivity*; *cause*, as contrasted with *effect*; that which is wholly *free*, as contrasted with that which occurs by *necessity*; that which is the *origin*, as contrasted with that which is the *product*. For example, he writes: "God . . . is never passive, and cannot be affected by any other being, because he is the first efficient cause of all. . . . Since Substance is [the cause] and origin of all its modes, it may with far greater right be called an agent than a patient."[10]

When Spinoza thinks of God as a Creative Power, he borrows from the theistic conception of God not only the notion of creativity but also the notion of God as *indivisible into parts*. He insists

[9] Spinoza, *Ethics*, Part I, Prop. 24, Corrol.
[10] Spinoza, *Short Treatise*, 28, 30.

that Substance cannot be divided.[11] "As regards the parts in Nature," he writes, "we maintain that division . . . never takes place in Substance but always and only in the modes of Substance. Thus, if I want to divide water, I only divide the mode of Substance, and not Substance itself. And whether this mode is that of water or something else it is always the same."[12] Only modes can be divided, being composite. But God or Substance is simple and indivisible. It is clear that if we are to think of God as an indivisible Creative Power, we are no longer thinking of God or Nature as an all-inclusive Individual Whole—for the latter *is* composed of its various parts, and so *can* be divided. The indivisibility or absolute simplicity of God is not only connected with Spinoza's conception of God as an Absolute Creative Power, but with his conception of God or Substance as a *Summum Genus*. Of the latter, too, one can say that it cannot be defined, that is, assigned various essential properties. For this would involve the appeal to other wider, more inclusive generic concepts or kinds. However, the concept of God is not further analyzable into more fundamental conceptual components.

It is by using the Creative Source model that Spinoza seeks to incorporate within his own system the traditional distinction between God and the World. While God is no longer an Immaterial Spirit, Lawgiver, Craftsman, Providence, Judge, or Designing Intelligence, God is nevertheless an absolute Creative Power. This Power is to be thought of in terms of the operation of free, immanent, efficient causality. Unlike the traditional theistic view of God—according to which God is separate and distinct from the world—God is not to be thought of as separate from the corporeal World. How then does Spinoza overcome this traditional dualism? One device he uses is the distinction between *Natura naturans* and *Natura naturata*. In the *Short Treatise*, where Spinoza introduces this distinction, he writes:

[11] Spinoza, *Ethics*, Part I, Props. 12, 13.
[12] Spinoza, *Short Treatise*, 29.

We shall . . . divide the whole of Nature . . . into *Natura naturans* and *Natura naturata*. By *Natura naturans* we understand a being that we conceive clearly and distinctly through itself, and without needing anything beside itself . . . that is, God. The Thomists likewise understand God by it, but their *Natura naturans* was a being (so they called it) beyond all substances.[13]

In the *Ethics*, Spinoza restates this distinction as follows:

. . . by *natura naturans* we are to understand that which is in itself and is conceived through itself, or those attributes of Substance which express eternal and infinite essence, that is to say . . . God insofar as He is considered as a free cause. But by *natura naturata* I understand everything which follows from the necessity of the nature of God, or of any one of God's attributes, that is to say, all the modes of God's attributes in so far as they are considered as things which are in God, and which without God can neither be nor can be conceived.[14]

As Spinoza formulates it, the distinction clearly identifies the traditional conception of God with what in his system is also called "God," but is now understood as *natura naturans*. Similarly, what in the traditional conception was called "the World" is now characterized as *natura naturata*. In this way, God and the World together are complementary aspects of one and the same underlying reality. This warrants Spinoza's use of the phrase *Deus sive Natura*, God or Nature. They are one and the same, a unity.

The unity of God or Nature is at the heart of Spinoza's world-picture. This unity can be formulated and established in several different ways. We have just seen how that unity can be expressed in terms of the complementary relation between the world as seen

---

[13] Ibid., chap. 8, p. 56. For the historical background of this terminology, see H. Siebeck, "Ueber die Entstehung der Termini natura naturans und natura naturata," *Archiv für Geschichte der Philosophie* 3 (1889-1890), 370-378.

[14] Spinoza, *Ethics*, Part I, Prop. 29, Schol.

from the vantage point of *natura naturans*, on the one side, and *natura naturata*, on the other. They are two sides or aspects of one and the same reality.

Another way in which the doctrine of the unity of God and Nature can be approached is by seeing how Spinoza's philosophy undertakes to challenge and replace a dualism at the heart of traditional theism. That dualism consists in upholding the radical ontological distinction between two types of fundamental substances: the immaterial substance that is God and the material substance that is the physical universe and all that it contains. On the traditional view, the two substances have different properties or attributes. God's substance is eternal, necessary, beyond space and time, free, uncaused, and marked by the infinite perfections of omnipotence, omniscience, and absolute goodness. As distinct from God, the world as a totality is dependent on God both for its existence and its properties. Whether regarded as a totality or in terms of the aggregate of its finite parts, the world lacks the perfections of God. The essential relation between the substance of God and the substance of the world is that of Creation: the world is created by God. Spinoza's attack on this fundamental ontological dualism seeks to overthrow it by rational arguments. He would show that there cannot be two distinct major types of substances—the immaterial substance of God and the material substance of the world. If we clearly understand the nature of substance, there can be only one Substance. It is a matter of indifference whether we call this one Substance "God" or "Nature." For these are but two different names for one and the same reality. With this realization goes an abandonment of the conception of Creation as consisting in the relation between two distinct substances. For if there are not two substances but only one Substance, then if the concept of creation is retained, it needs to be reinterpreted. This can be done, for example, by means of the distinction between *natura naturans* and *natura naturata*. These are two complementary ways of regarding one creative power: God or Nature. It does not stand for the relation between two separate substances.

There is, finally, another major route to understanding the importance of the doctrine of the unity of God or Nature in Spinoza's philosophy. The notion of unity, in general, contains at least two separate meanings. According to one of these meanings, to speak of "unity" is another way of referring to *identity*. We express this notion of unity by saying that what we might otherwise think are two distinct entities are in fact identical: they are *one and the same*. This is the meaning of "unity" we have explored so far. The unity of God or Nature means that these are one and the same reality, even though we might use two different names to refer to this one and the same reality. There is, however, another meaning of unity besides that of identity. "Unity" can also stand for *uniqueness*. To say that there is a unity of God or Nature, with this second sense of the term "unity" in mind, is another way of saying that there is *one and only one* God or Nature. There cannot be more than one ultimate reality or Substance. And this aspect of the unity of Substance, its uniqueness, is for Spinoza an equally fundamental way of conceiving it.

To see what supports this doctrine of the unity or uniqueness of God or Nature, we need simply recall what we had established earlier in reviewing Spinoza's treatment of the concept of Substance. We saw that, for Spinoza, we can use at least three different models for understanding the nature of Substance. One of these exploits the concept of the relation of part and whole and the closely related notion of the spatial meaning of "in." On this approach, Substance is regarded as an absolute Individual Whole. It is that which contains everything else as its parts, and in which everything is situated. However, in being the absolute whole and container, Substance is not itself contained in anything more inclusive. It is not situated in any larger whole. On this analysis of what it means to speak of an Absolute Individual Whole, there can be one and only one such absolute whole. We can properly use the term "the" here to signify this uniqueness. There is or exists only *the* absolute Individual Whole. A second model of Substance, for Spinoza, is the use of the terminology of genus and species. On this approach, when we track the hierarchy or nesting of a species within a genus, and that of a given genus within a still wider genus, we are led, ultimately, to recognize that there must be a *Summum Genus*, one in which all other genera and species are subsumed, but which itself is not subsumed under any more inclusive genus. This *Summum Genus* must be understood or conceived in terms of itself, not in terms of another. On this view, once again, it is clear that if we are to think of a *Summum Genus*, there can be at most one such genus, by virtue of the very meaning of *summum* (the highest): there cannot be more than one "highest." It is unique. And so we are led by this route, too, to say that Substance, that is, God or Nature, as a *Summum Genus*, is unique. The third model that Spinoza employs for describing Substance rests on the notions of efficient causality and the way this concept is integrated within the notion of creation. When seen in terms of their causal relations to one another—as science progressively discovers these patches of causal connectedness, and the way science integrates these patches in ever more inclusive deductive networks—we are led, finally, to envisage as the goal of science what Spinoza calls *scientia intuitiva*. It would represent the culmination of a completed scientific, rational understanding of Nature. In such a system, everything would be explained as a necessary consequence of certain axiomatic principles. These principles would not themselves be deduced from anything more fundamental. An understanding and knowledge of their truth and necessity, their self-evidence, would be the understanding of the ultimate cause. Everything would flow rationally from this cause the same way as a theorem in a mathematical system follows necessarily from its axiomatic premises. This notion of ultimate cause, for Spinoza, replaces the anthropomorphic concept of God as Creator who operates by design and by means of a wholly mysterious power of bringing the world into existence "out of nothing." It also replaces the concept of God as a Creator, when this is understood in terms of the property of being a First Cause. For Spinoza, this notion of God as a Creator and First Cause is otiose. We are led to a proper notion of God as Creative Power and as First Cause when we follow the deductive, scientific concept of causal relations, not the anthropomorphic one employed in traditional theology. And when one has understood and accepted this more satisfactory concept of a First Cause, once again we see that this concept leads to the notion that such a cause, in being "first," entails the notion that there can only be one such cause. The very concept of what it is to be absolutely first or primary means that there cannot be more than one such cause. Substance, as First Cause and Creator, is unique. Taken together, then, all three routes lead to the same conclusion: "Substance," which is another name for God or Nature, is unique. And for Spinoza this is another important direction or level in which we can understand the unity of God or Nature.

THE UNIVERSE AS EXISTENT

Our earlier discussion of the concept of intelligibility pointed to a fundamental contrast between two ways of interpreting this concept. On one approach, intelligibility is regarded as an inherent property of a subject matter. It consists in the presence in the subject matter of a determinate structure independently of, and prior to, all human inquiry. To set out to understand a subject matter amounts to wanting to *disclose* what that inherent structure is. Perfect knowledge would be equivalent to a matching between a conceptual means of representation and the structure already present in the subject matter. If known completely, truth, as a property of the means of representation, would consist in a perfect correspondence between the means of representation and the "facts as they are." There is only one way for such an ideal correspondence to be stated, since there is only one determinate structure that inheres in the subject matter. Truth is like the solution to a puzzle for which there is only *one* correct solution.

On the contrasted approach to the concept of intelligibility, the emphasis falls, in the first place, on the availability of multiple, humanly devised linguistic rules and conceptual schemes for *conferring* intelligibility on some subject matter. Competing conceptual schemes are not merely verbally different ways of saying the same thing, are not simply translatable or mutually reducible into one another without conceptual remainder. Between any two genuinely rival conceptual schemes there is some ineliminable *incommensurability*. The merit of a conceptual scheme is to be judged pragmatically by comparing the relative advantages—for purposes of description, explanation, or prediction—of applying one scheme over available alternatives. There are genuinely different ways of accomplishing these goals. It is not presupposed that there is only one true or correct way of conferring intelligibility. For example, scientists will hold on to a preferred way of stating what is known about the subject matter until a *better* way comes along.

Traditional schemes of theistic philosophy were dominated by the first, or realistic, conception of intelligibility sketched above. For orthodox theism as a dualistic world view, God is a substance possessed of His own inherent essence and attributes. The world He creates also has its own imposed, fundamental, and inherent set of properties. Man's desire to know the truth involves the attempt to disclose the inherent essential traits of both realities—that of God and that of the created world. Various methods are available—faith, revelation, reason. Different forms of theological doctrine will champion one or another, or a combination, of these methods, depending on what the target of inquiry is. For example, as the supreme reality, God has His own inherent essence and set of attributes, and in this sense is "intelligible." By one method or another (faith, revelation, mystical experience, rational argument), man may assure himself *that* God exists, and may even claim having some limited or, at best, analogical knowledge of some of God's attributes. However, it would commonly be claimed that man's powers of understanding are forever insufficient to know God's essence in any full and literal way. God's intelligibility remains forever shielded from complete human understanding. On the other hand, many versions of traditional theology allow that, in using various appropriate God-given human faculties—for example, observation and reason—man may come to understand and know, at least in certain directions and to some degree, the inherent intelligible structure that God imposed on *the world* at its Creation.

When Spinoza laid down his challenge to traditional theology, his main attack centered on the ontological dualism of that world view, its insistence on separating God and Nature (the world). In his own naturalistic world view, Spinoza would abandon that ontological dualism. For him, God and Nature are the same. However, in championing this reorientation in world view and in supporting the reliance on human reason to disclose the intelligible structure of Nature, Spinoza's own philosophy *retained* the traditional realistic approach to intelligibility. In his rationalistic version of this realism, Spinoza rejected the appeal to either faith or revelation. He placed his entire confidence in the power of human reason to find out progressively the truth about the world. Since God and Nature are the same, even God's essence is in principle progressively discoverable by man. This is equivalent to saying that by the use of scientific reason, men gradually come to understand the causal interconnections and structure of Nature in its various parts—its events, objects, and processes. And by appeal to what he calls *scientia intuitiva*, Spinoza would say that man even has an anticipatory intuitive sense of what Nature as a single, integrated, totally intelligible order is like, if this were ever to be completely known.

If one were to adopt a Spinozistic type of world view as a metaphysical framework in terms of which to make sense of the pursuit of scientific cosmology, one would say that the goal of cosmology is to disclose progressively the objective order of the universe as an intelligible whole. At any particular stage of cosmological inquiry, the account of the known universe is a step in the direction of the final truth. The final truth would consist in man's having a cosmological model that succeeds above all others in disclosing the structure of the universe as it is "in itself."

On this view, the goal of cosmology would be to achieve a state of understanding in which there are no further horizons to be overcome. Ideally realized, the known universe would coincide with what the universe "really is." *If* our knowledge of Nature were final and complete, the universe could be described from an epistemological point of view as the Boundless, precisely because under those conditions there would be no further cognitive horizons to be overcome. As known, the universe would be without conceptual bounds.

From a Spinozistic perspective, the universe would also be described as the Boundless, not only because there would be no conceptual bounds, if it were known completely, but also because there is no other reality beyond the universe that in some way places limits on it—for example, by enclosing it within spatial, temporal, physical, causal, or any other types of bounds.

What, however, can we say about the concept of the Boundless once we abandon a realistic approach to intelligibility? It is obvious that we should no longer be able to adopt a Spinozistic type of world view in terms of which to construe the goals of cosmology. The question, however, I wish to raise is this: Can we still make use of the concept of the Boundless if we were to adopt a pragmatically oriented view of intelligibility—one that takes seriously the type of insights Kant first achieved in epistemology, or those embodied in the later philosophy of Wittgenstein? In response to this suggestion, it might be held by some that such a project is a misconceived one, since if our goal is to make sense of the pursuit of cosmology, there is no need to make use of the notion of the Boundless. It is sufficient, it might be said, to examine the concepts and procedures of the cosmologist as he goes about constructing and testing various models of the universe. If we do so, we should find that at no stage of his inquiries does he appeal to the notion of the Boundless.

In response to this criticism, I should grant that the normal technical concerns of the cosmologist lie either within the domain of securing and interpreting observational data, performing mathematical calculations, or considering the relevance and advantages of using one or another set of physical laws and the concepts of some physical theory in solving various problems. At no point in fulfilling these kinds of interests does the scientific cosmologist need to introduce the notion of the Boundless, if it does not fall within the vocabulary of one or another of these types of interests. However, if one sets out to deal with the broader philosophical aspects of the pursuit of cosmology, as I am doing in this book, the foregoing objection cannot be taken as a block to further analysis, or as a damaging enough reason to deny the possible advantages and importance of raising questions of an ontological sort. If we do raise such questions, I wish to suggest, we should find the notion of the Boundless of central relevance. At any rate, this is what the ensuing discussion will seek to establish. The central question then becomes: If it is important to incorporate this concept of the Boundless in our philosophy, how might this be done?

One entry point to our analysis is provided by considering one use of the expression "existent." In order to qualify as an existent, in the sense in which I shall be using this expression, each of the following three conditions must be satisfied. Each is a necessary condition, and, taken together, they are sufficient. An existent is an individual that (1) can be described by the application of one or more general terms; (2) is nonfictional; (3) has a temporal beginning and end.

One common use of the term "exists" is to assert (or in some cases to question, in other cases to deny) that *there is* something that exemplifies or possesses some specified property or group of properties: "Mountains exist on the other side of the Moon"; "Does there exist a human being who weighs one thousand pounds?"; "Physicists came to agree that the luminiferous ether filling all of absolute space doesn't exist." And so on.

As modern quantificational logic has taught us, one use of the expression "exists," from which we can derive the nominative expression "existent," is thus conveyed by a formula whose general form is: "There is an x, such that x has the property P (or the combination of properties, P, Q, R . . .)." As shown by this formula, one use of the words "there is" conveys the sense of "exists." On this approach, "exists" is not itself a general term of description— it does not describe a property—in the same way in which we use the letters P, Q, R, as general terms of description to represent properties of some entity. If it can be established as true that there is at least one instance or individual example from the class of individuals over which the variable x ranges, of which one or more general terms of description—*P, Q, R*—is true, then that individual will satisfy one condition for being recognized as an existent. Let us use the symbols *a, b, c*, etc., as names to designate the individuals of which it is true to say that such an individual possesses the property or properties in question—that it can be truthfully described by the general predicates conveyed by *P, Q, R*, etc. Then *a, b, c*, can serve as names for individual existents. Proper names, or other ways of referring to individuals, need to be distinguished from general terms. The latter are not names of individual entities. A term of description (*P, Q, R*) is general if it might be applied to more than one individual. Consider the sentence "Buildings that are more than 1,000 feet tall exist." When rewritten to satisfy a modern logician's way of parsing this sentence, we should say: "There is an *x* (some individual that belongs to the class *x*) that has the properties both of being a building and having a height of more than 1,000 feet." Let us suppose this sentence is confirmed as true: one can find at least one individual that meets this description. In this case, the individual so referred to and identified satisfies a necessary condition for being an existent. Thus the name "Empire State building" is a name for such an existent.

A second, closely related use of "exists" is as a synonym for "real." This term is used, with this special emphasis in mind, in those contexts where one is concerned to draw a contrast between what is fictional and what is nonfictional. To say something is nonfictional is to assert that what is being referred to is not to be identified simply by means of an exercise of the imagination. Rather, what the name denotes can be confronted observationally in some way, is part of the world of objects and events in space and time, and is publicly confirmable as having such a location and status. In its ordinary usage, something is said to be real or to exist if it is known to be part of the known universe, whatever its location in space or time, its material composition, its place in some evolutionary scheme, or its value as considered from a human point of view. It is with this special interest in contrasting reality with fiction that we use the term "exists" in the following sentences: "The Taj Mahal exists"; "The Wizard of Oz does not exist";

"Did King Arthur exist?" On this stipulation, the Taj Mahal is an existent, but the Wizard of Oz is not an existent. The author Conan Doyle wrote stories containing the character Sherlock Holmes. Sherlock Holmes is not an existent, but Conan Doyle is, as are the acts of reading the stories or enacting them.

A third use of "exists" is found wherever we wish to single out individuals that have a temporally bound duration: a beginning and an end. There are countless examples of such entities. Your life and mine, this table, the planet Earth, the ancient city of Babylon, Socrates, World War II, yesterday's concert by the New York Philharmonic—all exist in the sense of being temporally bound objects or events, and so satisfy another necessary condition of being classified as existents.

If we accept the foregoing stipulations with respect to the use of the term "existent," shall we say that, in addition to examples drawn from ordinary experience, the universe too is an existent? Let us recall the principal distinctions we worked out earlier about the use of the term "universe"—as designating that which is observable, intelligible, or known. For purposes of the present discussion, we may confine our attention to the known universe. It incorporates the observable universe and relies on a model to render the universe intelligible that is accepted by the community of experts as warrantedly assertible. With respect to the known universe at the present stage of cosmological inquiry, cosmologists are in broad agreement on the need to adopt some form of evolutionary model. On the basis of these considerations, it would seem wholly appropriate to give an affirmative answer to the question whether to classify the known universe as an existent, for all three conditions mentioned earlier are satisfied. As the subject of predications, the known universe exemplifies the combination of general predicates set out in the cosmological model that renders the universe intelligible. Insofar as the current model is accepted as warrantedly assertible, this is because it is believed *there is* something that has the properties described by the model. Furthermore, the universe is real, that is, nonfictional. The fact that the known universe includes at least the observable universe assures us of this fact. Indeed, as the maximally intelligible known whole, the universe includes within itself all other nonfictional individual entities. Finally, the universe is an existent according to the third criterion mentioned earlier. If we rely on the accounts of recent evolutionary cosmology, the universe, too (like any temporally bound object, process, or event within the universe), had a beginning and will have an end. According to the criteria we have laid down, the foregoing considerations support the conclusion that the known universe is an existent. They point to the similarities between the known universe and other entities we classify as existents and among which are found the very paradigms for the use of this expression. Despite this, a more careful examination brings to light major *differences* between the universe and other existents.

One such difference can be noted in connection with the application of the notion of what it is to be real or nonfictional. Consider ordinary examples of real objects, events, and processes: the Statue of Liberty, the boiling of water in a kettle at a particular moment, Socrates, the Andromeda galaxy, World War II, and so on. In each case, there is a wider background into which any one of these real entities can be fitted. Any one can be located in some spatial, temporal, causal, human-historical, astronomic, or other network and collection of objects, events, and processes. It is because this wider background (the furniture in a room, New York harbor, Greek history, the local cluster of galaxies, etc.) is regarded as real that the smaller unit, which belongs to it as a part, is also accorded the status of being real. The reality of a commonly acknowledged, noncontroversial example of any existent consists in our ability to find its nonfictional place within some wider, noncontroversial, real, comparative whole. Indeed, the same analysis can be applied to the comparative whole itself: it too is but a part of a still wider and more inclusive nonfictional whole. If carried through to still wider and more inclusive real wholes, this nesting process will only terminate when we reach the bounds of the known universe. It is as part of the known universe that reality belongs to any subordinate part, whatever the latter's size, duration, value, or physical composition. In short, each existent is so classified because it is ultimately a bona fide part of the known physical universe and not simply a product of the imagination.

But what of the known universe of which every other existent is a part? Can we say it is real for the same reason we give for any existent that is part of it? Obviously not. The known universe is not real because it belongs *as a part* to some wider whole. A particular accepted cosmological account of the known universe does not include any reference to some wider whole, much less a claim to knowledge concerning such a whole. Indeed, to use the very expression "known universe" disallows any such reference. For the known universe is grounded in the use of a cosmological model— a statement of the conceptual bounds and physical characteristics of the intelligible universe as a whole. Each cosmological model specifies, in its own terms, the nature of the absolute whole taken to constitute the universe and whose properties the model would set out in detail. If we do recognize the known universe as real, the notion of reality cannot include the notion of "being a part of some wider whole," as this is used in connection with ordinary existents. Because the universe is unique in this respect and wholly different from any other (real) existent, the notion of reality, if it is applied to the universe, has to be stated negatively: The known universe is *not* part of some wider, known whole.

Consider, next, the matter of being temporally bound, of having a beginning and an end, as this holds for existents that are everywhere to be found within the known universe. The length of the "lifetime" of an existent between the bounds of its "birth" and "death" will, of course, vary for different types of entities—for example, an ordinary main-sequence star, a human being, a subatomic particle. Moreover, whether the duration of its lifespan is long or short, every temporally bound existent within the known universe can be located in a temporal order of some kind with respect to other existents, themselves similarly situated within the known universe and temporally bound. There are numerous schemes used for accomplishing these temporal orderings. They range from the crudest to the most sophisticated, from those stated in simple qualitative terms to those resting on precisely stated quantitative techniques and principles, including those guided by the demands of accepted physical theory. (Think, for example, of the requirements for specifying the simultaneity of distant events according to special relativity theory, or of the need to satisfy the Uncertainty Principle in quantum mechanics.) By laying down rules for determining the relations "earlier than," "later than," or "simultaneous with," a temporal ordering scheme of some kind can be devised and applied to assign a place to a particular entity within a temporal sequence that includes *other* entities. As ordinarily encountered in everyday experience or in sciences other than cosmology, no individual existent is lacking in a surrounding temporal framework in which are located other events, objects, and processes. In specifying the *beginning* of duration of a particular event, process, or object, there are other entities to be found whose beginnings antedated that of the given particular. No entity, whose *end* can be assigned, is such that there are no other entities whose temporal durations extend beyond its own. Finally, there are an indefinitely large number of other events, processes, or objects whose temporal spans overlap or are *simultaneous* with that of a given object, event, or process. All of this is simply another way of making the obvious point that any given existent begins its career, endures for a finite temporal stretch (however long or short), and comes to an end in the context of a world that contains, along with itself, other existents. In short, the beginnings and endings of objects, events, and processes can be arranged in accordance with the deliverances of ordinary experience or the accepted laws and theories of science, so that the position and duration of a particular existent can be fixed in its relation to the temporal positions and durational spans of other existents. For existents of various types, the results will not be totally unlike—only enormously more complicated than—the determinate pattern of entrances, overlaps, and endings of the several parts of a Bach fugue.

As distinguished from specifying the temporal properties of all other existents, the project of determining the temporal properties of the known universe, according to an evolutionary model, does *not* depend on embedding the known evolving universe in a wider framework of other existents that themselves have temporal properties. For there is no known collection of existents of a more inclusive *temporal* scope than the universe itself. Its temporal properties—in particular its beginning and ending—cannot be related to other existents whose beginnings antedated its own beginning or that will endure after its own ending.

Another, related way of bringing out the difference between the temporal properties of existents within the known universe and the temporal properties of the universe, is this. In the case of existents within the known universe, a temporal ordering scheme, once settled on and applied, is used over and over again to place individual objects and occurrences with respect to one another. With the availability of the rules of such a scheme—particularly one that has been repeatedly applied in a successful way—it is the beginnings, durations, and endings of individual entities that might be settled by appealing to the rules of temporal ordering. What need to be settled are the assignments of positions and durations of particular objects and occurrences within a shared temporal order. In other words, in dealing with "ordinary" existents within the universe, it is *their* beginnings, durations, and endings that are normally under consideration, not that of the temporal ordering scheme itself.

In the case of the universe, however, as interpreted by an evolutionary model, the situation is markedly different. For to say that the known evolving *universe* had a beginning and will have an end is tantamount to saying that the *temporal ordering scheme itself* had a "beginning" and will have an "end." As an existent, the universe is not located *within* the same temporal order as other existents of more restricted scope. The so-called "temporal bounds" of the universe—its "beginning" and "end"—are *conceptual bounds*, not ordinary temporal bounds as normally assigned to existents within the universe. For, in the case of the universe, the problem of determining its temporal properties is not one of relating the temporal status of the universe, as one existent, to other existents within a commonly shared temporal order. In referring to the temporal "beginning" and "end" of the universe, one is actually referring to the conceptual breakdown of the temporal scheme employed in describing the universe. It is the temporal scheme, as applied to the universe as a known whole, that has a "beginning" and "end." And this is another way of saying that the temporal scheme is inapplicable for describing whatever physical or any other occurrences there may be at the "points" so labeled. In this respect, the known universe cannot be said to have a beginning and an end in the same way in which we use these expressions in connection with objects, events, and processes within the universe. For them, the terms "beginning," "duration," and "end" are reasonably well-defined in terms of some accepted temporal ordering scheme. In the case of the universe, it is the temporal ordering scheme one proposes to use that comes into question and exhibits its own bounds of applicability. Once again, we must conclude that the known universe, according to an evolutionary model, is different from other existents. Unlike other existents, the universe does not have a beginning or an end in the same sense in which these terms are ordinarily used. The terms "beginning" and "end" have a negative significance. They signify the unavailability—for example, of the four-dimensional space-time ordering scheme of general relativity, and its specialized grammar—for the use of the expressions "before" and "after," if one should raise questions about what happened *before* the big bang, or what will happen *after* whatever physical situation in an open or closed universe is taken to mark the end of the known universe.

As one of the necessary conditions for the use of the term "existent," I stipulated earlier that there be at least one individual of which it is true to say that some general predicate holds: that it has the property described by that predicate. When this condition is satisfied, the individual can be referred to as an existent relative to the predicate in question: it exemplifies or instantiates that predicate. Thus Socrates is an existent relative to the predicate "wise." The question I wish to consider now is whether, or to what extent, the known universe can be regarded as an existent from this point of view. Does the known universe qualify as an existent with respect to the instantiation of general predicates in the same way that other individuals do? In what follows, I shall point to a crucial respect in which the universe *differs* from other existents in meeting this requirement.

What makes a predicate general is its repeated applicability. The same predicate could be used over and over again to describe the property of any individual that satisfies the combination of marks (the definition or list of criteria) specified by the rule of use of the predicate as a general term. The terms "white," "soluble," "three feet long," "contains carbon in its chemical composition," and a host of others serve as general predicates in this way. There are many individual existents that fall under each of these general terms. Furthermore, the terminology of "instantiation" or "exemplification" can be used not only to describe the relation between a general predicate of ordinary language (such as those just mentioned) and any instance of it, but also to characterize the relation between a scientifically established law and one or more individual instances of the law. A law may be thought of as the empirically confirmed statement of a *general* pattern among various quantities (constants and variables) relevant to understanding a certain type of phenomenon. As a statement of an observed and confirmed regularity, the law can be applied to individual occurrences and situations whose properties fall within the scope of the variables appearing in the law, for purposes of description, prediction, or explanation of the individual case in question. For example, the general gas laws that state the relations between the volume, pressure, and temperature of a gas can be applied to, and exemplified in, an indefinitely large number of individual cases in the laboratory or elsewhere.

In cosmology, the principal conceptual tool for describing and explaining the properties of the universe as a maximally intelligible system is a cosmological model. From a logical point of view, this conceptual scheme may be regarded as containing—in addition to various constants and observational data concerning particular occurrences, processes, or objects—a complex string of general predicates. Among these predicational components are not only general predicates taken from ordinary language, but also various physical laws and theoretical principles taken from one or another of the major branches of physics: classical Newtonian mechanics, Maxwellian electromagnetic theory, thermodynamics, statistical mechanics, general relativity theory, quantum theory in its various forms, particle physics, and so on. For the sake of convenience, let us imagine that in setting out the distinctive conceptual content of a particular cosmological model, the terms drawn from one or another of these sources are listed as components in a conjunctive string of predicates that marks off that model from others. Of course, an essential requirement is that the component predicates in such a string be compatible with one another. Their use in some very long and complicated predicational statement must not harbor any inconsistency, otherwise their combined use could not have any actual or possible applications and exemplifications. To use Leibnizian terminology, the combination of general predicates must be *compossible*. Each model will be identified by its own distinctive conjunctive string of compossible, general predicates. While some predicates will undoubtedly reappear in several models (perhaps even in all seriously entertained models at a given stage of inquiry), there will be differences among competing cosmological models to the extent that no two models consist of exactly the same set of general predicates. For example, some models may appeal to, and incorporate, some recent theory of particle physics; but not all cosmological models need do so. Some models may employ a modified version of Einstein's principle of general relativity, whereas other models may use Einstein's original version. Some models may postulate a general homogeneity in the universe from the very beginning of its career, while others may posit an initial chaotic state. And so on. (If there were more than one model that had exactly the same set of predicates, these would not be logically distinct, but only verbally different versions of the same model.) Thus, let the predicates of one cosmological model be represented by P, Q, R, whereas another may have predicates

P, M, T, and a third *M, L, T.* And so on. By definition, each cosmological model purports to deal with the universe as a maximally intelligible whole. They differ in the set of general predicates (the properties) they assign to what they take to be the maximally intelligible whole. However, there is no single, independently identifiable subject matter—the universe in itself—that is the common target or subject of these different models. Each model defines its own version of what the universe as a whole is. This definition is comprised in the set of general predicates that a particular model incorporates and makes use of. When the status of a particular intelligible model is converted from being merely a proposed but not yet confirmed hypothesis (one that is still in competition with rival models) to being an account of the known universe, we can express this change of status by saying: "There is an *x* which has the properties set out in the now confirmed and preferred model (those, say, conveyed by *P, M, Z*)." The entity that meets these predicational requirements—the individual value of *x*—is the known universe. The known universe is the existent that instantiates or exemplifies the predicates *P, M, Z.*

So far, the situation I have described points to a similarity between the known universe as an existent and other existents. Each is an individual that instantiates one or more general predicates. There is, however, a crucial difference between the way in which the known universe, as an existent, instantiates its set of general predicates and the way in which any other existent instantiates its own set of general predicates. The crucial difference is this. Since every component predicate of a string of general predicates is general, the entire string of general predicates is also repeatedly applicable. In the case of all sciences other than cosmology, the appeal to any one general predicate or a conjunctive set of general predicates allows for the possibility that there may be more than one instance of it. A true existential statement asserts there is at least one case of exemplification of the predicate(s) contained in that statement. There is at least one *x* of which it is true to say it can be described by such-and-such general predicates. Even if there is only one actual example that has been thus far observed or otherwise identified, it would still be possible, in all sciences other than cosmology, to allow that there may be other instances of the same set of general predicates. While, in fact, only one instance may have been found, thus far, that instantiates a given set of general predicates, there is nothing in the statement of the laws of a science to prevent there being other actual instances elsewhere or in the future that might also be described by the same set of general predicates. Indeed, in the normal situation where empirical laws have been established, there is a plurality of individual instances in which a general pattern is exhibited. There are many examples of atoms, molecules, cells, stars, galaxies, human beings, human cultures, volcanic eruptions, eclipses, supernovae explosions, business cycles, snowstorms, pollenization, radioactive decay, idiot savants, crater formation, marriage ceremonies, and so on. However relatively unique or distinctive an individual belonging to one or another of these classes of entities or phenomena may be, as encountered in ordinary experience or in any of the natural or social sciences, that individual belongs to a class of other individuals similar to it in some respects. There are other musicians besides Mozart, other diamonds besides the Kohinoor, other mountains besides Everest, and so on. Any ordinary individual existent is given as embedded in a context of other individual existents that have some properties in common with it.

However, the universe is not given as embedded in a context of other universes. Indeed the universe is not "given" at all. Rather, it is conceived by means of a constructed cosmological model. Given the string of general predicates that make up a cosmological model, there is not only at least one instance, but at most one. By definition, the universe is the maximally intelligible whole. There cannot be more than one known universe, as established at a particular stage of cosmological inquiry. Unlike other sciences, therefore, in which there can be and normally are a plurality of existents that exemplify some law or other set of general predicates made use of in the conceptual tools of the science, cosmology is different in that the general predicates it falls back on for its descriptive and explanatory purposes can have at most one instance. In the case of an accepted cosmological model used to represent the known universe, there is at least one and at most one individual that instantiates the general predicates that distinctively characterize that model. The known universe is that existent. It differs from all other existents in being absolutely unique in its exemplification of the predicates used to describe it.

To sum up this phase of our discussion: As a scientific discipline, the pursuit of cosmology represents the human drive to obtain satisfactory knowledge of the widest and most comprehensive subject matter open to investigation. In obtaining knowledge of the universe as a whole, cosmology promises to yield this sought-for knowledge. I have sifted some of the possible views about the nature of intelligibility in the field of cosmology and have given reasons for opting for a type of approach that owes much to a Kantian heritage. Intelligibility in cosmology, I have argued, is the result of applying a humanly constructed conceptual scheme for picturing the universe as a whole as a maximally intelligible pattern of physical phenomena. The intelligibility thus achieved need not be taken as disclosing what may be thought of as some antecedently existing structure inherent in "the universe in itself." Instead, the intelligibility achieved in cosmology takes the form of a knowledge-product: the universe-as-known. In understanding what goes into the realization of this product, moreover, we are forced to take note of its conceptually bound character. How the currently known universe is conceptually bound is seen, in particular, in the way in which it is described as having a temporal beginning and end. However, there is no reason to believe that any other cosmological model—for example, one that might supersede those currently preferred—will be any the less conceptually bound in its own way. In the pursuit of scientific cosmology, the conceptual boundedness of any cosmological model is an inescapable feature—the price one pays for the achievement of intelligibility. Furthermore, our examination of the question to what extent we are to describe the universe-as-known as an existent has revealed a number of special features that show its absolute uniqueness as an existent.

The conceptual boundedness of any cosmological model, and the absolute uniqueness of the known universe as an existent, conspire to insure the endless search for better and better cosmological models. Both these features account for the endlessness of search for cosmic intelligibility. This endlessness of search is due in part to the fact that the universe, as an existent, cannot be compared with anything else. Its uniqueness as an existent has the consequence that in trying to render the universe intelligible, one does not have the advantage, as in the case of other existents, of examining multiple instances, and on the basis of a generalization learned from their shared or common features, of applying this knowledge to predict or explain what is still unknown in the individual case at hand. There are no other universes from whose study one can derive a general law of universe-behavior that would help to understand our universe. Nor, indeed, even in the absence of a law about universes, can one at least directly inspect the "given universe." For the universe as a whole is not given. In place of a law applied to an individual instance, one can only construct a model of the universe as a unique, maximally intelligible physical system. Once constructed, moreover, the model cannot be compared with the universe itself to see how close it comes to matching the various features of "the universe itself." The latter expression has no identifiable referent. The cosmologist constructs a model of an "entity" he is neither able to observe and inspect directly, now or at any future time, in order to see how closely his model matches what "it" is. He can only test his picture step by step as he goes along by appealing to such pragmatic criteria as success in predictive capacity with respect to parts of the universe that can be observed or inferred with some reasonable confidence, or on the basis of internal consistency and comprehensive, systematic power. In the construction of his model, he can only use analogies, invent special principles, or apply laws he has already discovered from the observation of other lesser systems and existents. He can put together these bits and pieces in conceiving what the universe as a unique whole is like. If a particular model falls by the wayside because of one or another shortcoming, all that can be done is to persist and to try to construct a better model. But of course a new model will not have any special advantages of confronting "the universe itself" more closely than other models. For the testing of any given cosmological model will always suffer from the same type of limitations that confront any other model. All that can be done is to continue the process of search in the hope that as one continues one will get better and better models. But the process is an endless one. For every conceptual horizon transcended, new horizons loom, and so on endlessly.

To the foregoing one might object that the picture of the endlessness of inquiry in cosmology is no different, in this respect, from the situation in any other science. Surely there is no reason to believe there will ever be an end to the search for better and better theories in physics, chemistry, biology, psychology, and so on? One reply might be that while this may be granted, there is an important difference between cosmology and other sciences. As the other sciences advance in the understanding of their respective subject matters, they do so by seeing various interrelations among their discipline and others. However, one overridingly important method of achieving this result is to see this growing network of interrelations within the context of the structure and development of the universe. As it advances, each science is gathered up within the conceptual framework of a more and more sophisticated cosmological model. The findings of various empirical sciences become parts of a comprehensive theory of the universe, not the other way around. A good recent example of this is the way in which theories of particle physics, such as GUTs or supersymmetry theories, become themselves better understood as they are seen to describe different types of physical states and phases in the temporal development of the universe as a whole. And, of course, other sciences—such as galactic or stellar astronomy, geology, chemistry, biology, and all the sciences having to do with man—are themselves enriched and better understood when seen in the wider context of cosmology. Therefore, if the process of search for intelligibility in cosmology is endless, this gives an added reason for saying that the search for scientific understanding of whatever exists has no final bounds. The endlessness of the search for intelligibility of the universe as a whole affects the search for intelligibility in all other disciplines, because the universe as a unique existent, in encompassing all other existents, cannot ever be made itself wholly and finally intelligible.

BOUNDLESS EXISTENCE

The ineliminable presence of conceptual bounds in the use of any cosmological model, however successful a particular model may be, provokes attempts to overcome the horizons of understanding enforced by those conceptual bounds. At any stage of inquiry, the known universe points beyond itself. Despite the advances made over earlier models, the raising of fresh questions and the confrontation of new, unsolved problems, brought into view with improved ways of thought, stimulate the drive to find a still more adequate picture of the universe as a whole. Since this situation keeps recurring, no matter how much progress has been made, there is an interminable search for ways of achieving increased intelligibility of cosmic scope—for ways of pushing back the horizons of the known universe. There is consequently no reason to believe that the series of descriptions of the known universe will have a final stage (however long cosmological inquiry may be continued), a stage in which a perfect and complete model will have been realized that exhibits no bounds, poses no problems, and satisfactorily answers all questions. If by "boundless," in one of its senses, is meant "endless," then cosmological inquiry is fated to be boundless, since the means for carrying on such inquiry—the use of cosmological models—will always be conceptually bound.

If this conclusion is accepted, then reflection on the endlessness of cosmological inquiry poses a further question. Given these features of the pursuit of cosmology, we are prompted to ask: If every account of the known universe is bound, and its horizons can only be overcome by moving into the conceptual bounds of a different cosmological model (a new picture of the known universe), is there a way of "breaking out" of this endless boundedness of cosmology? In view of the endlessness of cosmological inquiry, should we not be prepared to recognize a type of boundlessness altogether different in character from that of the endlessness of search for cosmological intelligibility? Should we not consider the possibility that there is a level or dimension of reality "beyond" any account of the known universe (or any of its contents), of which one can have a mode of awareness that is not hemmed in by the constraints and ever-present horizons of cosmological knowledge? If all that cosmological inquiry can look forward to, no matter how long pursued, is the replacement of one model by another, is it not the case, perhaps, that the very reason for this endlessness of cosmological search is due to the fact that the known universe, however construed, is connected in some way with a more profound, ultimate boundlessness or indeterminability at the very heart of reality?

In what follows, I shall bring forward a number of considerations in support of this proposal. We shall see what can be said in behalf of recognizing a level of transcendent reality of which we can have a direct mode of awareness that is without conceptual bounds or horizons. If we are prepared to pursue this line of philosophic speculation, we may see in the boundlessness of the search for cosmic knowledge a clue to the boundlessness (in another sense of this term) of Existence itself. According to this way of thinking, Existence, as ultimate reality, would neither be conceptually bound in the way the known universe is, nor, in being ultimate, would it be bound by anything beyond itself. To signify this double sense of "boundlessness," I shall hereafter use the expression *Boundless Existence*.

Although no stage reached in the pursuit of cosmology will by itself ever lead to *knowledge* of Boundless Existence, at any stage the known universe provides the best foothold from which to become *aware* of Boundless Existence. The known universe offers a "route to," a "glimpse of," and serves as an "embodiment" or "exemplification" of Boundless Existence. Boundless Existence is disclosed to us in a special, heightened form of awareness by an act of "bracketing" the known universe as an existent. What is left is not nothing, but Existence itself.

"Bracketing" represents an act of the mind whereby one is able to suspend natural attitudes and interests in order to be able to dwell exclusively on a selected feature of a total complex situation—a feature that comes into sharpened focus as a result. To bracket is to disregard, to disconnect, to suspend normal interests, in order to give heightened attention to what remains and is thereby detached. To bracket the known universe as an existent is to put out of attention the fact that it is an all-inclusive whole that possesses a variety of contents and has the overall structure ascribed to it by a particular cosmological model. Detached from attention is the fact that it has a spatial or temporal structure at all, as well as the makeup of its various physical contents (from subatomic particles to clusters of galaxies), along with the evolutionary or other patterns and properties that describe the individual existents that belong to this all-inclusive whole. In addition to suspending all interests of a cosmic scope of the sort that interest the cosmologist, the act of bracketing that concerns us also, of course, involves suspending the normal kinds of interests, responses, and modes of interaction that would preoccupy a person or social group in the course of ongoing daily affairs and experience, whether in action, making, or thinking. Existence is not anything to which attention is given in everyday practical affairs or in science. One could go through life without being aware of Existence as such, since such awareness is not necessary or relevant to carrying out the tasks that we have as members of social groups, as biological creatures engaged in fulfilling various needs and desires, as practitioners of the arts, or as scientific inquirers. All such natural and normal human concerns are suspended for the duration of the experience in question, however brief or intermittent this may be. To bracket all these is to drop them out of the center, indeed out of the entire field of consciousness.

To bring Boundless Existence into awareness is not to exercise the senses, imagination, or powers of conception. The target of such awareness is not anything one can point to in the field of observation, or of which one can form an image. Nor is what we are aware of something that can be conveyed by a concept-word (a general predicate), since the term "Existence" does not apply by way of description of a property to one or more individuals. What the term "Boundless Existence" denotes is utterly unique. Hence the ordinary powers of the mind (whether of perception, imagination, or concept-formation) are not engaged in its awareness. Nor can an awareness of Existence be communicated, if by "communication" is meant the use of propositional discourse of a conventional sort. Of someone who does not have this awareness, one might say that such a person suffers from a certain type of "blindness." One can only hope to awaken in such a person the required sort of awareness by reliance on various metaphors, clues, signposts, and so on. But there is no guarantee that any of these will work. And to one who fails to share in that awareness and so remains unresponsive and untouched by that experience, there is no argument or evidence that might be offered to succeed where other techniques have failed.

To forestall possible objections, it is necessary to insist that there is no intention in the foregoing proposal to use the expression "Boundless Existence" as a name for a type of object or entity. Such use would be altogether misleading in the present context. The expression "Boundless Existence" is not a proper name, as this grammatical category is ordinarily understood, for there is no object or entity to serve as its referent. Nor does it have a sense, if by this is meant supplying a description—an analysis of component parts or list of criteria—by which to guide and justify its application. Boundless Existence cannot be pointed to and is not conceptually accessible in any way. No standard use of language— whether as found in everyday discourse or in any of the sciences, including cosmology—can accommodate the term "Boundless Existence" within its ordinary grammatical categories. We shall be driven, consequently, and at the end, to silence, although the "talk" on the way, if at all helpful, will have had its value in making the silence a pregnant one, and indeed the occasion for having an overridingly important type of human experience. If at all successful, our discussion of the role to be assigned to this expression will have brought into sharpened focus an awareness of something of such transcendent uniqueness and philosophic importance that all attempts to assimilate or compare what it signifies to other ranges of experience, objects of linguistic reference, description, or analysis must ultimately fail.

Although the route we are following as a means for becoming aware of Boundless Existence is through the known universe as an existent, it is important nevertheless not to regard them as identical. For there is a crucial ontological difference between Boundless Existence and the known universe. As an existent, the known universe is distinguished from all other existents by virtue of the fact that it is the all-inclusive whole that incorporates all of them within itself. The fact that the known universe is a real, maximally comprehensive intelligible system nevertheless does not change its status as an existent, though—as an all-inclusive whole—it is an absolutely unique existent. Even the known universe as a maximally intelligible comprehensive whole of all existents still falls short of being identical with Boundless Existence as such.

What holds true of the universe as an existent does not apply to Boundless Existence. In an earlier phase of my discussion, I stipulated as necessary conditions for the use of the expression "existent" that anything so classified has a temporal beginning and end, is describable by the use of general predicates, and is nonfictional. On these criteria, the known universe is to be considered an existent, especially if we bear in mind the outlook of currently favored evolutionary models of the universe. By contrast with the known universe as an existent, Boundless Existence is not a whole of any sort whatever, whether maximally comprehensive or otherwise; does not have a temporal beginning or end; is not real, in the limited and special sense of being nonfictional insofar as it has a publicly acknowledged observational basis; and cannot be described at all, whether through the use of general predicates or laws of any kind. If Boundless Existence were identical with the known universe as an existent, then cosmology would offer an account of

Boundless Existence. However, this would land us back in the results we had already found in connection with the pursuit of cosmology, whereas we are interested in transcending that type of inquiry to reach a level of reality different from that of any version of the known universe. In coming to know the universe, cosmology makes use of complex conceptual structures. Any cosmological model is therefore conceptually bound. Awareness of Existence, however, is not achieved by means of a cosmological model. Boundless Existence is not anything of which one can have knowledge, to the extent that knowledge is bound up with the use of concepts. If access to Existence is not via concepts, then awareness of Existence is not conceptually bound. For this reason, unlike the endlessness of inquiry in cosmology, awareness of Existence is not endlessly protracted. Instead, it is available at any time in a direct, self-contained, and complete experience. If Existence is not conceptually bound—if it is boundless in this sense—then no description can be given of "it." No ordinary categories apply to "it." In short, if we are prepared to affirm that there is a more fundamental level of reality than the known universe, then Existence is not an existent, not even the known universe as a unique existent.

All ways of describing the transition we make in becoming aware of Boundless Existence are either negative or metaphoric. We speak of "making a leap," of an "act of transcendence" (of "jumping over" the bounds in the use of ordinary language or the conceptual schemes of science), of "coming into the clearing" of Boundless Existence, of having it "revealed" to us, of an "insight" into it, and so on. Not only must one admit to the need of falling back on metaphoric language, but one must also admit that if one is going to describe the mode of "access" to the Boundless or "what" it is, again it is necessary to use negatives, to say constantly "not this, not that." Thus one must deny that the way to reach Boundless Existence is by way of faith or rational argument. To those who have an intensified awareness of Boundless Existence, it is the most obvious fact of their experience. It needs no further underpinning, no further appeal to evidence or argument to support that awareness. Indeed, everything else—every other mode of evidence, belief, experience, or justification—in some way presupposes or rests upon that awareness. In some ways, the awareness of Boundless Existence is reminiscent of traditional appeals to the Ontological Argument in support of a belief in God—although, if properly understsood, the Ontological Argument is, strictly speaking, no *argument*. It declares, rather, the acceptance of a starting point from which everything else follows, but which itself does not follow from anything more fundamental.

Once reached, Boundless Existence can only be said to stand in some "relation" to that from which we took our point of departure, in ways borrowed from the world of existents. We say that ordinary existents "exemplify" Boundless Existence, or they are "parts" of it, or that Boundless Existence is "inexhaustible" and "infinite," or that existents "share" in some way in the "property" of Boundless Existence, or that Boundless Existence is an "infinitely creative source," "produces," or "brings into existence," or is the "ultimate" or "First Cause" out of which everything "arises" and of which it is its "effects." And so on. Yet all of these terms of description, halting and analogical as they must be, fail. Boundless Existence can only be "characterized" in negative terms. It is not a complex whole composed of parts. It is not "in" space or time, nor does it have any spatial or temporal structure. It has no history: neither a past, present, nor future. Nor is it spread out in space or have any location or shape. It does not have any structure at all. The term "Existence" is not a general term that can be defined or analyzed. It cannot be used to describe individuals. Nor can any general terms be used to describe "it." It does not refer to an individual that can be observed or inferred. It is not an individual that lies beyond the range of observation, since it is not an individual at all. It is not an agency, cause, source, generator, producer, or creator. It has no mind, purpose, value. Nor is it a mind, purpose, or value. Nor is it anything material, decomposable, or transformable into something else. It has neither extension nor thought, nor any other attributes, properties, or qualities. One cannot make any literal object-language predications of it that would describe it in true sentences. There are no laws, generalizations, or patterns that can be confirmed as holding of it. Boundless Existence is so totally unique (again a misleading analogical term!) that all similarities with anything in our ordinary experience must fall short and be inadequate. For example, it is so "unique" that one cannot even form a negative of it. "Absolute Nothing" or "Pure Non-Being" are expressions for which no satisfactory analysis has ever been given.

Boundless Existence "shines through" the known universe as an existent but is not identical with it or any other existent. In a way that is wholly unintelligible and unknowable, Boundless Existence "underlies" the existence of the universe and all that it contains. It is the wholly unknowable "reason" for the inexhaustibility of any knowledge to be had of the universe.

In the foregoing, I have stressed the approach to Boundless Existence by contrasting it, and our awareness of it, with the known universe as an existent and our knowledge of the universe. However, there are other routes to becoming aware of Boundless Existence. One such route is by way of understanding the contrast between the experience of knowing *what* the universe is said to be, on the one hand, and the awareness or experience *that* it exists, on the other. Boundlesss Existence is what is pointed to in focusing on the awareness of the "thatness" aspect of the known universe as an existent. Such awareness of "thatness" is not a conceptual matter. It cannot be explicated by means of propositions that set out the *properties* of the known universe.

Another way of coming upon Boundless Existence is through coming to recognize there is no known or knowable reason for the existence of the universe. In my book *The Mystery of Existence*, I have examined this route in detail. And there are other routes as well. In the end, they all converge on the same outcome—the realization that there is a dimension of Reality that is beyond all actual or possible conceptual analysis and rational comprehension.

SEVEN

Human Existence

THE COUPLING OF MAN AND THE UNIVERSE

Does recent cosmology throw any light on the origins, sources, and conditions of human existence in the universe? To what extent does recent cosmology have anything fresh and important to add to what other sciences—for example, planetary astronomy, geology, chemistry, and biology—have already contributed to our understanding of life? That cosmology might provide such a fresh perspective is related to recent discussions of the *anthropic principle*.[1] One version of this principle calls attention to certain special circumstances of a cosmological character necessary for the very existence of life. When examined in this perspective, the an-

[1] Cf. George Gale, "The Anthropic Principle," *Scientific American* (December 1981), 154-171; B. J. Carr and M. J. Rees, "The Anthropic Principle and the Structure of the Physical World," *Nature* 278 (1979), 605-612; R. H. Dicke, "Dirac's Cosmology and Mach's Principle," *Nature* 192 (1961), 440-441; Brandon Carter, "Large Number Coincidences and the Anthropic Principle in Cosmology," in M. S. Longair, ed., *Confrontations of Cosmological Theories with Observational Data* (Dordrecht: Reidel, 1974), 291-298; J. D. Barrow, "The Lore of Large Numbers: Some Historical Background to the Anthropic Principle," *Quart. J. Roy. Astr. Soc.* 22 (1981), 388-420; idem, "Anthropic Definitions," *Quart. J. Roy. Astr. Soc.* 24 (1983), 146-153; M. J. Rees, "Large Numbers and Ratios in Astrophysics and Cosmology," *Phil. Trans. Royal Soc. Lond.* A 310 (1983), 311-322; J. Leslie, "Anthropic Principle, World Ensemble, Design," *American Philosophical Quarterly* 19 (1982), 141-151; J. Barrow and F. Tipler, *The Anthropic Cosmological Principle* (Oxford: Oxford University Press, 1986).

thropic principle undertakes to make clear why it is that without these special cosmologic conditions, life would not exist at all. The very same principle, however, has also been used in order to show that the fact of human existence illuminates special features of the actual universe as compared with other possible universes. It is not simply that certain properties of the universe throw light on human existence, but the reverse also holds. The universe and human life are coupled. If we are to understand either, we need to move in both directions: from the universe to man and from man to the universe, since they are mutually involved in a very special way.

Brandon Carter was among the first to make important contributions to this topic. He introduced the expression "the anthropic principle" and characterized it, briefly, as saying that "what we can expect to observe must be restricted to the conditions necessary for our presence as observers."[2]

Taken in one way, this might be regarded, at first glance, as a mere tautology. For does it not simply say that if something is to be observed it needs the presence of observers? In this case, it does not make a factual statement at all and cannot possibly contribute to our knowledge of the universe, man, or anything else. Far from being the illuminating statement it supposedly is, we might be inclined to dismiss it out of hand as not worthy of further consideration. Of course, Carter did not intend to make a trivial tautological assertion. On the contrary, he intended to make a factual claim, one that is informatively true (and not merely grammatically a priori necessary). It might, therefore, be false. The anthropic principle is saved from being a tautology because Carter, along with many others, thinks of it as allowing all sorts of predictions and explanations to be derived from it. If confirmed, these could be used to add to our knowledge (however insecurely) of certain matters of fact. And a tautology could not, by itself, ever do this.

The reason Carter thought in these terms is that, like most other cosmologists, he can be seen to adhere to a *realist* philosophy. He

[2] Carter, "Large Number Coincidences," 291.

believes, in other words, there exists—independently of, and antecedently to, human observation or any other mode of cognitive response—a universe that already has a set of determinate properties. He proposes to use the anthropic principle to discover and explain certain facts about the properties of this independently existing entity. The route he proposes to follow is to examine certain facts about the existence of human observers, and to use them to deduce the character of *other* facts, namely, those having to do with certain properties of the independently existing universe itself—properties that "we can expect to observe."

In what follows, we shall examine some leading interpretations and examples of the appeal to the anthropic principle. A fundamental classification, proposed by Brandon Carter, distinguishes the *weak anthropic principle* and the *strong anthropic principle*. To clarify this distinction is our first task.

When considered from the perspective of their diverse types of physical structure, the phenomena of nature are found to be distributed over an extremely wide range of scales. The range extends from the universe as an inclusive physical system, at one end, down through succeedingly smaller scales typically associated with such objects as clusters of galaxies, individual galaxies, stars, planets, living organisms, cells, molecules, atoms, and finally subatomic particles, at the other end. Aside from their internal structural properties, these various types of entities differ from one another in terms of size and mass. For example, galaxies have a typical size of 10^{21} meters, as compared to the typical size of 10^7 meters for a planet, 10^{-10} meter for an atom, and 10^{-15} meter for nuclear particles. Similarly, the range of masses is equally wide. For example, the mass of a cluster of galaxies is 10^{43} kilograms, whereas the mass of a nuclear particle is on the order of 10^{-27} kilogram, with many intermediate values belonging to objects lying between these extremes. Each specialized scientific discipline is devoted to discovering the laws that describe and explain the behavior of the particular group of entities it selects for intensive study. These entities belong to one or another scale of size and mass.

Despite the wide range of scales and variety of structures, it is a familiar fact that natural phenomena of the most diverse types are interrelated with one another in many ways. For example, an understanding of the global structure and evolution of the universe requires, among other matters, an application of the laws of elementary particle physics. The shining of the stars is explained by the laws of atomic and nuclear physics. The chemicals necessary for life are the products of supernovae explosions. The functioning of cells depends on the chemistry of molecules. The gross phenomena of electricity, magnetism, and light are linked with the internal structure of atoms as described in quantum physics. It is a commonplace, too, that the origin and continuance of human life depends on all sorts of astronomic, physical, chemical, meteorologic, biological, and social conditions.

It is less commonly recognized that underlying all the many diverse conditions for life, and indeed, more generally, underlying all physical, chemical, and astronomic phenomena, there is a small set of fundamental physical constants without which the entire superstructure and network of nature would not itself be possible. In addition, then, to the manifold interrelations among the phenomena studied by the several sciences, fundamental physics provides strong evidence of an underlying systematic unity in nature due to the pervasive presence of certain universal physical constants. These are: G (the gravitational constant); c (the speed of light); $\hbar$ [$\hbar = h/2\pi$] (Planck's constant); and e (the electric charge of the proton and the electron). These constants determine the gross features of the different scales of size and mass that differentiate the great variety of objects in the universe. These universal physical constants determine—to within an order of magnitude[3]—

[3] The order of magnitude of a quantity is represented by the symbol $\sim$. It stands for the property of a number, within one or two powers of 10, that most nearly expresses the value of the quantity. For example, the number representing the ratio of the mass of the proton (m_p) and the mass of the electron (m_e) is 1836. This number is of the same order of magnitude as the number representing the ratio $\hbar c/e^2$,

why galaxies, stars, planets, atoms, and atomic nuclei have the typical sizes and masses they do.

For example, while the detailed laws of physics explain the shining of stars as due to the burning of nuclear fuel, the sizes and masses of stars that make possible such burning are themselves determined by fundamental constants. Were these constants different, or if there had been any significant changes in the values of the constants G, $\hbar$, c, and e from the ones that actually obtain in the universe, this would have had major repercussions of all sorts. For example, it would have affected the structure and evolution of stars and therefore also indirectly the very existence of biological phenomena. In short, the values of the universal constants link the domains of the cosmic, the biological, the human, and the microphysical in a tight network of interdependencies.

We shall briefly review some aspects of this role of the universal constants in order to see how they bear on the very existence of life in the universe. We begin by considering the aforementioned small number of fundamental constants and some of their interrelations. First, it is worth bearing in mind that a *fundamental constant* is to be distinguished from other types of constants. For example, at the surface of the Earth, the value of the acceleration of gravity, g, is 9.81 m/sec². The value of g is different at the surface of the Moon, on Jupiter, and so on. In short, this type of constant does not have the same value throughout the universe. It is not, therefore, a *fundamental constant*. The latter has the *same* value throughout the universe. This is the case, for example, with G, the fundamental Newtonian gravitational constant. This constant appears in the Newtonian inverse square law:

$$F = -Gm_1m_2/r^2.$$

Here F is the gravitational force between two masses, m_1 and m_2, and r is the distance separating them. The negative sign indicates that there is a force of attraction between them. The value of G is determined experimentally. The numerical value of the constant

which is 137. On the other hand, numbers such as 10^{20}, 10^{40}, or 10^{-35} are of wholly different orders of magnitude. The symbol $\cong$ signifies an approximate equality (roughly within a factor of two) between two quantities.

depends on the basic units for measuring mass, length, and time. In one such widely adopted system (cgs), the value of G is:

$$G = 6.7 \times 10^{-8} \text{cm}^3/\text{g sec}^2.$$

In addition to the universal gravitational constant, there are several other fundamental constants that help determine the distinctive physical properties of objects at different scales. One of these is the constant e, involved in all electromagnetic and atomic phenomena. It represents the electric charge on protons and electrons. By convention, the charge on the proton is positive, that on the electron negative. Other fundamental constants are: c, the constant representing the velocity of light; Planck's constant, $\hbar$, which appears in all formulae of quantum physics; m_p, the rest mass of the proton; and m_e, the rest mass of the electron.

Given this small group of fundamental constants, other constants can be derived through various combinations. As we shall see shortly, these derived constants and their relations prove to be of great importance in explaining the properties of objects and processes at different scales. One of these derived constants, represented by α, is the *electromagnetic fine structure constant*. When dealing with subatomic processes involving the interaction of electrons and nucleons, a major interest of quantum physics is to describe in detail the various ways in which energy changes within the atom are associated with the absorption or emission of photons. Since the physics is of a quantum character, the Planck constant $\hbar$ plays a fundamental role. Similarly, the behavior of light particles (photons) is governed by c, the fundamental constant for the velocity of light. And since what is involved is the electric charge on the proton and electron, the constant e also plays a crucial role. These three fundamental constants—$\hbar$, c, and e—are combined in a single formula that shows the ratio among them. It is represented by the symbol α, and is defined as follows:

$$\alpha \equiv e^2/\hbar c \sim 1/137.$$

The numerical value of this ratio, $1/137$, is a pure, natural, or dimensionless number, since it is independent of arbitrary or conventional units of measurement. Just as the ratio between the mass of a proton (nucleon) and the mass of an electron, $m_p/m_e = 1836$

$\sim$ 1800, independently of whether the mass is measured in terms of grams or kilograms, so, too, the ratio representing the electromagnetic fine structure constant, $e^2/\hbar c$, is a natural or dimensionless number. It is independent of arbitrary units of measurement for expressing c, $\hbar$, and e. The value $1/137$ for this ratio is such a natural number.

Another important derived constant is the *gravitational coupling constant*. As the name suggests, it involves the use of the gravitational constant G. In the case of atomic phenomena, electrical forces are enormously larger than gravitational forces. The force of gravity within a hydrogen atom is some 10^{40} times weaker than the electromagnetic force. The ratio of the electric and the gravitational forces in a hydrogen atom is

$$e^2 \text{ (electrical force) } /Gm_p m_e \text{ (gravitational force).}$$

Its value is $\sim$0.2 $\times$ 10^{40}, showing that the electrical force is far stronger than the gravitational force. Gravitational forces are only relevant where large masses are involved. Since the universe contains equal numbers of positive and negative electric charges, these cancel one another wherever the physical systems are of larger dimensions than atoms or molecules. Electrical forces tend to neutralize one another, whereas gravitational forces are cumulative and cannot be neutralized. As the number of particles in a system increases, the gravitational force of attraction becomes increasingly important, whereas electrical forces play a relatively negligible role. In stellar or galactic systems, the gravitational force is dominant, while on the scale of the universe considered as a single system of galaxies, it is the strongest force.

A formula that conveys the relationship between the gravitational constant, G, the mass of the proton, m_p, the Planck constant, $\hbar$, and the velocity of light, c, is a ratio of the strength of gravitational to electromagnetic forces between protons. This defines the quantity α_G, known as the *gravitational coupling fine structure constant*. The defining formula for α_G is

$$\alpha_G \equiv Gm_p{}^2 \, / \, \hbar c \simeq 5 \times 10^{-39}.$$

Once again, the number representing α_G is a dimensionless or pure number. Its numerical value is of the order of magnitude 5 $\times$ 10^{-39}.

The importance of the foregoing data concerning fundamental physical constants is that this data can be used to determine, within an order of magnitude, the size and mass of entities such as nucleons, atoms, stars, and planets.[4] Consider, for example, the case of *atoms*. Here it is the combination of the constants e, c, $\hbar$, m_p, and m_e that are relevant, since electrons are bound to the nucleus by electromagnetic forces. To obtain some indication of the approximate size of atoms, one needs a measure of length. This can be obtained by combining some of the fundamental constants in an appropriate way—a way that gives the dimension of length. This is accomplished by combining the constants $\hbar$, m_e, and e to give the units of length (size). In doing so, one obtains a value for the Bohr radius. This is the lowest electron orbit of a hydrogen atom. It is symbolized by a_o, and its order of magnitude is conveyed by the following formula:

$$a_o \sim \frac{4\pi\epsilon\hbar^2}{m_e e^2} \sim 10^{-8}\text{cm}.$$

For atoms of greater atomic number than the hydrogen atom, the radius of the outer shell of electrons is of the same order of magnitude as a_o. Hence all atoms have approximately the same size. The value for the size of atoms arrived at on the basis of the above calculations, which make use only of the indicated constants, is confirmed experimentally.

Another illustration of the role of fundamental constants in determining, to an order of magnitude, the masses and sizes of objects, is the way this operates in the case of *stars*. Since life, as we know it, is attached to a planet belonging to the Sun as a typical main-sequence star, the analysis will make clear the way in which these constants control, within narrow limits, basic physical conditions for the very existence of human life. Stars are massive physical systems in which the gravitational constant plays a prominent role, in addition to the fundamental physical constants that characterize the structure of atoms. What distinguishes a star from other massive bodies—such as planets, in which gravitation is also of great importance—is that matter in the star exists in a gaseous

[4] Cf. Carr and Rees, "The Anthropic Principle"; P.C.W. Davies, *The Accidental Universe* (Cambridge, Eng.: Cambridge University Press, 1982).

state at extremely high temperature. This is evidenced by its luminosity. The compression of material (due to the action of self-gravity) raises the temperature of the system. Once having formed under gravity from a collapsing cloud of diffuse hydrogen, a star eventually reaches a state of equilibrium between the thermal and other forms of internal pressure, on the one hand, and its own self-gravity, on the other. The conditions necessary for thermonuclear reactions, found in a star, depend on the star's having reached a certain temperature. When the temperature is sufficiently high, it causes thermonuclear burning and the release, through radiation, of vast stores of energy. In order to radiate the quantities of energy it does, at temperatures of several millions of degrees, the star feeds on its own internal sources of nuclear fuel. This fuel is provided by the process of fusion and the conversion of the energy locked up in the proton masses of the particles of which the star is composed. The temperature a star can reach depends on the number of protons that make up the mass of the star. Based on the use of the fundamental physical constants, already mentioned, calculations point to the number of protons a star must have in order to reach the temperature essential to produce thermonuclear reactions. This number is arrived at by employing a formula constructed entirely out of a combination of relevant fundamental physical constants. The number of protons in a typical star is $\sim 10^{57}$. If we let M_* represent the mass of a typical star, then its order of magnitude is determined by the number of proton masses, N_*, which in turn is related to $\alpha_G{}^{-3/2}$.[5] The mass of a typical star is given by the following formula:

$$M_* \sim N_* m_p \sim \alpha_G{}^{3/2}\, m_p.$$

Stars have different masses. Only stars whose mass lies between the limits of 10^{56} and 10^{58} particles can turn into stable main-sequence stars. The luminosity of a star is proportional to the fourth power of its mass. The less massive a star, the slower its rate of converting hydrogen into helium, whereas the more massive the star, the faster the rate of burning. A normal main-sequence star

[5] Cf. Davies, *Accidental Universe*, 52.

goes through a typical life cycle. Having begun its career through a process of gravitational condensation from an interstellar cloud, it settles down to a process of steady nuclear burning of its hydrogen content. When the hydrogen supply in the star's interior is exhausted, a main-sequence star at first swells up into a red giant (a distended globe of gas that is relatively cool and strongly luminous). However, it eventually becomes a white dwarf (a type of star that is very dense but not very luminous) when nuclear reactions can no longer sustain its ordinary burning. Our Sun, as a typical, normal main-sequence star, has enough fuel to keep burning for approximately another 5 billion years, having already consumed its fuel supply at a relatively slow, steady rate for the past (roughly) 4 billion years.

From the foregoing it is evident that the lifetime of a star is an important aspect of its structure, which bears on the possibility of the existence and evolution of life on a habitable planet that may be attached to it. This stellar lifetime must be long enough to allow for the evolution of life to take place. In the case of the Sun, the rate of nuclear burning has remained constant over a period of at least 4 billion years. The rate at which our Sun consumes its nuclear fuel, and so provides the radiation necessary for the existence of life, depends in a crucial way on the value of the gravitational constant, G, and on the opacity of stellar material. The latter affects the rate at which photons are able to pass through the material in the interior of a star and emerge at the surface as radiation. This depends on the extent to which photons interact with free electrons or ions. And such interactions, in turn, are sensitive to the value of the electric charge, e, an electromagnetic constant. For example, were the value of the gravitational constant to differ by only a factor of ten, it would have drastic effects on the rate at which nuclear fuel would be consumed. Under such radically changed conditions, a typical star such as our Sun would accomplish its evolutionary development in a much shorter time. It would consume its supply of hydrogen at a much faster rate. This would have the consequence that the Earth could not serve as a suitable environment for the emergence and evolution of life, for the Sun would have undergone a transformation into its red giant phase in a much shorter time. In doing so, it would have consumed the Earth (along with other planets) long before life would have had a chance to develop.[6] The order of magnitude of the lifetime of a typical star can be arrived at by taking into account the way in which it is related to the gravitational coupling constant and the nuclear time scale (t_N). The latter is determined by the time required for light to traverse the length of a nucleon (proton). This is given by the expression: $t_N \sim h/m_p c^2$. From these quantities, the lifetime of a typical star, t_*, is found to be of the same order of magnitude as $\alpha_G^{-1} t_N$, namely 10^{40}.[7] Thus

$$t_* \sim \alpha^{-1} t_N \sim 10^{40} t_N.$$

This fact will be of importance in our later discussion of the anthropic principle. For, as we shall see, the lifetime of a typical star is of the very same order of magnitude as that of the age of the universe, where the latter is arrived at on the basis of the Hubble parameter, H.

Our examination, thus far, has focused on several interrelated matters. One has to do with identifying a small number of fundamental physical constants $(c, \hbar, G, m_p, m_e, e)$. A second concerns quantities that can be derived from various combinations of these fundamental constants—for example, the electromagnetic fine structure constant (α), the gravitational coupling constant (α_G), and the Bohr radius (a_o). A third is to note the roles these quantities and ratios play in determining physical properties of systems at different scales of nature. In the course of this examination, we encountered two main groups of natural or dimensionless numbers. One group—to which, for example, $1/137$ $(e^2/\hbar c)$ and 1836 (m_p/m_e) belong—has an order of magnitude that may be taken as unity. Another group clusters around numbers whose order of magnitude is 10^{40}: for example, the value of the gravitational coupling constant, the ratio between the electrical and the gravitational forces for a proton and electron in a hydrogen atom, and the ratio of the

6 *Ibid.*, 54-55.
7 *Ibid.*, 55.

strength of electric and gravitational forces between protons. These two groups of dimensionless ratios primarily concern relations among particles on a subatomic level of behavior.

Let us turn now from the subatomic level to the cosmological. In so doing, let us recall that an evolutionary cosmology uses the Hubble parameter, H (the expansion rate for the universe), to arrive at the order of magnitude for the present age of the universe (t_H). This is calculated to be of the order of 10^{10} years. It is important to remember that, from the perspective of an evolutionary cosmology, the age of the universe (t) is a variable: the age of the universe varies with time. Thus, at one time in the remote past—say, when very close to the big bang—the age of the universe was measurable in terms of seconds or minutes, whereas in the remote future the age of the universe will have a value greater than its present value of 10^{10} years. To repeat: the age of the universe, t, is a variable. Its present value, t_H, is the value of this variable at the present time.

Now for an intriguing discovery! Let us calculate the ratio between the *present* age of the universe ($t_H \sim 10^{10}$ years) and the quantity representing the proton Compton time, $t_N \sim 10^{-24}$ second. (The Compton time is the characteristic time for light to traverse a proton. It is derived from the quantity $h/m_p c^2$.) The ratio, so obtained, between the present age of the universe and the Compton proton time, t_H/t_N, has the value: $t_H/t_N \sim 10^{40}$. Furthermore, the inverse of the gravitational coupling constant, α_G^{-1}, that states the ratio between the electric and gravitational forces for subatomic particles, *also* has an order of magnitude of 10^{40}. In other words, both t_H/t_N and α_G^{-1} have the same order of magnitude, 10^{40}:

$$t_H/t_N \sim \alpha_G^{-1} \sim 10^{40}.$$

What is startling is this. In constructing the ratio that involves, as one of its components, a *cosmological* property—the present age of the universe—we obtain a large number of the *same* order of magnitude as that previously obtained when dealing only with constants relevant to the domain of *subatomic* particles. In other words, when one compares the present age of the universe, 10^{10}

years, with the time needed for light to traverse a subatomic particle such as a proton (the constant quantity 10^{-24} second: the proton Compton time), the ratio is the large number 10^{40}. And the
value of the inverse of the gravitational coupling constant, for subatomic phenomena, also yields the same extremely large number,
10^{40}.

This numerical coincidence is wholly unexpected from an
a priori point of view. The value for the age of the universe, t,
being a true variable and not a fundamental constant, according to
an evolutionary cosmology, could theoretically be any one of an
indefinitely large array of possibilities. The fact that its present age
($\sim 10^{10}$ years) is a value whose role, in the ratio constructed on its
basis, yields a quantity that matches the order of magnitude, 10^{40},
for numbers relevant to the subatomic domain, is altogether startling. Why, of all possible numbers that express the numerical ratios obtained from totally separate domains—the subatomic and
the cosmological—did they nevertheless turn out to be the same?
Does this coincidence have some explanation?

One of the first efforts at offering an explanation of the large-
number coincidence we have noted was made by the Princeton
physicist Robert Dicke.[8] It consisted in an appeal to what was later
to be named the "weak anthropic principle." Briefly, Dicke proposed that the existence of life on our planet is the link that explains the otherwise highly improbable presence of the same large
number 10^{40} in ratios obtained from the subatomic and cosmic domains. It is this *biological* fact that provides the clue to understanding the puzzling numerical coincidence in ratios connected with
these two distinct domains.

In order for life to have evolved on the Earth (a planet attached
to a normal main-sequence star such as our Sun), it is necessary
for certain *other* massive main-sequence stars to have *completed*
their own life cycle. The kind of star in question ends its career as
a supernova. At least one generation of such stars must have com-

[8] Dicke, "Dirac's Cosmology," 440-441.

pleted its life cycle and produced chemical elements (for example, carbon) necessary for life as we know it, *before* the Earth itself was formed. Since we are here, this shows that a supernova had already completed its life cycle. A supernova marks a gigantic explosion of energy that occurs on the average three times per galaxy every hundred years. During the very brief period of time that it occurs, it has a brightness so enormous that if it were at a distance from us of 4 light-years (the approximate distance of our nearest star, Alpha Centauri), it would appear as bright as the Sun. In the course of this outburst, a supernova spews out elements that could not have been produced by ordinary main-sequence stars such as our Sun. Unlike the Sun, this type of star—at progressively higher temperatures and densities—at first burned hydrogen into helium, then helium into carbon and oxygen, then carbon and oxygen into neon, magnesium, silicon, phosphorous, sulphur, and so on, up to nickel and iron, and finally the latter into elements heavier than iron. It was out of the scattered debris produced in the explosion of this star that "contaminating" materials, consisting of these heavier elements, were dispersed and introduced into other stellar-forming gaseous environments throughout the Galaxy. These scattered fragments became parts of the gaseous clouds out of which other stars were formed. It was from such a contaminated gaseous cloud that our own Sun was formed and, with it, our planet Earth, to serve as the habitat for life with its complex chemical structures.

A crucial point in all this is that the order of magnitude of the present age of the universe, 10^{10} years, could not be less than that of the shortest lived supernova if there is going to be a human being to take note of its age. If the present age of the universe had been shorter than that required for the completion of a supernova life cycle, life would not have had a chance to emerge and develop. The very fact of our existence points to a lower limit in the possible time slot in the development of the universe in which life might be found. On the other hand, the present Hubble age of the universe could not have been very much larger than the time needed for the lifetime of a typical main-sequence star and still support "observers." For the supply of hydrogen in a star, from which all other elements are synthesized, is finite, and the process of hydrogen consumption is irreversible. This means that there could only be a few generations of stars within a galaxy that can support life. Therefore, if the order of magnitude of the Hubble age of the universe were very much larger than the typical age of a main-sequence star, most stars—including those that have life-supporting planets attached to them—would have exhausted their fuel supply and died. The present age of the universe therefore has an order of magnitude that lies somewhere between the average age of a moderately large star such as a supernova, and, say, ten times that value. It is within this range of time values that life could exist. It is the fact that we find ourselves within this time slot that accounts for the fact that we are able to take note of the present age of the universe as having the Hubble value of 10^{10} years. The existence of life serves as a basis of selection from among all possible values for t (the variable in an evolutionary cosmology that encompasses all possible ages of the universe) and that "chooses" the particular value of the present age of 10^{10} years.

Since life does exist and requires that the present age of the universe is at least that of the same order of magnitude as that of a supernova, it follows that the ratios mentioned earlier have the approximate values they do. In our earlier discussion of the average lifetime of a moderately massive main-sequence star, t_*, we found that this lifetime has an order of magnitude that, when expressed in units of nuclear time (proton Compton time, t_N), is 10^{40}, and that this same order of magnitude also applies to the inverse of the gravitational fine structure constant:

$$t_* \sim \alpha_G^{-1} t_N \sim 10^{40} t_N.$$

It follows, therefore, that since the present age of the universe is of the same order as that of a supernova—$t_H \sim t_*$—that the same relations among orders of magnitude for the present age of the universe, when expressed in nuclear time scale, will be the same as that holding for the lifetime of t_*. This means that when we replace t_* with t_H, we obtain the *same* ratios and orders of magnitude—and this is in fact what we do find. This explains, therefore, the otherwise puzzling and improbable number coincidence of 10^{40} occurring both in ratios involving the present age of the universe and that holding for subatomic phenomena. What helps explain the coincidence and dissolve the mystery is the biological fact of the existence of life on Earth. The very existence of life, as manifested by the presence of physicists who can take note of the numerical coincidence under consideration, places restrictions on the value determined for the present age of the universe. That numerical value has biological constraints.

It is important not to be misled here. All that is being explained is a numerical coincidence—the occurrence of the same very large number 10^{40} in two different physical contexts (the cosmological and the subatomic). The existence of human observers serves as an explanation of this coincidence by giving a reason for the use of the present age of the universe in the numerical coincidence under consideration. There is nothing in the form of the anthropic principle used by Dicke that denies the numerous scientifically well-established facts showing that the existence of life has physical, chemical, and other causal conditions. Indeed, the use of the anthropic principle, in the form used by Dicke, supports and illustrates this very point. It shows that the occurrence of a supernova provides some of the necessary causally linked chemical conditions for the existence of life. The existence of life does not causally explain the present age of the universe, nor of course does it explain the existence of the universe. On the contrary, it is the concatenations of various physical and other conditions in the universe that causally explain the emergence of life. This point is in no way challenged or overthrown by Dicke's argument. The introduction of the fact of the existence of human beings into the argument only serves as the biological starting point in a series of logical links that connect the present age of the universe with the lifetime of a supernova, and—through the latter—a way of explaining a numerical coincidence. Neither the existence of the universe nor, indeed, the values for the fundamental physical constants or their derivations are thereby explained. In the present use of the (weak) anthropic principle, they are taken as given, as unexplained. It is not an argument for believing in some form of teleological design in the universe. Its own sole purpose is to explain the presence of a certain puzzling numerical coincidence. It has no metaphysical axe to grind and, if read that way, would go beyond Dicke's original argument.

Other physicists, however, believe one can make use of a type of anthropic principle to make a stronger claim than the one so far examined. The basic idea of the anthropic principle, in any of its versions, is that our human existence imposes a *selection effect* on what we could expect to observe with respect to the universe. In the version we have been examining (the weak anthropic principle), an application of this principle yields an explanation for a puzzling numerical coincidence. By showing that our human existence, as a form of life, is linked with the completed lifetime of a main-sequence star, and that this stretch of time is of the same order of magnitude as that of the present age of the universe, one accounts for the selection of the present age of the universe in constructing a ratio whose order of magnitude (10^{40}) is similar to that obtained for numerical ratios based on fundamental physical constants relating to subatomic phenomena. The selection effect resulting from the presence of human observers is able to account for a particular property of the universe—its present age—in establishing the puzzling numerical coincidence. This value for the present age, t_H, is one out of many possible values encompassed by the variable t—one of an indefinitely large array of ages that includes those of the past and the future.

One way of differentiating the strong anthropic principle from the weak anthropic principle is that whereas the latter makes reference to the particular value of a variable—the present age of the universe—the strong anthropic principle does not fall back on the use of the present age of the universe, as a particular value for a variable. The strong anthropic principle deals exclusively with *fundamental constants*. It seeks to show that the presence of life in the Universe[9] is linked, in an explanatory way, with these con-

---

[9] I use the capitalized expression "Universe," following Carter, who (as we shall

stants. It seeks to explain the constants themselves by reference to the presence of life in the Universe. Let us consider Carter's way of describing this principle.[10] He writes:

> ". . . *the 'strong' anthropic principle* [states] that the Universe (and hence the fundamental parameters on which it depends) must be such as to admit the creation of observers within it at some stage. To paraphrase Descartes, 'cogito ergo mundus talis est'."[11] (In his own summary of various "anthropic definitions," J. D. Barrow formulates the strong anthropic principle he attributes to Carter as follows: "*The Universe must contain life*. An equivalent statement would be that the constants and laws of Nature must be such that life can exist."[12]

If we take the foregoing brief statement by Carter as our point of departure, it is clear that a crucial point that calls for analysis is how we are to understand the term "must." What does it mean to say that human observers (or life) *must* occur? Is the use of the term "must," in this context, another declaration of acceptance of the Design Argument as employed in various forms of theistic philosophy? Does it mean that we can explain both the existence of the Universe and of human life by saying God's plan requires that hu-

---

see), in his version of the strong anthropic principle, makes use of the notion of an "ensemble of worlds" or "universes." On this approach, and in this terminology, the Universe is to be distinguished from other universes.

[10] In what follows, I shall expound Carter's views in his own realistic terminology, without undertaking to reinterpret what he has to say in terminology that I consider more philosophically appropriate, namely, that of a pragmatist philosophy, as earlier sketched in this book. I do so because I am concerned to extract from Carter's own account the central point he makes in connection with the strong anthropic principle, namely, that the existence of intelligent life is a privileged occurrence. This conclusion, and the evidence he offers to support it (based on the strong anthropic principle), is one that might, perhaps, with some effort, be restated and incorporated in the pragmatist approach to cosmology, and the way it construes the several distinctions among the observable universe, the intelligible universe, and the known universe. I do not, however, undertake to attempt this translation on the present occasion.

[11] Carter, "Large Number Coincidences," 294.

[12] Barrow, "Anthropic Definitions," 149.

man beings be brought into existence? One interpretation of Carter's position might take the "must" as expressing the conviction that the Universe is *designed* to include life. We could fall back on religious faith to explain the fact that the physical values for the constants, on which life depends, exist because God, as the infinitely powerful, benevolent, omniscient, and creative being, designfully and deliberately chose this world to be the way it is, in preference to other possibilities, so that human beings may be part of it. One form of such traditional Design Arguments is to be found in Leibniz's philosophy. According to his analysis, the actual, created Universe is one among various possible universes that God might have created. In creating our actual Universe, and in including human beings and other living creatures in it, God chose the universe with the greatest possible perfection—for example, the greatest amount of possible good in it and the least amount of evil.

Although some commentators have interpreted Carter's statement of the strong anthropic principle as pointing in this direction, it is a mistake to do so. Neither the Leibnizian nor any other form of Design Argument is present (or even hinted at) in Carter's statement: in it, no reference is made to a transcendent Designing Intelligence. Instead, the argument purports to be altogether scientific in character. There is another, preferable way to interpret the use of the word "must." In Carter's statement, the "must" links the presence of human beings with certain fundamental physical constants. By virtue of the interrelations among its various constants, the Universe is so finely tuned that any change in one constant would significantly bear upon its relations to the others and would thereby affect the character of the structures and processes dependent on their joint, cooperative functioning. In particular, if the constants and their relations had been different, life as we know it would not have emerged. Human beings, who are able to observe and come to understand the Universe, would not have been among its contents and products. The very existence in the Universe of human beings thus provides a clear basis for fixing on a particular set of values for certain fundamental physical quantities.

The existence of human beings enables the prediction to be made of what the values of certain constants in the Universe *must* be. The same logic that leads to this prediction also makes possible an explanation. Carter explains some features of the world, such as that it has a weak gravitational coupling constant, from the fact that human beings exist.

It thus needs to be made clear of *what* an explanation is being offered. The way Carter uses the strong anthropic principle, it is *not at all as a basis for explaining the existence of human beings.* It is the existence of human beings that, in his sense, "explains" *the physical constants* in question. One starts from the existence of intelligent observers and knowers; *their* existence is a selection factor that "chooses" certain combinations of values for the fundamental physical constants and excludes others. In other words, Carter is saying: The Universe "must" contain life *if* it is to be cognizable, that is, if it is to be observed and known. But only if the values for the fundamental physical constants are within a certain limited range will it be possible for life to exist. The Universe we inhabit does have fundamental constants in this range. As evidence for this, there is the fact that we exist as observers. The existence of intelligent life thereby explains, that is, allows, the inference to be made *from* the existence of human beings *to* the fact that such and such values for the fundamental constants are found in the Universe.

A further way in which the strong anthropic principle differs from the weak anthropic principle is that whereas the latter deals exclusively with the actual universe and its possible age values, the strong anthropic principle introduces the notion of an ensemble of worlds or universes of which our Universe is but one member.

Carter writes:

> The existence of any organism describable as an observer will only be possible for certain restricted combinations of the parameters, which distinguish within the world-ensemble an exceptional *cognizable* subset. A prediction based on the strong anthropic principle may be regarded as a demonstra-

tion that the feature under consideration is common to all members of the cognizable subset. Subject to the further condition that it is possible to define some sort of fundamental a priori probability measure on the ensemble, it would be possible to make an even more general kind of prediction based on the demonstration that a feature under consideration occurred in "most" members of the cognizable subset.[13]

In the foregoing, Carter asks us to conceive of an ensemble of universes, all of which are real or actual, but which differ from one another in terms of the various parameters defining fundamental physical constants. In any one universe of the ensemble, a fundamental constant would have a particular value that would differ from the value that parameter has in some other universe. For example, the gravitational coupling constant has a very small value in our Universe. In other universes, however, the coupling constant can take on quite different values ranging from the very weak to the very strong—although in each universe the value would be a particular constant for that universe; and so on—for each of the fundamental physical coupling constants. The combination of constants in any particular universe would be different from that to be found in other member universes of the ensemble. Carter maintains, however, that of all these possible, alternative universes only a subset, including our own Universe, is cognizable. Only those universes in which the combination of fundamental constants that turn out to be life-supporting can contain intelligent observers. Not every conceivable or possible universe allows for the presence of observers in it, since certain combinations of the parameters are incompatible with the existence of observers.[14] If one

[13] Carter, "Large Number Coincidences," 296.

[14] But can we say, for Carter, that the other universes can be known, in any way, by ourselves—living in our own Universe? It is not clear what Carter's answer to this question might be. Carter writes: "Although the idea that there may exist many universes, *of which only one can be known to us* [my italics] may at first sight seem philosophically undesirable, it does not really go very much further than the Everett doctrine (see B. S. De Witt: 1967, *Phys. Rev.* 160, 113) to which one is virtually forced by the internal logic of quantum theory. According to the Everett doc-

accepts this version of the strong anthropic principle, then we should need to say that the existence of our Universe, possessed of the requisite combination of fundamental physical constants supportive of life, makes a very special matter of human existence, apart from every other consideration.

In summary, then, it follows from both the weak and the strong versions of the anthropic principle (the latter with or without the appeal to the doctrine of an ensemble of worlds) that the presence of life—and of human life in particular—is the outcome of such a unique concatenation of physical and cosmic conditions that one can properly describe the status of life as privileged, even though it is not central in the way this was taken in pre-Copernican times. Even if one surrenders the traditional belief that life occupies a uniquely central spatial position in the universe, or a dominant role within a divinely appointed hierarchical order of creatures, this cannot prevent reinstating an appreciation that the existence

---

trine the Universe, or more precisely the state vector of the Universe, has many branches of which only one can be known to any well defined observer (although all are equally 'real'). This doctrine would fit very naturally with the world ensemble philosophy that I have tried to describe." (See Carter, "Large Number Coincidences," 298.)

Does the existence of any universe depend exclusively on its cognizability by intelligent beings existing *within* the universe in question? Are other universes real, even if not life-supporting, yet cognizable, that is, known on the grounds of theoretical inference, by intelligent beings like ourselves inhabiting a real life-supporting universe such as our own? The questions surfacing here are parallel to those found in connection with making sense of Everett's (highly controversial) "many-worlds" interpretation of particle behavior in quantum physics, in its efforts to interpret the significance of probability wave amplitudes in that branch of physics. (See B. S. De Witt and N. Graham, eds., *The Many-Worlds Interpretation of Quantum Mechanics* (Princeton, N.J.: Princeton University Press, 1973); P. Davies, *Other Worlds* (New York: Simon and Schuster, 1980); Gale, "The Anthropic Principle," 160ff.; Leslie, "Anthropic Principle, World Ensemble, Design," 141-151.)

Other questions with respect to the doctrine of an ensemble of worlds, whose answers are left unclear, include: how "large" the ensemble is; how "small" the subset is that allows for the presence of observers in each member of the subset; how the "probability" of the occurrence of a cognizable subset can be estimated.

of life, when regarded from the perspective of purely physical and cosmic considerations, marks a very special "gift."

THE SEARCH FOR MEANING

How do the foregoing results—of recent scientific cosmology in its picture of the evolving universe, the contributions of the anthropic principle, and my own ventures in assessing the epistemological and metaphysical implications of these scientific materials—bear on one's philosophy of life, on a judgment of the place of human existence in the universe? One way of classifying this kind of question is that it has to do with the meaning of life.

There are some who would dismiss this question as vacuous and spurious—to be dissolved rather than answered. To be sure, this type of question is sometimes stated in a diffuse and unfocused way. For example, one might ask: "What is the point of it all?" "What's life all about, anyway?" And so on. Yet however ambiguous in its own possible meanings is the use of the term "meaning" in the phrase "the meaning of life," and however loose and vague the statement of the question sometimes is, it nevertheless expresses a genuine human need, one that deserves serious analysis and positive satisfaction, not a contemptuous dismissal.

Sometimes the occasion for posing this type of question may arise during a major crisis in the life of a person. In this case, it voices an acute feeling of bewilderment and despair. Customary supports, habitual patterns of activity, and hopeful projects founder, losing their appeal and stabilizing effect. A classic example of this type of stimulus—conveyed with great power, honesty, and personal intensity—is to be found in a well-known passage of Leo Tolstoy's *My Confession*. He writes:

> Five years ago, something very strange began to happen with me; I was overcome by minutes at first of perplexity and then an arrest of life, as though I did not know how to live or what to do, and I lost myself and was dejected. But that passed and I continued to live as before. Then those moments of per-

plexity were repeated oftener and oftener, and always in one and the same form. These arrests of life found their expression in ever the same question: "Why? Well, and then?"

At first I thought that those were simply aimless, inappropriate questions. It seemed to me that that was all well known and that if I wanted to busy myself with their solution, it would not cost me much labour,—that now I had no time to attend to them, but that if I wanted to I should find the proper answers. But the questions began to repeat themselves oftener and oftener, answers were demanded more and more persistently, and like dots that fall on the same spot, these questions, without any answers, thickened into one black blotch. . . .

I felt that what I was standing on had given way, that I had no foundation to stand on, that that which I lived by no longer existed, and that I had nothing to live by. . . .

"Well, I know," I said to myself, "all which science wants so persistently to know, but there is no answer to the question about the meaning of life."[15]

According to some, a question of the kind Tolstoy raises is to be taken seriously, but only at bottom as a psychological symptom. It reveals a breakdown in mental health. The voicing of the question (aloud or to oneself) constitutes a cry of the psyche, not a genuine puzzlement of the mind. It is a symptom of emotional disturbance, a form in which anxiety manifests itself. Accordingly, it is the person that needs to be treated, rather than the question answered head-on. The posing of the question calls for a psychotherapeutic response, not a direct answer. What needs to be found is a program of alterations in behavior and modifications in emotional attitudes. Together, these might have the effect of lifting the mood of despair, uncertainty, and anxiety. If successful, these changes would allow the individual to go on in a more stable, reassured, and normal way. As he tells us in the rest of his *My Confession*, Tolstoy eventually found his own cure. For him, it

[15] From Leo Tolstoy, *My Confession*, trans. Leo Weiner (London: J. M. Dent and Sons, 1905), *passim*.

consisted in an ardent and renewed declaration of faith in, and practice of, the traditional message of a Christian way of life. That way of life, Tolstoy was convinced, is already widely exemplified in the lives of simple peasant folk, not in the lives of the aristocracy to which he himself belonged.

However, we need not assume that a breakdown in a person's mental or emotional life, of the sort Tolstoy experienced, is the only occasion for raising the question of the meaning of life. For that question can arise in a less dramatic or psychologically threatening form for all mature, healthy human beings. Even in its unfocused form, the question simply voices a normal human need to have a philosophy of life. When acquired, such a philosophy provides a framework of basic principles that helps guide a person's reactions to the crises and opportunities of life, to the universal facts of human existence—being born and dying, being a member of society, being part of a wider universe. To have a set of basic guiding principles, whether accepted from some external source or worked out for oneself, is an inescapable requirement for a human being. To take seriously this requirement—to take the question as calling for an answer, and not simply a response in the form of a course of psychotherapy or of redirected behavior—is a legitimate and important challenge that the sheer fact of being alive puts to philosophy or any other intellectual resource one hopes will be of possible help. Instead of being dismissed or sublimated by one or another techniques, the question needs to be directly confronted, reformulated, and refined. Accordingly, if pressed to clarify what they intend by asking the question about the meaning of life, many persons would say that they are looking for answers to a fundamental series of "Why" questions: Why does the universe exist at all? Why do human beings exist? Why do I exist—what value or purpose is there to my own life?

By taking the results of recent cosmology as a point of departure, is there anything that can be said in response to this series of Why questions? How do these results bear on the ever-present challenge to have a philosophy of life that represents our best efforts at coming to terms with the most fundamental aspects of the human situation? As beings conscious of our natural origins and our existential limitations, do these findings oblige us to alter our philosophy of human existence, or do they simply offer the occasion for reenforcing conclusions we may have already arrived at prior to, and independently of, these considerations?

Surely one crucial aspect of the results of recent cosmology that calls for thoughtful consideration is the widely accepted belief that the known universe had a beginning a finite time ago and will suffer its own death. Regardless of any uncertainties and differences in depth of understanding that current cosmology has of these matters, any philosophy of life that is sensitive to the best available scientific theories will start from these results, and will try to determine their implications for our view of the human situation. We cannot avoid being deeply affected by how we react to these twin features of the temporal structure of the universe. For example, must we surrender all notions of cosmic design? If so, does this render life absurd and the search for meaning in life itself futile and misguided? In formulating our reaction, we must be prepared to deal with three principal themes: (1) what to make of the use of the concepts of creation and the beginning of the universe; (2) what to make of current views about the end or death of the universe; (3) how answers to the foregoing questions affect our conception of the meaning of life.

In attempting to reply to the first of the above questions, I will begin by commenting on the uses of the term "creation." For present purposes, I propose to draw a twofold distinction. In what we may think of as a broad use of this term, it has to do with all the varied attempts to *explain* the very existence of the world. To "explain," here, means to give a reason—in one or another sense of "reason"—why the universe exists. A creation account (whether classified as a myth, scientific theory, theological doctrine, or metaphysical speculation) offers such an explanation. The term "creation account" may be used as a classificatory placeholder for all such attempts. (Incidentally, under this broad use of the term "creation," it is not necessary to suppose that every creation account must take the form of asserting that the creation of the world occurred a finite time ago.)

In addition to the foregoing broad use of the term "creation," we may identify a narrower use, one that is far more commonplace, especially in those cultures or historical epochs like our own, where there is a dominant world view that has at its core a belief in a personal God as Creator of the World. Such a theistic view uses the notion of creation to mark the relation between God and the world. The varied accounts of creation in Judaism, Christianity, and Islam take their point of departure from the Book of Genesis. They build upon, and add to, this account, according to the distinctive doctrinal commitments of a particular religious tradition or the degree of intellectual sophistication involved in their articulation. Characteristic of this narrower, theistic use of the term (but by no means invariant) is the view that the act of Divine Creation took place "in the beginning"—a finite time ago. Typical of the latter interpretation (that of Thomas Aquinas is a prominent example) is the view that belief in that event must ultimately rest on faith, since attempts to support this belief by rational argument must ultimately fall short of complete adequacy.

With the foregoing distinctions in mind, we must consider our response to the question whether a study of the fruits of recent scientific cosmology obliges us to make use of the concept of creation, in some form, in articulating a world view that seeks guidance from the best-available results of science.

First, let us ask whether, with the narrower use of the term "creation" in mind, we should not give it a central place in our philosophy, given the strong emphasis on the notion of a beginning of the universe in recent evolutionary cosmology. In recognizing a beginning to the universe a finite time ago, is not science reaffirming a truth proclaimed by religion long ago? Is not the term "beginning" another way of saying "creation"? Though coming from different starting points and employing different methodologies, are we not witnessing a convergence and rapprochement between science and religion on a crucial item in our world view? Our previous discussions have sought to provide the philosophic bases for saying that to think along these lines would be a serious mistake. For what scientific cosmology offers is no updated version of a Biblical theory of creation. Science may weave its own myths, but the big bang model, in any of its sophisticated versions, does not have a conceptual pattern whose content and evidential support has any link or overlap with the Biblical account. When currently favored models of the universe talk about the "beginning" of the universe, this expression is to be understood in the light of grammatical rules that have an altogether different configuration from those associated with the forms of life and systems of thought that nurtured traditional religious beliefs. There is no warrant for interpreting the concept of a beginning of the universe, in currently favored cosmological models, as referring to a unique event in the past that marked the coming-into-existence of the universe by a deliberate act of creation performed by a designful Divine Intelligence.

As it appears in current cosmological models, the notion of a beginning of the universe simply marks a conceptual boundary at which a particular model of the evolutionary development of the universe breaks down and is no longer usable. It does not signify that, in the continuing course of scientific theory construction, it will be impossible to find a model (or class of models) that will be able to overcome the conceptual bounds labeled "the beginning of the universe" in these other, more restricted accounts. Perhaps a new theory of "time" will be forthcoming, or perhaps a theory dispensing altogether with the relativistic conception of space-time, or, for that matter, dispensing even with an appeal to a quantum theory of time. If forthcoming, such theories might succeed in pushing back the conceptual horizons now labeled "the beginning of the universe," although, in doing so, new frontiers of understanding will no doubt come into view. In any case, whether one remains at the bounds of current horizons, by using the currently specified marks for the beginning of the universe, or pushes back the horizon to a new frontier, there is nothing in the vocabulary of physics that makes use of the notion of the creation of the universe as a purposeful, wholly mysterious act by a Divine Agent, or points to the need to invoke—or link up with—the system of thought that makes use of the concept of Divine Creation. If physics were to use such a concept, it would no longer provide a scheme of intelligibility for describing and explaining observational data and natural phenomena by relying on normal standards of empirical confirmability, mathematical cogency, or logical coherence with empirically established laws.

This, however, is not all that needs to be said. For, in exploring beyond the limits of a too-simple big bang theory, is there not the opportunity—indeed, the need—for using the concept of creation in the broader sense of this term? We must consider, for example, those directions of speculation in recent cosmology that have sought to penetrate behind the big bang in trying to understand the antecedent sources and conditions of the known universe. In earlier sections of this book, we canvassed some of these recent speculations. They include, for example, use of the notions of a primordial vacuum and superspace. In expounding their theories along these lines, cosmologists frequently employ such expressions as "chaos," "chance," "probability," "unpredictable fluctuations," "the nothing out of which space-time itself arose," and so on. Is it not the case that in these speculative hypotheses we find a possible context for the use of the term "creation" in its broad sense?

If we bring to bear the philosophical distinctions we worked out in earlier sections of this book, let us consider the way in which, in general, we might construe these or other examples of what we could take to be a search for a creation account in scientific cosmology. In the first place, it would be best to describe it as a search for an explanation of the existence of the *known universe*. For cosmology, this amounts to looking for ways of overcoming the conceptual bounds of a particular model, widely accepted at a given stage of inquiry. Since even such a model leaves various questions unanswered, the search for an explanation of the existence of the known universe amounts to looking for a more inclusive and satisfactory cosmological model. If found and adopted, this new model would not only answer questions left unanswered by the discarded model, but in offering a new and enlarged characterization of the universe as a whole, it might, in this sense, succeed in explaining the existence of the universe as previously defined and understood. If we think of the matter of giving a creation account in these terms, and if, furthermore, we accept the analysis given earlier of the conceptually bound character of *any* cosmological model of a scientific sort, it follows that any creation account, accepted by science, is a provisional and open-ended affair. No explanation of the existence of the known universe can ever be anything but a stage in an unending search for more and more adequate explanations of the known universe, however the content and structure of the latter is conceived at a particular stage of cosmological inquiry. If a creation account is sought in any stronger sense than this—as explaining the existence of the known universe in a final and unrevisable way, and as thereby terminating all inquiry—then, of course, no such creation account can ever be furnished by scientific cosmology. Putting the matter negatively, if to look for a creation account amounts to looking for a final explanation of the existence of the universe "as such" or in some loose and generalized sense, then such a question needs to be dissolved and repudiated rather than taken as stimulating a search for an acceptable answer. Scientific cosmology could never find, nor pretend to offer, an answer to such a question.

One final point. Insofar as we recognize the dimension of existence I have labeled "Boundless Existence," as transcendent of all conceptual characterization, it would follow that all attempts to build a bridge, via some conceptual scheme, between Boundless Existence and the known universe (as existent) must be futile. And this would include all attempts to explain the existence of the known universe, as an existent, by deriving it somehow—causally, deductively, teleologically, or in any other way—from Boundless Existence. If to give a creation account is to undertake to give an explanation of the existence of the known universe by linking it in one or another way with Boundless Existence, then the quest for such an explanation must also be dissolved. It is unanswerable by any conceptual means. No such putative account can sustain a meaningful conceptual explanation. Not only, of course, can science not yield such a sought-for explanation (it is totally beyond the scope of its possible competency)—but an ontology that appeals to a nonconceptual awareness of Boundless Existence cannot do so either.

In undertaking to draw the implications of the results of recent cosmology for our view of the place of human existence in the entire scheme of things, I have chosen to give special attention to the way in which evolutionary models of the universe normally include claims about the origin and death of the universe. For if these cosmic limits, at either end, are the most inclusive temporal bounds within which all existent parts of the universe are themselves located, they must be taken into account in examining, in particular, the status of human life in the cosmos and the search for its meaning.

In addition, then, to the way in which the question of cosmic beginnings is relevant to the search for meaning in life, the prediction that the universe itself will come to an end will also be of fundamental importance. It should be said at once, of course, that any discussion of the end of the universe is bound to be highly speculative (even more so than discussions oriented toward the creation of the universe), since the entire project of forecasting the long-range future of the universe is far less adequately supported by reliable evidence than inferences to its past. Put in terms of numbers alone (let alone with respect to the degree of comprehension of the physics involved), although there is general agreement that the origin of the universe, in one sense, took place some fifteen billion years ago—a number whose order of magnitude is represented by 1 followed by 10 zeros—recent predictions of the number of years into the future when the death of the universe will occur (in one of its possible forms) involve a number whose order of magnitude consists of 1 followed by 100 or more zeros! In judging the prospects for, and character of, life during such extended and remote time frames, terms like "optimism" or "pessimism" clearly lose their ordinary grounds of applicability and warrant.

In any case, there are two aspects of this topic that call for special consideration. First—quite apart from the question of meaning in life—what interpretation shall we give to discussions about the "end" or "death" of the universe? Secondly, if we accept the belief that the universe will come to an end, does this enforce the conclusion that the very existence of human life and all its accomplishments—for as long as it did endure on a collective or personal level—are reduced to meaninglessness and absurdity?

With respect to forecasting the end of the universe, we have seen that, at the present stage of inquiry, no clear decision among the experts has been reached as to what form that end will take. On the basis of theory, most cosmologists are in agreement that the actual mass-energy density of the universe is close to the critical density. However, in the absence of adequate empirical data concerning the exact amount of the actual density, it cannot be said at the present time whether the universe will eventually contract to a singularity (and so manifest a closed spatial geometry), or, on the contrary, will continue to expand in an infinite future (and so manifest an open geometry that is either flat or hyperbolic).

To speak of the "end" or "death" of the universe takes on different meanings, accordingly, and depends on which type of future is envisaged. If the end will come in the form of a singularity of gravitational collapse, it will have a different character from an end that comes by an indefinitely prolonged gradual disintegration of all complex material structures into increasingly separated elementary particles in an ever-expanding space. If the space of the universe is positively curved and therefore closed, the future occurrence of a singularity or extremely dense concentration of mass-energy will mark the stage that could be said to constitute the "death" of the universe. If, on the other hand—as many cosmologists are inclined to believe at the present time—the future course of the evolution of the universe is associated with zero spatial curvature, then the end of the universe will be identifiable with the phase in the remote future when all baryons will have decayed and all galactic-size black holes will have evaporated. While the universe will still contain whatever elementary particles or forms of energy have survived, no composite material structures (including all forms of life) will be found among its contents at this stage.

Whether the universe will have recollapsed to a singularity, or will have taken the form of an extremely dilute and decomposed mass-energy distribution, the end of the universe will not consist in a transition to absolute nothing. However characterized in physical terms, the event of cosmic death identifies a conceptual horizon of present cosmic understanding. It is only by contrast with earlier stages in which various types of entities had existed that one might say "nothing exists any more"—that the universe will have met its "death." To say that at its death the universe will be "followed by absolute nothing" not only lacks any clear sense, but would close off any possibility of scientific advance; hence it is not consistent with ongoing efforts of science to overcome present horizons of intelligibility.

Resignation to the inevitability of the death and permanent extinction of the individual self has always been a cornerstone for any naturalistic philosophy that bears on personal life. What is new and challenging in recent cosmology, in predicting the death of the universe, is that this entails the eventual extinction—along with everything else of a composite material sort—of mankind itself or of any other intelligent forms of life that may exist now or in the future, not only in other parts of our Galaxy but anywhere else in the vast reaches of the universe.

Some find it difficult to reconcile themselves to this inference and have speculated about ways in which some future, highly sophisticated, and technologically well-equipped civilization might find ways of coping with the overhanging threat and closer approach of final doom. A prominent spokesman for this point of view is Freeman Dyson.[16] He admits that if, indeed, the universe is closed and fated to recontract into a state of gravitational collapse, then there is virtually no chance that mankind can escape "being fried." He pins his hopes, instead, on the alternative pos-

[16] Freeman Dyson, "Time Without End: Physics and Biology in an Open Universe," *Rev. of Modern Physics* 51 (1979), 447-460.

sibility that we live in an open universe. He believes this option gives greater scope for envisioning a future in which intelligent beings might devise ways of transforming and adjusting themselves to live in the endlessly expanding universe of lower temperatures and reduced energy levels. One basis for taking his broadly "optimistic" view, according to Dyson, is to assume that current theoretical predictions of the phenomenon of proton decay will not be confirmed in ongoing experimental investigations. "The most serious uncertainty affecting the ultimate fate of the universe is the question whether the proton is absolutely stable against decay into lighter particles. If the proton is unstable, all matter is transitory and must dissolve into radiation. . . . On grounds of simplicity, I disregard these possibilities and suppose the proton to be absolutely stable."[17] Turning to biological considerations, Dyson points out, furthermore, that there is no necessary connection between the emergence of life or consciousness and their presence in organisms composed of flesh and blood—in creatures with a particular molecular structure. It is possible to conceive, in very general and highly speculative terms, of creatures possessed of life and consciousness embodied in altogether different material or energetic structures from those known at present, and therefore able to function under radically different conditions of much-lowered temperature and energy from those that prevail in life-supporting habitats we are now familiar with. For Dyson, it is sufficient to allow such possibilities in order to think of our universe as one containing "life surviving forever and making itself known to its neighbors across unimaginable gulfs of space and time."[18]

However, if the widely accepted predictions of current cosmology about the end of the universe are substantially true and will be sustained by further inquiry, then any expressions of hope for the future of intelligent life, of the sort Dyson voices, must be severely circumscribed. Of course, any dogmatism here about which predictions to rely on—Dyson's or those of others—is clearly out of

[17] Ibid., 450.
[18] Ibid., 459.

the question. To the bystander, if not to the active scientific investigator, suspension of judgment on these factual questions is the only reasonable stance.

In assessing the empirical data, theories, and predictions of recent cosmology, another, contrasted point of view to that of Dyson is expressed by Steven Weinberg. Taking his point of departure from the widely accepted belief that life in any form is fated to disappear in the future development of the universe, Weinberg voices his conclusions about what this suggests with respect to the question of the meaning of life. In this, he probably speaks for many in the following comments he makes at the end of his book *The First Three Minutes*:

> It is almost irresistible for humans to believe that we have some special relation to the universe, that human life is not just a more-or-less farcical outcome of a chain of accidents reaching back to the first three minutes, but that we were somehow built in from the beginning. . . . It is even harder to realize that this present universe has evolved from an unspeakably unfamiliar early condition, and faces a future extinction of endless cold or intolerable heat. The more the universe seems comprehensible, the more it also seems pointless.
>
> But if there is no solace in the fruits of our research, there is at least some consolation in the research itself. Men and women are not content to comfort themselves with tales of gods and giants, or to confine their thoughts to the daily affairs of life; they also build telescopes and satellites and accelerators, and sit at their desks for endless hours working out the meaning of the data they gather. The effort to understand the universe is one of the very few things that lifts human life a little above the level of farce, and gives it some of the grace of tragedy.[19]

[19] Steven Weinberg, *The First Three Minutes* (New York: Basic Books, 1977), 154-155.

We must ask: If the universe will come to an end, and with it all forms of conscious and intelligent life, does it follow that the universe is pointless, that human life has a predominantly farcical character, and that only the effort to understand the universe lifts human life a little above the level of farce?

To say something is "pointless"—whether the universe or human life—however, is another way of saying it is "without meaning." Since the term "meaning," in one of its meanings, signifies "purpose" or "value," to say the universe or human life is pointless is equivalent to saying it is without purpose and therefore valueless. The belief that because the universe will come to an end it is pointless, conveys a sense of disillusionment. Such a sense of disillusionment can occur only, however, if one is already committed to the truth of at least two distinguishable, though related, beliefs. The first is that there is an overall purpose to the existence of the universe, a purpose embodied in its structure and contents. The second is that the existence of human life within the universe occupies a designed position and role. Insofar as one accepts the foregoing beliefs, it would follow that if they were to be surrendered, the existence of the universe and of human life are "pointless." But what reason do we have to accept this twofold conjunction of presuppositions? Surely nothing in the pursuit of cosmology as a science, or the results it has achieved thus far, requires acceptance of either one of these beliefs. If built into a world view, these beliefs do not have their source in any results of scientific cosmology.

Their source is from the side of mythology, traditional theistic religion, various metaphysical schemes, and, in general, the human propensity to find meaning (purpose, value) in its existence, by looking for support and guidance beyond its own resources to that which is trans-human. Thus, according to traditional theistic world pictures in the West, questions about the status of human existence in the universe and the meaning of life are interrelated. They are derived from a conception of order in the world that is at bottom teleological. In understanding that order, it is necessary to think of it as a network of means and ends, of a hierarchical arrangement of parts fitting together to give meaning or value to the whole as well as to the parts. The notion of place is related to the kind of contribution made to the fulfillment of ends. Status or role carries with it a sense of relative rank and importance. Together, the ideas of place, status, and role determine the meaning of a creature's life in the wider scheme of things. On a theistic approach, the meaning of life is to be found in fulfilling God's purposes, in being guided by a faith in God's infinite goodness, mercy, love, and justice, and in taking these as supreme models for our own behavior. For traditional religious cosmogony, the universe was created in order that man, as part and pinnacle of creation, should be able to fulfill God's purposes. Man was brought into the world so that he may achieve the benefits and goods of life, as planned by God—that he may work out his salvation.

All that we have seen thus far of the approach and results of recent scientific cosmology have been entirely devoid of any such teleological notions. However much these teleological ideas may have been at the center of traditional religious cosmogonies, they are totally irrelevant to understanding the pictures of the universe drawn in modern cosmology.

However, if we surrender belief in a divinely grounded cosmic purpose that orders all things and in human existence, in particular, should we not agree with Weinberg that life becomes absurd? Or, is it possible that life might be provided with meaning by looking in other directions? For example, can meaning be found in ways supplied by man, on the basis of his own resources and accomplishments, rather than by conforming to a trans-humanly imposed design? In what follows, I shall defend one type of affirmative answer to these questions, and maintain that surrender of a belief in cosmic purpose does not require abandoning the project of finding an adequate replacement. Life can have "a point" even if the universe itself will suffer its own "death."

But what "point"? In sketching an answer, we can obtain important guidance from thinkers such as Democritus, Aristotle, and Spinoza in earlier epochs, and from George Santayana's *Life of Reason* and the writings of John Dewey in our own day. Despite important internal differences among these spokesmen, there is a broad consensus on certain fundamental principles. They would agree that the origins and conditions of human life are to be understood by relying on the best available theories and empirically established laws of science. Furthermore, although the existence of life as a biological phenomenon (as collectively realized in the human species or in the career of a single individual) is not the outcome of any form of cosmic purpose, and is, instead, entirely the result of the operation of natural causes, this does not preclude the possibility, in building on these natural origins and conditions, for a person's life to find intrinsic satisfactions and rewards that rescue it from meaninglessness and absurdity. It is by exercising man's creative imagination, aesthetic sensibilities, scientific understanding, practical intelligence, and the capacity for refined feelings of love for one's fellow creatures, that rewarding nodes of life experience can be realized. To the degree and amount in which these prevail and characterize the life of an individual between the limits of his birth and death, that life is meaningful and self-justifying. From this perspective, a life would indeed be absurd to the extent that it largely failed to achieve a modicum of such satisfactions of human potentialities or fulfillment of intrinsically worthwhile goals. According to this way of looking at things, life is not absurd because of the minuscule size of the human being or that of the Earth on which man lives as compared with the spatial vastness of the astronomical universe, because of the brief temporal span of a single life, or because of the inevitable termination in death of every life. For it is not a matter of the sheer bulk or size of the human organism, the durational span, or the temporal ending of life that makes life irrational. Life would not necessarily be more rational and meaningful merely by having an increase in size (spatial volume) or to have a limitless increase in its duration.

It is true that the elements of rationality or meaningful activity that can be realized in life rest on arbitrary, contingent, natural (physico-chemical, biological, historical, social, psychological) conditions. However, the success of reason and human intelligence consists precisely in starting with arbitrarily given, inherited, natural conditions and materials, and in being able to transform them into sources of self-justifying satisfaction. Life is not absurd because it contains arbitrary conditions and limitations. Achieving some modicum of happiness is not possible without arbitrary bases. To say there is a wedge between justification and realization that skepticism can always drive because all justifications are themselves grounded in what is arbitrary and contingent is to misread the situation of man in the world, a misreading that a sound philosophy would avoid.

Boundless Existence and the known universe are two dimensions of reality. As part of the universe, a human being undergoes various experiences in interaction with other existents. As a result of being exposed to existents, including the universe as the maximally comprehensive known existent, a person may be stimulated to become aware, through such exposure, of Boundless Existence itself. However, Boundless Existence is not identical with any existent. Boundless Existence is not an object; it is not an entity; it is not an existent. Nor is it the known universe—a whole of parts with a spatial, temporal, and compositional structure. The awareness of Boundless Existence is not anything to which scientific cosmology, as a search for intelligibility, need ever appeal. Boundless Existence is not anything that rational thought can comprehend, for it has no internal structure of its own that can be linked in some way with other structures that are conceptually accessible. Hence an awareness of Boundless Existence does not compete with, replace, or add to scientific understanding. Boundless Existence is beyond intelligibility, since intelligibility means allowing for the applicability of descriptive or explanatory concepts. Wherever concepts can normally be employed to describe or explain some situation or entity, it is by virtue of being able to find some basis of comparison with, or resemblance to, other situations or entities. However, there is no type, class, law, or recurrent pattern of which Boundless Existence is one instance among others. Boundless Existence is so utterly unique it is not an instance of anything whatsoever. Its uniqueness is not a numerical matter, but rather the fact that it is "wholly other." Therefore one cannot assert anything, whether descriptive or explanatory, of it. Nevertheless, it is not Nothing, although it is no thing. It is best to leave the recognition of Boundless Existence as a basic experience that cannot be analyzed into anything more simple or fundamental.

It follows from this, that Boundless Existence does not have the kind of content that a typical traditional theological system ascribes to the concept of God—for example, the attributes of omnipotence, benevolence, and omniscience. Thus, among other matters, a world-view that includes the notion of Boundless Existence does not provide a theory of creation. It leaves the "relation" between Boundless Existence and the universe-as-an-existent wholly inexplicable because it is not comparable to types of relations for which we already have conceptual characterizations and manifold examples. To specify this "relation" by appealing to faith, as is done in traditional theism, is one way of trying to make it intelligible. But just as reason fails in describing this "relation" (with its various proofs for the existence of God), so too must faith fail. For no leap of faith that ascribes a particular set of properties to transcendent reality can establish its superiority over some rival leap of faith that would fill in its concept of the transcendent in a different way, or to no leap at all.

Man has the twin capacities to respond to the two dimensions of reality—existents and Boundless Existence—and, in so doing, realizes an opportunity, as far as we know, wholly unique to human beings. To become aware of Boundless Existence is a level of human experience unlike any other. It does not arise from a biological need or consist in a satisfaction of such a need. It is not a mode of experience deriving from being a member of a social group or achieved in any form of interpersonal relationship. It does not belong to the sphere of the arts. It is not an intellectual experience such as one finds in science. It is not only *sui generis* among the goods and experiences of life, but precisely because its realization is not made available by means of instruction, habit, imitation, or training, it is likely to be absent from the life experiences of many persons. Even when present, it may be only fleeting, relatively superficial, and easily displaced by more pressing involvements and conventional activities. Nevertheless, some people can acquire and develop an intensified awareness of Boundless Existence. To have this intensified awareness does not require that a person dwell on it exclusively, or, in having it, think of ordinary worldly experiences as illusory or to be relegated to an inferior status. The intensified awareness of Boundless Existence is a spiritual good that—for those who possess it in some moderate or highly developed form—crowns the list of opportunities which the gift of human existence makes possible, and which in its own distinctive way helps give life an additional dimension of meaning.

A question that poses itself immediately is this: How is it possible for there to be any consequences from having an intensified awareness of Boundless Existence if, unlike the known universe or any of its parts, Boundless Existence has no properties? How can the awareness of something that has no properties lead to one rather than another result, indeed to any results whatsoever? How can awareness of Boundless Existence bring about any qualitative *difference* in a person's experience, as compared with a life wholly devoid of such awareness?

The foregoing question can be answered and the paradox it expresses can be dissolved once we take note of the fact that it is precisely because Boundless Existence is totally different from anything else that the awareness of this unique difference leads to whatever consequences it does. It is not any specific properties of Boundless Existence that yield differential consequences, since it has no properties. It is the very fact that Boundless Existence is unlike anything else whatsoever—in not having any properties—*this* is what produces, in one who has an intensified awareness of this absolutely basic ontological fact, the consequences it does. Of nothing else, neither of the known universe as a maximally intelligible physical system, nor of any constituent of the known universe, nor of any construct of human imagination or reason—for example, a character in a work of fiction or a mathematical concept—can we say that it does not have any properties. Any actual, imaginable, or conceivable entity has whatever properties we either discover it to have, or, by contrivance, attribute to it or endow it with. The tree facing me has a brown gnarled bark, a girth of ten feet at its base. The Euclidean triangle has whatever properties the initial postulates or derived theorems show it to have. Shakespeare's King Lear has whatever properties the author chose to attribute to him. But Boundless Existence is unlike any such entity. It has no properties or qualities. And this ontological difference between Boundless Existence and everything else stands out, above all, for our awareness, and accounts for such consequences that awareness may have for our attitudes and behavior. The *awareness* of Boundless Existence is different from any other experience. The presence of the awareness—and not of that to which awareness is directed—is a property of the person (an existent, a part of the universe) who has this awareness.

How can we determine whether someone does have an awareness of Boundless Existence? One type of answer must be immediately ruled out: that what we are to look for is an *image* of Boundless Existence. Even if in being aware of Boundless Existence it should somehow be established—for example, by the report of someone who claims to have such an awareness—that whenever he has such an awareness there is a certain image present to him in his mind, this would only tell us, at best, that such an image *accompanies* his awareness of Boundless Existence. It would not establish that the awareness *consists* in the having of an image, and that if there were no image of the kind in question there would be no awareness. Indeed, one can go further. To have an awareness of Boundless Existence precludes the having of an image *of* "it," as if "it" were something of which one *could* have an image, in the way, for example, one could have an image of an apple or of a person. Boundless Existence is that of which one could not have an image at all.

We come closer to an acceptable answer if one finds that the person having this awareness is able to make clear the grammar or grammatical rule for the use of the *expression* "Boundless Existence." He might supply the details along lines I myself proposed earlier. He might be able to show how the expression "Boundless Existence" is related to, and differentiated from, the expressions "the (known) universe" and "existent." A person would fail to understand that grammar if, for example, he were to attempt to employ the expression "Boundless Existence" as the subject of a sentence to which a descriptive predicate is attached. However, even if someone were to show competency in the use of the expression "Boundless Existence," this would not by itself show that he had an awareness of Boundless Existence, as distinguished from an ability to use the expression correctly. An awareness of Boundless Existence is not identical with, or reducible to, competency in explicating the grammatical rule concerning the use of the expression "Boundless Existence."

Apart from a linguistic test, how then can we establish whether someone does have an awareness of Boundless Existence? Since it is impossible to predicate anything of Boundless Existence in a sentence that has the latter as its subject, we are obviously prevented from making our awareness known to others by the use of such sentences. Our awareness of Boundless Existence is, in *this* sense, unutterable and incapable of being conveyed in language. The only proper response to Boundless Existence is *silence*. The term *surdus* in Latin (from which we get our English word "surd") means that which is "dull, deaf, or mute"; it is a rendering of the Greek term *alogos*. Since the term "logos" has to do at once both with the power of speech and of reason, this relevance of (*a-*)*logos* to both speech and reason is reflected in the use of the term "surd" in two of its more technical meanings. In mathematics, the term "surd" is used to describe a number or quantity that cannot be expressed in rational numbers, for example, $\sqrt{5}$. Again, in phonetics, a surd is a voiceless or breathed sound, one that does not involve a vibration of the vocal chords. In using the term "surd" by way of obvious metaphor and as added to more familiar examples, we might say Boundless Existence is the supreme surd. Boundless Existence *shows* itself. But having become aware of what is shown, we cannot provide a full, literal, descriptive statement of what has been shown: we cannot use language to describe Boundless Existence. And this is why, even though one might write entire books "about" Boundless Existence, strictly speaking this is all a sham and futile. The silence is enforced by the utter impossibility of saying anything informative concerning Boundless Existence.

The resultant pregnant silence can be filled with deep emotion. Yet, even here, to use language to convey the kind of emotion felt (awe, sense of the holy, fear, anxiety, surprise, and so on) would ultimately fail. For the use of emotive terms of one sort or another would be borrowed from their use in other contexts and on occasions other than an encounter with Boundless Existence. Insofar as Boundless Existence is wholly other, even the emotions aroused by it are *sui generis*. Any emotive language used for this purpose can be only analogical or metaphorical.

This is a way of asserting that the awareness of Boundless Existence is a type of mystical experience. However, this does not mean we need use the metaphors of *mystical union* or *mystical revelation* in describing that experience. There are other ways of undergoing a mystical experience than by saying it represents a mode of achieving union with a Supreme Reality or as having access to a special form of *knowledge* not otherwise available.

The chief effect upon a person's behavior and attitudes that an intensified awareness of Boundless Existence has is that it contributes to a feeling of underlying serenity in all that the person experiences and undergoes in the course of his life. However, the type of serenity that is the effect of this intensified awareness of Boundless Existence is different from the kinds of serenity that result from a religious faith in God or a scientific comprehension of the causal structure of the known universe. This difference in quality is due to the fact that, unlike traditional conceptions of God, Boundless Existence has no properties that make it a center of infinite value in itself or a source of value (meaning, purpose) in other finite entities. Nor is Boundless Existence possessed of an intelligible causal structure in the way the universe and any of its constituent parts are accessible to description and explanation.

The serenity of a religious believer derives from his unshaken faith in God's goodness, justice, mercy, and love—and the eventual triumph of God's purposes. It is these ultimate expressions of God's infinite benevolence that control whatever happens to oneself, to others, or to everything in the universe. Unlike theism, however, a world view that incorporates an intensified awareness of Boundless Existence does not offer a basis for hope, love, or moral guidance. Boundless Existence has nothing to offer in the way of these qualities. The only genuine grounds for their realization in life are those made possible by exclusively relying on and developing *human* capacities and resources. Again, for one whose serenity derives fundamentally from a scientific comprehension of the causal (but not providentially designed) structure of the world—what Spinoza called "the intellectual love of God"—peace of mind arises from recognizing and accommodating to the causally necessary concatenation of all natural events. In understanding the inevitable sequence and pattern of events, man can achieve the serenity that comes through this understanding. However, the contribution made to serenity by an intensified awareness of Boundless Existence does not result from any exercise of rational comprehension of a causal structure. For, unlike the known universe, Boundless Existence has neither a causal nor any other type of intelligible structure.

Seeing things from the vantage point of Boundless Existence makes possible a self-transcending perspective, a perspective on our own personal life and death, the life and ultimate extinction of mankind, the status of everything else in the universe, and the known universe itself. In using the expression "seeing things from the vantage point of Boundless Existence," I am, of course, using a figure of speech. In lacking all properties, Boundless Existence does not yield any foothold from which to obtain a specific vantage point of valuation or of understanding in terms of which to look at the universe, at any of its contents, or at human life. It is *we*, as human beings, located in the universe, but also as equipped with the power of awareness of Boundless Existence, who can bring to bear the latter awareness in responding to the gift and opportunities of life.

Precisely because Boundless Existence is a surd, all emphasis on finding meaning in life falls on what can be achieved by the individual person between the limits of his birth and death, and for mankind at large before the final extinction of the human species as set within the framework of the death of the universe itself. The oblivion of death that faces all existents and casts its shadow on all that can be realized before its occurrence makes all the more important, serious, and urgent the full attention given to what the gift of life opens up in the way of possibilities for the realization of goods. Insofar as our awareness of Boundless Existence permeates our lives, it introduces some quality of the negations—the quality of being a surd—that "characterizes" Boundless Existence itself. To the extent that this is the case, our awareness of Boundless Existence relieves us from being *exclusively* involved as existent parts of an existent universe. As existents, we develop our purposes, suffer defeats, celebrate and enjoy our successes. Our awareness of the absence of any qualities in Boundless Existence, however, can affect the way in which we think of our life—its opportunities, defeats, accomplishments, and satisfactions. The qualitylessness—the total absence of purpose and intelligibility—in Boundless Existence "shines through" into our lives and qualifies such elements of purpose and rationality as we are able to confer upon, and bring into, existence. In being deeply affected by this realization, the intensity of the joy, agony, hope, and fear that fill our lives are trimmed, lessened, and qualified. Through this realization, to some extent, we can be lightened and freed. The absence of any meaning, purpose, or intelligibility in Boundless Existence spills over into, and permeates, our dealings with or attitudes toward existents—ourselves, other persons, natural events, the universe itself. It affects the way we regard our own personal lives, our death, and the fate of mankind as a whole. All of these are bathed in a sea of no meaning, no intelligibility, no hope, no fear.

As parts of the universe, we are aware at the same time also of Boundless Existence, and, in this sense, stand at the intersection of both—the universe and Boundless Existence. We are affected by this double exposure. The result in our attitude to all that happens in our life is a mixture that reflects our being accessible to both aspects of reality. To some degree, life can be made rational. However, Boundless Existence is a surd. It ultimately defeats and qualifies all efforts at rationality. We should therefore take life with less than total seriousness. We can "smile" at it and take it "lightly." And this combination of seriousness and lightness is what underlies the serenity born of an intensified awareness of Boundless Existence. In the degree in which we can succeed in achieving this balance of attitudes is born one important avenue to the peace of spirit possible to man.

Index

Library of Congress Cataloging-in-Publication Data

Munitz, Milton Karl, 1913-
Cosmic understanding.

Includes index.
1. Cosmology. I. Title.
BD511.M78 1986   113   86-91546
ISBN 0-691-07312-0 (alk. paper)